Adel Al-Hezmi

Efficient Session-based Multimedia Content Delivery in NGNs

Adel Al-Hezmi

Efficient Session-based Multimedia Content Delivery in NGNs

Efficient Session-based Multimedia Content Delivery in Next Generation Networks

Südwestdeutscher Verlag für Hochschulschriften

Impressum/Imprint (nur für Deutschland/only for Germany)
Bibliografische Information der Deutschen Nationalbibliothek: Die Deutsche Nationalbibliothek verzeichnet diese Publikation in der Deutschen Nationalbibliografie; detaillierte bibliografische Daten sind im Internet über http://dnb.d-nb.de abrufbar.

Alle in diesem Buch genannten Marken und Produktnamen unterliegen warenzeichen-, marken- oder patentrechtlichem Schutz bzw. sind Warenzeichen oder eingetragene Warenzeichen der jeweiligen Inhaber. Die Wiedergabe von Marken, Produktnamen, Gebrauchsnamen, Handelsnamen, Warenbezeichnungen u.s.w. in diesem Werk berechtigt auch ohne besondere Kennzeichnung nicht zu der Annahme, dass solche Namen im Sinne der Warenzeichen- und Markenschutzgesetzgebung als frei zu betrachten wären und daher von jedermann benutzt werden dürften.

Verlag: Südwestdeutscher Verlag für Hochschulschriften GmbH & Co. KG
Dudweiler Landstr. 99, 66123 Saarbrücken, Deutschland
Telefon +49 681 37 20 271-1, Telefax +49 681 37 20 271-0
Email: info@svh-verlag.de

Approved by: Berlin, TU, Diss., 2011

Herstellung in Deutschland:
Schaltungsdienst Lange o.H.G., Berlin
Books on Demand GmbH, Norderstedt
Reha GmbH, Saarbrücken
Amazon Distribution GmbH, Leipzig
ISBN: 978-3-8381-1262-6

Imprint (only for USA, GB)
Bibliographic information published by the Deutsche Nationalbibliothek: The Deutsche Nationalbibliothek lists this publication in the Deutsche Nationalbibliografie; detailed bibliographic data are available in the Internet at http://dnb.d-nb.de.

Any brand names and product names mentioned in this book are subject to trademark, brand or patent protection and are trademarks or registered trademarks of their respective holders. The use of brand names, product names, common names, trade names, product descriptions etc. even without a particular marking in this works is in no way to be construed to mean that such names may be regarded as unrestricted in respect of trademark and brand protection legislation and could thus be used by anyone.

Publisher: Südwestdeutscher Verlag für Hochschulschriften GmbH & Co. KG
Dudweiler Landstr. 99, 66123 Saarbrücken, Germany
Phone +49 681 37 20 271-1, Fax +49 681 37 20 271-0
Email: info@svh-verlag.de

Printed in the U.S.A.
Printed in the U.K. by (see last page)
ISBN: 978-3-8381-1262-6

Copyright © 2011 by the author and Südwestdeutscher Verlag für Hochschulschriften GmbH & Co. KG and licensors
All rights reserved. Saarbrücken 2011

Acknowledgments

Praise be to Allah, who helped me to finalize this work. Throughout my research years, a lot of people supported me professionally, as well as personally. Without their help, I would not have accomplished this thesis. I would like to thank everyone who have supported me throughout the recent years.

First of all, I would like to thank Thomas Magedanz who has supervised my entire academic career at Fraunhofer FOKUS as well as from the start to end of my research work. My respects go to Hans Schotten and Alex Küpper for their valuable suggestions during my frequent research discussions and for reviewing my research work.

I thank all members of Fraunhofer Institute FOKUS for their technical support in my research project at FOKUS and throughout the compilation of this dissertation. In these projects and my daily work I was supported by a team of active and aspiring colleagues, especially Christian Riede, Jordi Jaen Pallares, Oliver Friedrich, Stefan Arbanowski, Hakan Coskun, Bogdan Harjoc, Jose Simoes, Alice Motanga, Andreas Bachmann, Simon Dutkowski, Lajos Lange, Abdulrahman Al-Wsabi, Mohammed Al-khameri and Frank Schulze.

Many thanks to my wife Sara for giving much time to me and to our children, suspending her job and sparing me for the research. Thank you for being so appreciative, especially in the last two years.

I am very grateful to my friend Ashraf Sattar for supporting through this thesis and for valuable feedback and reviewing this research work.

My mother and the whole family, specially my brothers Mohammad, Ahmad and Yahya have been very supportive in the last years helping me to reach my goal. I hope that this achievement makes you proud of your son.

Abstract: The demand for various multimedia services over the Internet and *Next Generation Networks* (NGN) has been increasing rapidly and made feasible through the rapid advances in broadband networking technology. The NGN is the evolution of the classical telecommunications network defined by the ITU-T and ETSI TISPAN as an IP-based network architecture following the layered approach and with support of guaranteed service delivery.

There are two main challenges for efficient multimedia content delivery in the NGN. First, there is a lack of mechanisms to support the delivery of multimedia content according to user context and preferences from multiple sources to a large number of end-users over various communication channels. Second, multimedia streaming in NGN is based on several signaling and transport protocols each of which has several functions and related methods - the challenge here is to determine the optimal blend of protocols and the specific methods to use for efficient multimedia delivery. This essentially means that *the most efficient interaction models for multimedia content delivery are those that can effectively minimize use of network resources.*

This thesis addresses both of these challenges. To address the first challenge, this work proposes a methodology to integrate a user-centric multi-domain architecture that orchestrates amongst several players. The *EffiCient SessiOn-baSed MultImedia Content* (COSMIC) delivery methodology is proposed for the NGN environment that enables smooth interaction between the content provider, the service provider, the network operator and the users. To address the second challenge, this thesis develops a formalized model of NGN streaming protocols, in particular the *Session Initiation Protocol* (SIP) and its associated interaction models. In order to achieve this, several models associated with different multimedia scenarios are evaluated and analyzed to enable us to understand the impact on the NGN and provide guidelines for selecting the appropriate interaction models when developing carrier grade multimedia applications.

The contribution of this research is fourfold: First, the analysis of existing multimedia content delivery approaches in terms of efficiency; Second, the classification of multimedia content delivery approaches and the associated interaction models; Third, the design of a reference architecture for efficient multimedia content delivery in the NGN environment; Fourth, a prototype implementation of the major components of the reference architecture together with its validation.

Zusammenfassung: Der ständige Anstieg der Nachfrage nach Multimediainhalten zeigt, dass die Evolution des Next Generation Network (NGN) weitgehend von den Anforderungen der Übertragung der Multimediainhalten angetrieben werden wird. Das NGN ist die Evolution des klassischen Telekomnetzes, die von der ITU-T und ETSI TISPAN als IP-basiertes Netzwerk in einem mehrschichtigen Ansatz und mit Unterstützung von QoS definiert wurde.

Es gibt zwei wesentliche Herausforderungen für eine effiziente Übertragung von Multimediainhalten in NGN. Zum einen fehlen Mechanismen zur Verteilung von Multimediainhalten von verschiedenen Quellen zu einer großen Anzahl von Endnutzern über verschiedene Kommunikationskanäle. Zum anderen wird Multimedia-Streaming in NGN durch mehrere Signalisierungs- und Transportprotokollen ermöglicht, von denen jede mehrere Funktionen und verschiedene Methoden haben kann. Die Herausforderung besteht darin, für eine effiziente Übertragung die optimale Kombination aus Protokollen und spezifischen Methoden zu finden.

Beide genannten Herausforderungen werden in dieser Arbeit behandelt. Als Resultat ist ein Session-basiertes Inhaltsübertragungsprinzip (COSMIC) hervorgegangen. Zum einen löst COSMIC die Bereitstellung der Multimediainhalte über verschiedene Domänen durch ein integratives Referenzmodell, das die Inhaltsanbieter, die Dienstanbieter und die Netzbetreiber in den Dienstleistungsvorgang einbezieht. Zum anderen werden die Interaktionen zwischen den NGN Komponenten effizient gestaltet. Hierfür wurden unterschiedliche Multimedia-Szenarien analysiert und anhand der Nutzung der Netzwerkressourcen ausgewertet. Hervorgegangen ist ein formalisiertes Modell der NGN Streaming-Protokolle, das als Grundlage das Session Initiation Protocol (SIP) hat und Richtlinien für die Auswahl der geeigneten Interaktionsmodelle bei der Entwicklung von Multimediaanwendungen für ein Carrier-Grade-Netzwerk bereitstellt.

Diese Arbeit hat vier Hauptbeiträge geleistet: Erstens, die Analyse der vorhandenen Ansätze für die Übertragung von Multimediainhalten hinsichtlich Effizienz; Zweitens, die Klassifizierung der Übertragung von Multimediainhalten und die damit verbundenen Interaktionsmodelle; Drittens das Design einer generischen Referenzarchitektur für eine effiziente Übertragung von Multimediainhalten im NGN Umfeld; Zuletzt, eine prototypische Realisierung der beschriebenen Hauptkomponenten der Referenzarchitektur, die im Zusammenhang mit verschiedenen Szenarien validiert wurden.

Contents

1 Introduction   1
    1.1 Motivation 1
    1.2 Problem Statement 3
    1.3 Classification of Multimedia Content Delivery 5
        1.3.1 Un-Managed Delivery Platforms 6
        1.3.2 Managed Delivery Platforms 7
    1.4 PhD Scope 8
    1.5 Major Contribution 11
    1.6 Methodology 12
    1.7 Thesis Structure 13

2 State of the Art   15
    2.1 Introduction 15
    2.2 Fundamentals of Multimedia Content Delivery 15
        2.2.1 Transmission Modes 15
        2.2.2 Control Delivery Models 16
        2.2.3 Content Delivery and Supported Protocols 18
    2.3 Network Architecture 24
        2.3.1 Access Technologies 25
        2.3.2 Transport 27
        2.3.3 Real-time Multimedia Content Control in Next Generation Network (NGN) 29
        2.3.4 Service Environment 35
    2.4 Related Work 43
        2.4.1 IMS-based Streaming Platforms 43
        2.4.2 IMS and Peer-to-Peer Integrated Architecture 44
        2.4.3 Session Establishment 44
        2.4.4 Multimedia Content Delivery 45
    2.5 Discussion 46

3 Media Delivery Core Requirements   49
    3.1 Introduction 49
    3.2 Content Delivery Properties of Key Interest 49
        3.2.1 Real-time Delivery Properties 49
        3.2.2 NGN Architectural Properties 53
    3.3 Core Functionalities 56
        3.3.1 Multimedia Content Management 57

		3.3.2	Multimedia Session Management	58
		3.3.3	Content Delivery	59
	3.4	Summary		61

4 Major Design Aspects for Session-based Multimedia Content Delivery — 65

- 4.1 Introduction 65
- 4.2 Overall Architecture 65
  - 4.2.1 Multimedia Content Delivery Life-Cycle 66
  - 4.2.2 Evaluating the Interaction Models of Content Delivery 68
  - 4.2.3 IMS core Functions 68
  - 4.2.4 Content Information Provisioning Function 69
  - 4.2.5 Content Management 74
  - 4.2.6 Multimedia Session Management 77
  - 4.2.7 Media Delivery Function 82
- 4.3 Analysis of Efficient IMS-based Content Delivery Network .. 86
  - 4.3.1 Basic Service Profiles 86
  - 4.3.2 Message Flows 97
- 4.4 Protocols Evaluation 110
  - 4.4.1 SIP vs. HTTP 111
  - 4.4.2 Streaming over UDP vs. TCP 112
- 4.5 Discussion 113

5 Design and Specification of COSMIC — 119

- 5.1 Introduction 119
- 5.2 Content Delivery Core Components 119
  - 5.2.1 Content Information Provisioning Enabler 121
  - 5.2.2 Content Management Enabler 127
  - 5.2.3 Session Management Enabler 129
  - 5.2.4 Media Delivery Function 133
- 5.3 Summary 136

6 Implementation of Multimedia Content Delivery Core Enablers — 139

- 6.1 Introduction 139
- 6.2 Multimedia Service Enablers 139
  - 6.2.1 Content Information Provisioning Enabler 140
  - 6.2.2 Content Management Enabler 142
  - 6.2.3 Session Management Enabler 143
  - 6.2.4 Media Delivery Function 150
- 6.3 Discussion 152

Contents 9

7	**Validation and Evaluation**	**155**
7.1	Introduction	155
7.2	COSMIC Deployments	155
	7.2.1 Testbeds	155
	7.2.2 Projects	160
7.3	Performance Evaluation	164
	7.3.1 Test Environment	165
	7.3.2 SIP Transactions Evaluation	169
	7.3.3 End-to-End Signaling Evaluation	171
	7.3.4 Multimedia Service Enablers	176
	7.3.5 Media Delivery Control	182
7.4	Discussion and Comparison with other Solutions	187
	7.4.1 Standardization Bodies	187
	7.4.2 Research Community	189
8	**Conclusions**	**195**
8.1	Summary and Impacts	195
8.2	Outlook	198
9	**Acronyms**	**201**
	Bibliography	**207**
A	**IMS Interfaces**	**219**
A.1	IMS Logical Architecture	219
A.2	IMS Interfaces	219
B	**Evaluation of IMS-based IPTV Transactions**	**223**
B.1	Multicast Switching	223
B.2	Push Delivery Method	224
C	**Specification of Multimedia Service Enablers**	**227**
C.1	Content Information Provisioning Enabler	227
	C.1.1 CIPE Use Cases	227
	C.1.2 CIPE Message Flows	227
	C.1.3 External Entities	228
	C.1.4 Interfaces	230
	C.1.5 Multimedia Content Information Data Model	233
C.2	Content Management Enabler	235
	C.2.1 Use Cases	235
	C.2.2 CME Message Flows	236
	C.2.3 External Entities	238

	C.2.4	Interfaces	238
C.3	Session Management Enabler		240
	C.3.1	Use Cases	240
	C.3.2	Message Flows	241
	C.3.3	External Entities	243
	C.3.4	Interfaces	244
C.4	Media Delivery Function		246
	C.4.1	External Entities	246
	C.4.2	Interfaces	247

D IMS MBMS Integration 249

List of Figures

1.1	Stakeholders of multimedia content delivery applications . . .	3
1.2	Multimedia content delivery concerns in converged networks .	4
1.3	Taxonomy of multimedia content delivery	6
1.4	Overall multimedia service and content delivery research framework	9
1.5	Workflow of the research	13
2.1	Overall IMS logical architecture	31
2.2	Application server interfaces	37
2.3	Parlay and Parlay-X architecture	40
2.4	TISPAN IMS-based IPTV Architecture	42
4.1	Network delivery phases	67
4.2	Content Information Provisioning functional entities	72
4.3	Consumer, service and content relationship	75
4.4	Media Delivery Functions	84
4.5	SIP registration flow	98
4.6	User-initiated invite request for unicast delivery mode	99
4.7	User-initiated invite request for multicast delivery mode	101
4.8	User-initiated multicast switching request via SIP Re-Invite .	102
4.9	User-initiated multicast switching request assisted with SIP Info	103
4.10	User-initiated multicast switching request assisted with Subscription-Notification	104
4.11	User-initiated multicast switching request assisted with presence server	105
4.12	Application-initiated unicast session	107
4.13	Application-initiated multicast session	108
4.14	Event-induced session flow	109
5.1	Generic framework for multimedia content delivery in NGN environment	120
5.2	Content Information Provisioning Enabler architecture	122
5.3	Content information data model	126
5.4	Content Management Enabler architecture	128
5.5	Session Management Enabler architecture	130
5.6	Media Delivery Function architecture	134

6.1	Content Information Provisioning Enabler reference implementation	140
6.2	Content management Enabler reference implementation	142
6.3	Content Management Enabler activity diagram	144
6.4	Session management Enabler reference implementation	145
6.5	Live Content Streamer activity diagram	147
6.6	Stored Content Streamer activity diagram	149
6.7	Media Delivery Function reference implementation	150
6.8	Message flows of integrating all multimedia service enablers	153
7.1	IMS-based DVB-H and UMTS integrated streaming scenario	157
7.2	Message flow of the IMS-based DVB-H and UMTS integration	158
7.3	Media Interoperability Lab testbed setup	159
7.4	Session Mobility Application	160
7.5	Sharing Multimedia Activities	160
7.6	IMS-MBMS integrated architecture	162
7.7	Message flows of the IMS-MBMS session	163
7.8	Test environment	166
7.9	Relationship between the number of UEs and generated request over the time	167
7.10	Delay of several SIP transactions at rate 25 cps	170
7.11	End-to-end message flows of a live content session	172
7.12	Application-initiated content delivery	177
7.13	Delay of user-initiated session at 3 cps	179
7.14	Delay of user-initiated session at 5 cps	179
7.15	Delay of user-initiated session at 7 cps	179
7.16	Delay of user-initiated session at 10 cps	179
7.17	Delay of application-initiated session at 5 cps	181
7.18	Delay of application-initiated session at 7 cps	181
7.19	Push-mode signaling delay over various call rates	182
7.20	Message flows of the MDF relay function	185
7.21	MDF prepare for relay performance measurement results based on calls/1s	185
7.22	Triggering relay function at 1 cps	186
7.23	Triggering relay function at 10 cps	186
A.1	3GPP IMS logical architecture	221
C.1	CIPE content provider use case maintaining own content list	227
C.2	CIPE content information provisioning use case	228
C.3	CIPE message flows for maintaining content list by content provider	229

List of Figures

C.4   CIPE Content provider publishing new content information related to his content list 230
C.5   Content Information Watcher Subscription, single domain . . . 231
C.6   Information Watcher Subscription, multi domains 232
C.7   The use case of content management enabler interacting with the content provider 236
C.8   Relationship between an application and the content management enabler 236
C.9   Setup between the CME and CP, push method 237
C.10 Session setup between the CME and CP, pull method 237
C.11 Session termination between the CME and the content provider 238
C.12 Use case of delivering multimedia content triggered by a consumer 240
C.13 Use case of delivering multimedia content triggered by an application 240
C.14 Relationship use case between the SME and the CME 241
C.15 Message flows of session setup for delivering stored multimedia content 242
C.16 Message flows of session termination for delivering live multimedia content 243
C.17 Message flows of session setup for delivering stored multimedia content 244
C.18 Message flows of session termination for delivering stored multimedia content 245
C.19 Pushing live multimedia content triggered by 3rd application . 246

D.1   IMS-MBMS integration, session activation 251
D.2   IMS-MBMS integration, start transmission 252

List of Tables

1.1	Characteristics of Content Delivery Networks	6
2.1	SIP basic methods	20
2.2	SIP request codes	21
2.3	Type defined by SDP	22
2.4	SIP JSRs	37
2.5	Relationship of the presence enabler and the NGN core	40
4.1	Evaluation of provisioning methods	74
4.2	Evaluation of session setup methods	80
4.3	IMS registration profile	87
4.4	Multicast and unicast session profile	89
4.5	Multicast switching profile	90
4.6	Event framework profile	92
4.7	SIP transactions of registration flow	97
4.8	SIP transactions of user-initiated Invite unicast mode	99
4.9	SIP transactions of user-initiated invite request for multicast delivery mode	100
4.10	SIP transactions of user-initiated multicast switching request via SIP Re-Invite	101
4.11	SIP transactions of user-initiated multicast switching request assisted with SIP Info	103
4.12	SIP transactions of user-initiated multicast switching request assisted with Subscription-Notification	105
4.13	SIP transactions of user-initiated multicast switching request assisted with presence server	105
4.14	SIP transactions of application-initiated unicast session	106
4.15	SIP transactions of application-initiated multicast session	108
4.16	SIP transactions of event-induced session flow	109
4.17	SIP vs. HTTP Features	111
4.18	Evaluation of streaming via UDP vs. TCP	112
4.19	Content and Service Provider use case relationship	115
4.20	Evaluation of multicast switching options	116
4.21	Service Provider and consumer use case relationships	117
7.1	Switching delay from LAN and UMTS to DVB-T	158
7.2	SIP transactions evaluation	170
7.3	End-to-End evaluation test cases	172

7.4	Total end-to-end signaling delay of user-initiated multimedia session	174
7.5	Performance measurement use cases	176
7.6	MDF performance test cases	183
7.7	Comparison between current multimedia delivery frameworks and COSMIC	188
7.8	Rating of multimedia delivery approaches	193
A.1	3GPP IMS Interfaces	220
B.1	IPTV service profile	223
B.2	Nr of SIP SUBSCRIBE and NOTIFY messages of an IPTV Service	224
B.3	Number of SIP transactions for IPTV multicast switching	224
B.4	Push method service profile	224
B.5	SIP transactions of different types of unicast and multicast sessions	225

CHAPTER 1
Introduction

1.1 Motivation

The success of the Internet as a packet-based technology has convinced the operators of telecommunications networks, as well as cable TV network operators worldwide to migrate their core networks towards IP. Four factors are of significance for this evolution: The first is related to the nature of the IP network as a distributed architecture allowing network intelligence to be distributed among the endpoints instead of being centralized within a set of dedicated nodes. The second is the ability of end nodes to offer a wide range of services to customers while incurring low capital investment and operational costs; known as Capital Expenditures (CAPEX) and Operating Expenses (OPEX), respectively. The third refers to the open nature of the Internet that enables any user of the Internet services to act either as a content consumer or as a content producer. Fourth is the facility of the end points to communicate using various types of communication models (client-server, peer-to-peer or master-slave) and to make use of different transmission modes (unicast, multicast or broadcast).

Recent developments in IP-based technologies have changed the way we consume multimedia content (which is the combination of different forms of media such as text, audio, image, video and interactivity). In particular, the current growth in the demand for IP-based streaming applications shows that the evolution of IP networks will be largely driven by the delivery requirements of multimedia content. Nowadays, multimedia content is delivered and distributed over three different types of networks, as depicted in Figure 1.1: (1) traditional broadcast and digital TV networks, (2) on-demand bidirectional fixed and mobile networks and (3) the public Internet. It is envisaged that in the near future, the fixed and wireless broadband access networks will provide the means to share and distribute multimedia content and services with superior quality and support of personalization. In order to enable this vision, new signaling & transport protocols, new multimedia encoding schemes and content adaptation mechanisms are required.

Next Generation Network NGN is the evolution of the classical telecommunications network defined by the International Telecommunication Union,

Telecommunication Standardization Sector (ITU-T) and European Telecommunications Standards Institute (ETSI) Telecoms & Internet converged Services & Protocols for Advanced Networks (TISPAN). The *NGN is defined as a layered architecture with an IP-based transport layer that has built in resource control mechanisms to guarantee a certain level of Quality of Service (QoS) for different types of traffic* [1, 2]. Although there are other interpretations of the term NGN in the industry, this is the definition considered in this dissertation. The IP-based NGN transport layer enables the provisioning of multimedia services over several broadband access technologies. However, the heterogeneity of broadband access technologies provides new challenges for the design of service awareness in IP networks. Within this context, enhancements of the IP core with QoS, autonomous behavior and mobility support are currently research subjects that are being conducted worldwide.

Currently, the Internet enables the delivery of live and stored multimedia content worldwide based on Web technology or Peer-to-Peer (P2P) overlay networks with best effort delivery [3]. This type of delivery is unable to provide any guarantee of quality of service and reliability. However, the Internet offers tremendous multimedia content that is generated by professional and amateur content providers and users can upload or download content to/from targeted hosts connected to the Internet at any time.

With the objective of overcoming the Internet's current limitations, the NGN enables the delivery of multimedia content applications with support of a certain level of QoS. However, in the context of this research, one of the most challenging services to support over the NGN is the delivery of multimedia services (e.g. TV) along with telecommunications services over various access networks. For instance, delivering TV services over IP (termed IP Television (IPTV)) currently has significant focus from both the research and standardization perspectives. In fact, nowadays, several proprietary IPTV solutions are deployed in closed operator domains. However, there are various Standards Development Organizations (SDOs) such as ETSI TISPAN [1], ITU-T [2], Alliance for Telecommunications Industry Solutions (ATIS) [4], the Open IPTV Forum (OIF) [5], and the Digital Video Broadcasting (DVB) Forum that are working on the specification of the IPTV standards.

The provisioning of multimedia applications will involve different stakeholders in the value chain ranging from consumer, network operator, content provider up to service providers. The steady increase in bandwidth offered through various access technologies, aligned with the improvements on the IP layer, will enable end users to access a wide range of services that are offered by providers of their choice. Multimedia content streaming can be offered by a telecommunication service provider or Over-The-Top (OTT) service providers who offer their own services and content over the service providers

1.2. Problem Statement

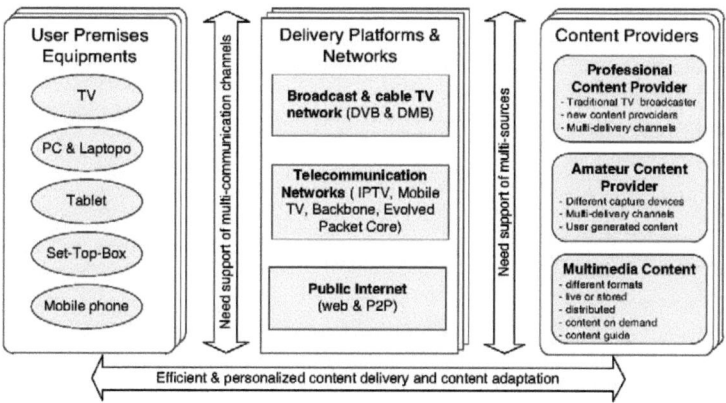

Figure 1.1: Stakeholders of multimedia content delivery applications

networks. However, users are no longer restricted to being mere consumers of content but are increasingly becoming involved in the creation of multimedia content. This will impose new requirements on the related delivery platforms and introduce additional challenges. Ultimately, these players have to interact smoothly to fulfill the task of providing an enjoyable multimedia experience to the end user.

The related requirements should be derived from an abstract view of the involved network entities as depicted in Figure 1.1, which illustrates the various stakeholders involved during the delivery of any multimedia applications. These players are the content provider, the service provider, the network provider and the consumer. All or parts of these players - among others - are jointly involved in the value chain of multimedia applications. However, the business relationship between these players can vary from business model to business model.

1.2 Problem Statement

The vision of the future network is to enable the delivery of multimedia content that are designed, constructed and marketed in ways that is highly adapted to current and future human needs (e.g. the need to socialize, for new sensations and entertainment, for ease of use anywhere and anytime, to mitigate the need to travel and save time and energy etc.) [3]. To enable this vision, the above described evolution in technology ranging from the network layer to the

Chapter 1. Introduction

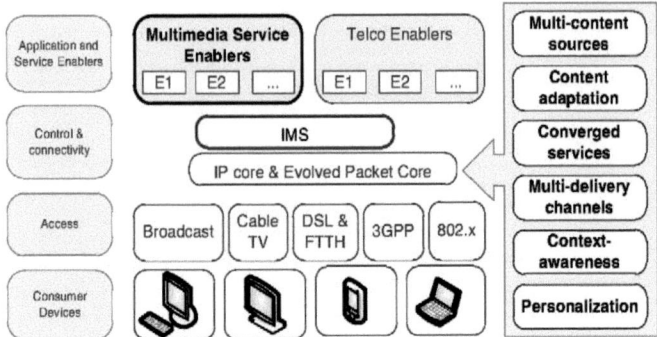

Figure 1.2: Multimedia content delivery concerns in converged networks

control and service layers, imposes changes for operators as well as service and content providers. Figure 1.2 provides an overview of the issues and concerns that content providers, multimedia service providers and operators need to cope with in a growing market of multimedia services.

In fact, there is a strong market demand for more sophisticated integration levels that will enable the delivery of converged multimedia and telecommunications services in an efficient manner. However, the challenge is to deliver multimedia content from multiple sources to end-users over various communication channels and be adapted according to user context and preferences. Nowadays, the main limitations are:

- From the application perspective, there are a number of interaction models, communication styles, signaling and transport protocols that can be applied for content delivery; push, pull and event-based. However, changing the interactions models of an application can have more impact on performance and efficiency than the communication protocol used for that interaction. A formalized description of such models in NGN is currently missing. This essentially means that *the most efficient interaction models for multimedia content delivery applications are those that can effectively minimize use of the network resources when it is possible*, as defined in [6] but with a few modifications applied in respect to our research work.

- Current NGN-based delivery platforms do not support multi-communication channels covering unicast, multicast and broadcast capabilities that are an important feature for content delivery, especially for large-scale live content streaming or community-based applications.

- Content processing and adaptation functionalities in the NGN architecture are only limited to support telephony applications with features like playing audio announcements, executing IVR (Interactive Voice Response) applications and providing conference bridges. However, capabilities like linear streaming (e.g. live TV), on-demand streaming (e.g. VoD) and content adaptation (e.g. rate-scaling or transcoding) are also essential for multimedia services.

- There is lack of a basic set of multimedia delivery capabilities accessible through simple interfaces that allow service developers to effectively integrate the multimedia content streaming component as part of the service logic, irrespective of the underlying signaling and transport protocols or selected access technologies.

To cope with these challenges, the next subsection discusses the scope of this dissertation which deals in detail with problems related to the increasing variety of technologies on multimedia content delivery, the analysis of interaction models in NGN, the convergence of multimedia streaming applications with telecommunications services and the delivery of personalized and context-aware multimedia content from multiple sources to several users through a myriad of communication channels.

1.3 Classification of Multimedia Content Delivery

As mentioned above, multimedia content is distributed over IP through several delivery types of infrastructures. A comparison of three types of exiting multimedia content delivery platforms is shown in Table 1.1. As most of these platforms lack multiple advanced features that are challenged, either by the Internet applications or available as propriety solution, it is important to indicate these features as requirements for this research work. *A multimedia content delivery platform is defined as a set of distributed functional components that enable the delivery of multimedia content from content provider to consumers with a dedicated business model.*

Multimedia content delivery can be categorized into two general classes, unmanaged and managed content delivery network, as depicted in Figure 1.3:

State-of-the-art	Description
Classical broadcast	Content is broadcasted over the air with lack of personalization, adaptation and interactivity.
Public Internet	Content is distributed over the Web or peer-to-peer networks. Users can acquire multimedia content at any time. Content delivery lacks reliability, QoS and efficiency due to limited support for multicast delivery. It supports different interaction models (client-server, peer-to-peer and event-based)
Managed IP-based networks (NGN, Next Generation Mobile Network (NGMN) and digital TV)	Content is distributed through a managed network infrastructure with support of certain level of QoS. Content delivery lacks support of context-awareness and has limited support of personalization. It supports different interaction models (client-server, peer-to-peer and event-based).

Table 1.1: Characteristics of Content Delivery Networks

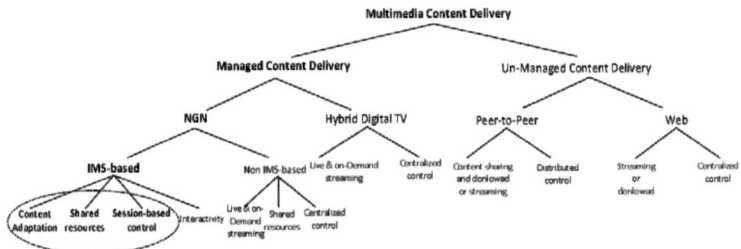

Figure 1.3: Taxonomy of multimedia content delivery

1.3.1 Un-Managed Delivery Platforms

Multimedia content streams (e.g. TV, news, e-learning, user generated content, etc.) are delivered across several domains and without ensuring Service Level Agreement (SLA) in between. Such delivery usually leverages the public Internet to transfer multimedia content among Internet users with best effort. Therefore, network nodes are not aware about flow characteristics and thus, do not guarantee delivery of the content. Content is distributed through the Web (e.g. content provider portal, YouTube or social networks) or the P2P networks. From the telecommunications operator perspective, the associated providers are considered as OTT service providers that provide rich multimedia content and often telecommunications type services with a lower degree of Quality of Experience (QoE) for the end user.

1.3.2 Managed Delivery Platforms

Multimedia content streams are delivered through a managed network where the content is delivered over an end-to-end controllable infrastructure ranging from source, aggregation, processing nodes, access nodes up to content receiving devices, where the delivery path may traverse one or more operator's administrative domains. Therefore content delivery should be governed by intra- and inter-domain SLAs among all involved operators, where the SLAs guarantee QoS parameters (e.g. delay, jitter, packet loss, committed rate, etc.), security, privacy and Digital Rights Management (DRM).

In contrast to un-managed content delivery, the managed NGN and cable TV networks deliver content streaming (e.g. live TV and on-demand content) over an infrastructure, which is typically owned by a single service provider (or telecommunications operator) that has contracted with several players like TV broadcasters and video content providers, in order to ensure high quality and professional content sources. Owning the networking infrastructure allows the operators to engineer their systems to support the end-to-end delivery of high quality content. In the NGN, there are two streaming subsystems being defined by the SDOs; first an IMS-based (IP Multimedia Subsystem) and a non-IMS-based streaming subsystem.

The IP Multimedia Subsystem (IMS) is expected to form the foundation of future telecommunications service delivery infrastructures. All IMS related standards activities are being conducted under the supervision of the 3rd Generation Partnership Project (3GPP) to generate a single set of IMS standards to the development of which all the other main SDOs (including 3GPP2, TISPAN, ITU-T and Packetcable) are making direct contributions. In comparison to Internet-based applications, the IMS is currently accepted by the SDOs as a single common centralized subsystem for controlling the delivery of multimedia converged applications in NGN environments.

Therefore, those concerned with the IMS-based content delivery framework must pay particular attention to the importance to this research for the following reasons:

- First, as discussed above, there are several players involved in the value chain of multimedia content provisioning and the corresponding SDOs play an important role for specifying the required reference points between these players. However, due to domain distinction of these players, the standardization process may take a long time to come up with consensus for the related interfaces.

- Second, the IMS-based content delivery framework is expected to embrace the heterogeneity arising from the different service control, transport or access technologies, so that a multimedia service appears homogeneous to the potential customer.

- Finally, IMS offers advanced capabilities to enhance existing services or create new services through combination of existing ones. Service composition is realized by invoking a set of basic services in an appropriate sequence, in accordance with defined filter criteria stored in the user profile.

As a consequence of such constraints, the service logic of a multimedia application is tightly coupled with concrete IMS signaling and transport protocols. Although the Session Initiation Protocol (SIP) is the main signaling protocol in the IMS, it supports various methods following several communication styles. For this reason, the analysis and evaluation of these models are in scope of this dissertation. Furthermore, this work will limit the scope to this category of content delivery as depicted in the most left side of Figure 1.3.

1.4 PhD Scope

The main goals of this research work are to define a model for understanding multimedia content delivery mechanisms in the NGN network, identify ways to deliver multimedia content efficiently and present solutions to enable the support of personalization and interactivity. By examining relevant requirements for a target platform managing the delivery of multimedia content within a converged NGN infrastructure, a set of basic key components are identified for providing network-centric control and processing functions. With this regard, only the managed content delivery network is considered in this research rather than un-managed content delivery networks. To allow the delivery of rich multimedia applications in converged and heterogeneous networks, the following major aspects are to be considered:

1. Multiple sources of multimedia content

2. Various channels for content transmission to multiple devices with different modalities

3. Session-based delivery control and session management

4. Management of interactivity, personalization and related metadata

5. Understanding social multimedia services and predicting user behavior and preferences

1.4. PhD Scope

As the first three points represent the core functionalities for multimedia content delivery, they are the main subjects of this research, while the last two research aspects are not subject to discussion in this dissertation, as they are considered in a parallel dissertation [1]. Figure 1.4 illustrates the overall research framework that follows the NGN layering approach defined by the ITU-T and ETSI TISPAN. However, the scope of this dissertation is depicted in the lower and the upper half of Figure 1.4. The session-based multimedia content delivery will be applied for multimedia content delivery from multiple content sources to several end users. *A session-based content delivery model enables the user or the application to initiate a multimedia content delivery session then invoke a series of transactions and finally either the user or the application terminates the session.*

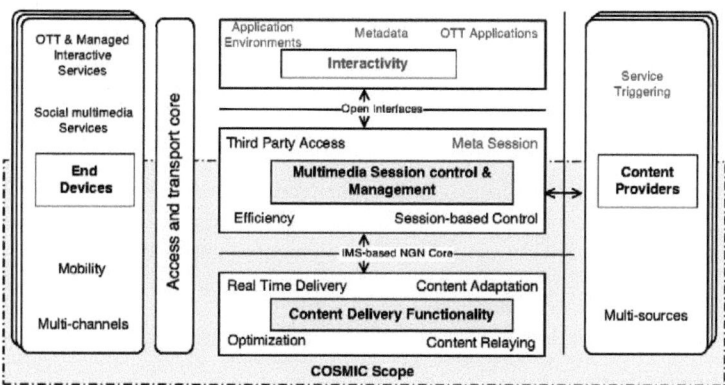

Figure 1.4: Overall multimedia service and content delivery research framework

Initially, the work will define a model for understanding the relationship between the content provider, the service provider, the content delivery system and the consumer. It will then focus on efficient content delivery using different IMS controlled transport modes along with support of interactivity and personalization, as depicted in Figure 1.4. Since the IMS supports an individual bidirectional communication channel to each IMS subscriber, the realization of the interactivity and personalization will be feasible. On the other hand, although the IMS enables the delivery of seamless converged multimedia services over fixed and mobile access technologies, it currently only

---
[1] Please refer to "An integrated interactive application environment for session-oriented IPTV systems enabling shared user experiences" by O. Friedrich

supports unicast content delivery rather than multicast or broadcast transmission modes, by means of which content delivery gains much more efficiency.

Efficiency is described in the Webster[2] dictionary in three definitions: 1) as the ratio of the useful energy delivered by a dynamic system to the energy supplied to it; 2) the effective operation as measured by a comparison of production with cost (as in energy, time, and money); 3) the ability to do something or produce something without wasting materials, time, or energy. Fielding [6] defines the network efficiency as the ability of a network-based application to effectively minimize use of the network. With respect to our research work, *the efficiency is defined as the ability to deliver multimedia content with minimum usage of network resources*. In this regard, real-time delivery properties such as delay and packet loss, as well as the architectural properties such as network performance, user-perceived quality and scalability will be considered.

This dissertation focuses on an *EffiCient Session-based MultImedia Content Delivery in Next Generation Networks* effiCient sessiOn-baSed MultImedia Content Delivery in Next Generation Network (COSMIC). Figure 1.4 illustrates the three research topics that are of significance in this research:

1. **Multimedia Session Control and Management**: The main objective of this topic is to examine and analysze the interaction and communication models for the delivery of multimedia content in an IMS-based network. Further it will define control and content delivery mechanisms from content provider to the consumer through the IMS session by taking into consideration real-time requirements in terms of optimizing session setup delay and efficient content delivery by making use of several transmission modes (unicast, multicast or broadcast) whenever possible, i.e. based for example on terminal capabilities and network conditions. Within this context, specific standardized mechanisms will be applied. Session setup delay and processing performance are criteria for the efficiency of this component. While the realization of interactivity and personalization will be based on session management and context-awareness of user activities, the related-research aspects will not be considered in this dissertation.

2. **Content management**: The objective is to develop new mechanisms that enable the service provider to obtain or receive multimedia content from multiple sources which include professional and/or amateur Content Providers. User generated content will play here an important role. Therefore, discovery and control mechanisms for content delivery from

---

[2]http://www.merriam-webster.com/

content provider to service provider and content storage is the focus of this topic.

3. **Media Delivery Functions**: In order to support multiple sources and various channels content delivery, network-centric content adaptation functions are in the scope of this work. With this regard, mechanisms for controlling media delivery and adaptation functions that follow a centralized session control paradigm are considered as well. Although the distribution of content delivery and adaptation functions are important for large networks, the distribution pattern is not in the scope of this dissertation.

These three key functionalities are still missing and a common integrated solution at the point of writing was not available. Figure 1.4 illustrates the roles of these three functionalities and their interactions within the IMS network. Furthermore and as stated above, this dissertation will concentrate only on IMS protocols and their dependences. The proposed solutions presented within are specially targeted towards the NGN network; however, they might be also applicable for other kinds of IP-based networks. Also, the scope is directed to the IMS network level: Implementation errors or user errors are not considered. This dissertation will focus on dedicated IMS related multimedia applications, and does not consider common IP-based applications. The design of the architecture as well as the related components will follow the Service-Oriented Architecture (SOA) paradigm and enable service openness towards third parties in order to make use of the multimedia content delivery functions through open interfaces easily.

1.5 Major Contribution

The work explores a junction on the frontiers of two research areas: multimedia applications and centralized content delivery network. In summary, this dissertation makes the following contributions:

1. Classification and discussion of several delivery and interaction models for IMS-based multimedia applications based on the architectural properties they would induce when applied to the architecture for delivering real-time multimedia services;

2. Analysis of existing multimedia content delivery approaches in terms of efficiency;

3. The design and development of basic core functionalities for delivering real-time multimedia content streams from multiple sources to various

user devices capable of connecting and communicating with different types of access networks. With this regard, this work relies on the NGN subsystem-oriented architecture which allows the integration or the extension of new functionalities without modifying the existing subsystems. The dissertation proposes enhancements to the NGN session procedure with the required extensions.

4. Providing reference implementation of the core functionalities and disseminating the results through publications and workshops and contributing to the related standardization organizations.

These topics are discussed throughout this dissertation and the related results are summarized in the final chapter.

1.6 Methodology

This dissertation will provide a fivefold approach for addressing problems within the above described scope as follows:

1. Study and analyze existing content delivery approaches and related technologies, in particular for existing NGN-based networks and identify the main issues that prevent the efficient multimedia content delivery.

2. Identify the key properties for real-time content delivery defined in the literature and then define the requirements of multimedia services for generalized multimedia delivery functions from the perspective of content provider, service provider, connectivity provider and user.

3. Model an end-to-end framework addressing our identified functions with the related network entities and/or corresponding enhancements. Based on this model and specific IMS-based service profiles, several interactions and delivery models are to be studied and the related impact on efficiency, user and network performance are evaluated. Therefore, the work will explore existing delivery mechanisms available in literature and advance them where needed or define new methods targeted for efficient content delivery.

4. Efficient multimedia content delivery requires mainly three core functionalities: content management, session-based delivery control and media handling. The recommended delivery mechanisms will guide the work to design the targeted media delivery core architecture and to specify the related interfaces and dependencies. As a result of the analyses, a reference implementation will be developed.

1.7. Thesis Structure

5. Finally, end-to-end system functionalities and component basic functions are going to be validated and evaluated by conducting performance measurement on specific component or interfaces.

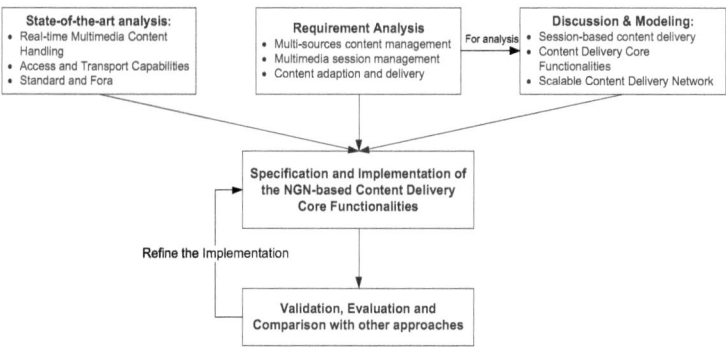

Figure 1.5: Workflow of the research

Figure 1.5 illustrates the necessary steps to be followed in this dissertation showing the basic core functionalities for delivering rich multimedia content applications in an NGN-based infrastructure in an efficient manner.

1.7 Thesis Structure

The dissertation is structured in seven main parts:

1. Chapter 2 provides an overview of the relevant technologies and standards in the context of this dissertation and with regard to multimedia content delivery.

2. Chapter 3 identifies detailed requirements of the basic core functionalities for efficient real-time content delivery in the NGN infrastructure.

3. Whereas chapter 3, defines the requirements, chapter 4 discusses these requirements and analyzes the interaction and delivery models in an IMS-based network. Then, it provides recommendations for the design of the targeted architecture.

4. Chapter 5 describes in detail the design of media delivery core functionalities that are of interest within the research framework according to the discussion taking place in chapter 4.

5. Chapter 6, explains the reference implementation and applied tools and technologies.

6. In chapter 7, the validation of the implementation carried out at Fraunhofer FOKUS and in industry and research projects is presented. Further, end-to-end evaluation and interface or component specific performance measurements are discussed and dissertation results are compared with other approaches in current and past research activities.

7. Finally, chapter 8 gives a summary of this dissertation and introduces open research questions and future works.

CHAPTER 2
State of the Art

2.1 Introduction

This chapter gives an overview of the available technologies that impact directly or indirectly the delivery of multimedia content. The most promising applications of our era deal with aspects of real-time, collaboration and user generated content (production, distribution, consumption) regardless of the network used (wired, wireless).

In the first section we give an overview of the delivery modes; namely unicast, multicast and broadcast. Then the different architectural models for controlling content transmission are discussed followed by the associated signaling and transport protocols. Section two represents current network architectures for multimedia content delivery and related standards whereas fixed and mobile access and transport technologies are introduced followed by NGN core control and finally the service environments. Last section discusses the summary of the state-of-the-art technologies.

2.2 Fundamentals of Multimedia Content Delivery

2.2.1 Transmission Modes

Multimedia content has to be sent from one or multiple sources to one or more recipients, whereas data packets (e.g. multimedia packets) are usually transmitted from a content provider to consumers via a dedicated network technology. With this context, there are three modes for content transmission, as introduced in the following subsections.

2.2.1.1 BroadcastMode

Multimedia content is transmitted from a single source over a unidirectional broadcast channel. Every recipient of the broadcast signal can receive and possibly render the multimedia packets. Content is primarily broadcast on the access network such as the DVB or 3GPP MBMS.

2.2.1.2 Multicast

Multimedia content is transmitted from a single source to n users. There are several approaches for the realization of multicast content transmission:

1. **The access layer**: The DVB and the MBMS support content delivery to dedicated users each of which shall join or be aware of the multicast group address.

2. **The IP core**: Routers create optimal distribution paths for multimedia packets sent to a multicast destination address spanning tree in real-time. Interested users should join the associated multicast group, following the IP multicast protocols.

3. **The application level**: An application-based overlay network is in charge of the transmission of multimedia packets by replicating multimedia packets among different members. The application-based multicast approach is not efficient as IP multicast due to data duplication on the application layer that requires more resources compared to IP multicast. The nodes organize themselves in some well-defined manner (e.g. into mesh or tree structures) [7] and [8].

While the multicast transmission improves the efficiency of content delivery, multicast-awareness on the application server is mandatory in order to support interactivity and personalization features.

2.2.1.3 Unicast

In unicast transmission mode, multimedia packets are usually sent from a single source to a single destination. The transmission relies on interactive bidirectional transmission channel. This mode is mainly used in most web-based Internet and mobile applications. Protocols that support this mode of transmission are known as unicast protocols.

2.2.2 Control Delivery Models

Most of the content delivery platforms require an infrastructure in order to be able to manage the delivery of multimedia content from the content provider to users with support of adaptability and personalization. The related control functionalities can be centralized, partially or fully decentralized, according in particular to their locations: in the network nodes and/or in the end-user devices. In these regards there are three classes of control models that are introduced in the next subsections.

2.2. Fundamentals of Multimedia Content Delivery

2.2.2.1 Centralized Control

The centralized control model is the most frequently encountered of the control model for Internet-based applications. There are two classes of this model:

1. **Client-Server control model (CS)**: A server, offering a set of services, listens for requests upon those services. A client, desiring that a service be performed, sends a request to the server via a defined protocol. The server either rejects or performs the request and sends a response back to the client. The basic form of client-server does not constrain how the application state is partitioned between the client and the server. It is often referred to by the mechanisms used for the protocol and application logic, such as a web browser or a VoD application using the Hypertext Transfer Protocol (HTTP) or the RTSP (Real Time Streaming Protocol), respectively.

2. **Master-Slave control Model (MS)**: A controller is the master giving commands and the slave is the processing node performing actions, such as a media server or a media gateway in an NGN. As the master often controls a set of slaves, this model may decrease the performance of the controller. For this reason, the number of the slaves shall not exceed a specific number. However, it is application dependent.

In MS model, the slave is always tightly-coupled with a dedicated master, in contrast to the client in the CS model in which the client can select to initiate request to any server at any time. Both models are widely used in NGN due to their ease of implementation.

2.2.2.2 Decentralized Control Model

Decentralized control is based on mesh topology connection or follows the peer-to-peer (P2P) model, where nodes build a structured or unstructured overlay topology, which is significant autonomy from central server, such as BitTorent [7]. P2P distribution has emerged as a practical solution due to its ease of deployment, low cost of operation and scalability.

The advantage of P2P content distribution over the client-server model is that it enables offering of more resources to clients by effectively turning each one of them into a secondary server that offers the same content (or live content stream) from the original server. Nevertheless, P2P network have shown a clear lack of mechanisms to ensure efficient and fair utilization of network resources [3].

2.2.2.3 Session-based Control Model

Session-based control model is a variant of the centralized client-server model, in which the client establishes a session on the server then invokes a series of services on the server and finally either the client or the server terminates the session. The application state is shared between the client and the server. This model is typically used in VoIP or IMS-based IPTV sessions [9] and [10].

The advantages of the session-based control model are that it is easier to centrally maintain the services on the server, reducing concerns about inconsistencies in deployed clients when functionality is extended, and improves efficiency if the interactions make use of extended session context on the server. The disadvantages are that it reduces scalability of the server, due to the centralized service control, unlike the p2p model.

2.2.3 Content Delivery and Supported Protocols

In an NGN environment, multimedia content delivery protocols are primarily based on Internet protocols defined by the IETF (Internet Engineering Task Force). These protocols can be classified into three categories:

1. Signaling protocols responsible for controlling multimedia session or processing nodes such as SIP or H.248.

2. Transmission Protocols used to transfer media stream or data such as RTP or HTTP protocol.

3. Resource Management protocols used to carry authentication, authorization and accounting messages such as Diameter.

As there are several protocols used in or that support the delivery of multimedia content, the following subsections describe only those protocols related to this work.

2.2.3.1 Session Initiation Protocol

The Session Initiation Protocol (SIP) is an application layer protocol defined by the IETF for controlling and managing any multimedia session. It is designed to establish, modify or terminate a session among two or more partners. The session may include one or more types of media traffic (e.g. audio, video, messaging, interactive gaming, etc.).

According to the IP paradigm, SIP is an end-to-end signaling protocol following the *session-based control model*, in which each SIP entity may act as a client and as a server concurrently. SIP is a text-based protocol influenced

2.2. Fundamentals of Multimedia Content Delivery

initially by the HTTP [11] and Simple Mail Transfer Protocol (SMTP) [12], and it still uses some of these functionalities, e.g. Uniform Resource Identifiers (URIs) and many message header fields such as "To" and "From". SIP is highly extensible, and thus multiple RFCs and other documents can define new extensions to the SIP specification [13].

SIP is supposed to control sessions rather than the transmission of media traffic (e.g. voice packets). Description and transport of content are managed by other protocols, which are run in conjunction with SIP such as the SDP or RTP, respectively, and will be outlined in the next subsections. SIP defines four types of logical entities that may act as a client by initiating requests, as a server by responding to requests or both. A set of logical entities may be implemented on one single entity. These entities are:

User Agent (UA) : The endpoint entity that initiates and terminates a SIP session. It contains user agent client and user agent server.

SIP Proxy (SP) : Responsible for routing SIP messages between SIP entities. It is in charge of request validation, user authentication, forking requests, address resolving, or canceling pending sessions.

Registrar : It maintains the user location (IP and SIP ID). Therefore it accepts user registration requests and stores this information in location service for further reference.

SIP Redirect Server : It accepts SIP requests and responds with the redirection message that refers the client to contact another SIP address.

The SIP proxy, registrar and redirect server are mostly implemented on one physical server with a local or distributed database to store user subscription and registrar information. However, the SIP proxy server is transparent to the UAs and thus it is not allowed to modify SIP messages.

SIP messages are plain text and are either a request or a response referring to a SIP method or a SIP state code, respectively. A SIP message consists of three parts:

- Start Line which includes message type (SIP method or response code) and protocol version. The start line is called Request-Line for request and Status-Line for responses. The Request-Line covers a request URI indicating the target user or service. The core SIP specification defines six SIP methods as summarized in Table 2.1. The Status-Line includes the numeric Status-Code and its associated textual phrase, as shown in Table 2.2.

- Headers: SIP header fields are used to convey message attributes and to modify message meaning. They take the format <name> : <value>;

- Body: A message body is used to carry session description information. For instance, in a VoIP session, the message body includes both end's IP addresses, ports and supported audio codecs, or the message body may cover textual or binary data related in some way to the negotiated session.

Method	Description
INVITE	Initiating or modifying a session
ACK	Confirming the final response for an INVITE message
BYE	Terminating a session initiated with an INVITE dialog
CANCEL	Canceling session establishment initiated by an INVITE message
OPTIONS	Queries the capabilities of the other side
REGISTER	Registering SIP user with the location service

Table 2.1: SIP basic methods

Additional SIP methods have been defined in numerous specifications produced by the IETF in different RFCs. From the point of view of this research, it is essential to consider the event framework as one of SIP extensions for the core specification. The RFC 3265 defines the SUBSCRIBE and NOTIFY methods which provide a general event notification framework for SIP [9]. This framework includes procedures for creating, refreshing, and terminating subscriptions, as well as the possibility to fetch or periodically poll the event resource. This event framework is one of the more convenient mechanisms when compared to e.g. HTTP, which is based on *request-response model*.

In order to use the event framework, extensions need to be defined for specific event packages. An event package defines a schema for the event data and describes other aspects of event processing specific to that schema. An RFC 3265 implementation is required when any event package is used. Therefore there are several events packages defined in different RFCs. For instance, the RFC 3680 defines the SIP Event Package for Registrations that enables the detection of changes in registration status, or the RFC 3856 defines an event package for the indication of user presence (status, activity, mood, etc.) [14]. Moreover, the RFC 3903 defines the PUBLISH method used by all event packages as mechanisms for pushing an event into the system [15]. The first application of this extension is for the publication of presence information.

Because the majority of the NOTIFY messages generated by the subscription refreshes do not indicate any change of the event state, and the subscriber usually is in possession of the event state already, the RFC 5839 [16] defines

2.2. Fundamentals of Multimedia Content Delivery 21

Class	Description
1xx	Provisional messages - used by the server to indicate progress, but they do not terminate SIP transactions (searching, ringing, queuing, etc).
2xx	Success answer
3xx	Redirection message
4xx	Request failure (client mistakes)
5xx	Server failure
6xx	Global failure (busy, refusal, not available anywhere)

Table 2.2: SIP request codes

an extension to RFC 3265 to optimize the performance of notifications. When a client subscribes, it can indicate what version of a document it has, so the server can skip sending a notification if the client is up-to-date. It is applicable to any event package.

Further SIP extensions have been defined in several RFCs for either a specific purpose or targeted application. The RFC 5411 [13] gives a good summary of these extensions that, unlike the core specifications, are not used for every SIP session or registration.

In the SIP session, message exchanges that last a certain amount of time are classified in SIP as either dialog or transaction. A dialog is a peer-to-peer SIP relationship between two UAs that persists for some time. A dialog is established by SIP messages, such as a 2xx response to an INVITE request. Such a dialog can be terminated with a BYE message at a later time. Depending on the type of session, dialogs can exist for a considerable amount of time, e.g. during a voice session or a video transmission. SIP transactions consist of a single request and any responses to that request, which includes zero or more provisional responses and one or more final responses. As such, any dialog is created from individual transactions. Transactions have a client side and a server side whereas a transaction builds a hub-by-hub relationship between each UAC and UAS, contrary to the dialog.

2.2.3.2 Session Description Protocol

The Session Description Protocol (SDP) is an application layer protocol defined by the IETF in RFC 4566 [17]. It is commonly used to describe multimedia sessions in real time in conjunction with the SIP or the RTSP (Real Time Streaming Protocol) protocol. It does not actually define a network protocol, as it does not have a transport mechanism or any kind of parameter negotiation. It defines a simple message format. It follows the *Offer-Answer model* where, for each received request (offer), a response (answer) must be created. Thereby the description of the multimedia session and the negotiation of the necessary parameters required for this multimedia session are realized. SDP is a text-based protocol like SIP and consists of a set of lines following the form type = value. The types are identified by a single letter and the format of the value depends on the type. Some lines in each description are required and some are optional but all must appear in exactly the same order. Table 2.3 lists most of the types defined in the SDP protocol.

Type	Description	Type	Description
v	Protocol version	b	Bandwidth
o	Owner of the session and session identifier	z	Time zone adjustments
s	Session name	k	Encryption key
i	Session information	a	Attributes
u	URL containing a description of the session	t	Time interval when the session is active
e	E-mail address to obtain information about the session	r	Repetition time
p	Phone number to obtain information about the session	m	Transport protocol information (media line)
c	Connection information		

Table 2.3: Type defined by SDP

2.2.3.3 Media Processing Control Protocols

In order to make use of media server functions, a controller, an application server or a user agent can request a function via a dedicated control protocol. Currently, there are two control protocols for controlling the media server used in the industry, H.248/MGCP and SIP. In a VoD session a user agent may also use the RTSP (Real-Time Steaming Protocol) to control media stream, as follows:

1. **Real-Time Steaming Protocol (RTSP)**: The RTSP is an application layer following client-server control model as defined by the IETF in RFC2326 [18]. It is designed to control the delivery of multimedia streaming data such as the VoD it establishes and RTSP is the "network remote control" between the server and the client. It provides remote control functionality for audio and video streams, such as play, pause, fast-forward, reverse, and absolute positioning. The data source can be live or stored content. It is designed to work with other protocol like SDP, RTP and RSVP to provide a complete streaming service over IP-based network.

2.2. Fundamentals of Multimedia Content Delivery

2. **H.248**: This protocol was initially defined by the IETF with the name MEGACO in the RFC2805 [19] and then published by the ITU-T in different recommendations. It is used to control the media gateways following the master-slave control model in which the controller issues commands to be executed by the slave (media gateway). It is primarily specified to support media processing functions within a VoIP session, in particular between IP-based network and PSTN network.

3. **Basic Network Media Services with SIP**: The initial media processing control protocol that is based on SIP is the Basic Network Media Services with SIP, which is defined in RFC 4240 and is known as Netann [20]. It describes how to invoke only three simple operations in a media server using SIP, without any modification on SIP protocol, by using the user address or the left-hand-side of the URI as a service indicator. These three services are announcements, simple conferencing and scripted Interactive Voice Response (IVR).

4. **Media Server Control Markup Language (MSCML) and Protocol**: The MSCML is defined in RFC5022 as an alternative to Netann to partially address two of Netann's deficiencies, namely the unscripted IVR and advanced conferencing [21].

2.2.3.4 Real-time Transport Protocol

Real-Time Transport Protocol (RTP) is an end-to-end streaming protocol defined by the IETF in RFC 3550 [22]. It provides various mechanisms for the transmission of multimedia content such as video and audio streams. It is network and transport protocol independent; however, it is mostly used over UDP and thus can rely on unicast or multicast transmission modes.

Due to the unpredictable delay and jitter on IP networks, RTP provides a time stamping mechanism and packet numbering in order to ensure sequential packet rendering. Further, RTP defines payload type identifiers to specify the type of data being transmitted.

Since RTP is content and transport protocol independent, there is no guaranty that RTP data packets will arrive in order as they were sent. Packet reconstruction has to be done in the application level by using the information provided in the packet header.

While RTP does not provide any mechanisms for obtaining feedback on the quality of data transmission and information about participants in the on-going session, these issues are addressed by the control protocols like Real-Time Control Protocol (RTCP), RTSP or SIP. When an application requires a certain level of quality of service, RTP application can rely on any QoS mechanisms like the Resource Reservation Protocol (RSVP) [23]. Nevertheless, the RTCP is defined in conjunction with the RTP in RFC 1889 [22] in order to control the quality of the RTP media streams, so RTCP packets are sent periodically to all of the participants in the session. RTCP packets are stackable and are sent as a compound packet that contains at least two packets, a report packet and a source description packet.

2.2.3.5 Resource Management Protocols

DIAMETER was defined by the ITEF in RFC 3588 [24] as a successor for RADIUS [25] with additional extensions and improvements. The Diameter is defined in terms of base protocol and set of applications. The base protocol provides an extensible framework for the use of Authentication, Authorization, and Accounting (AAA) services. Each application is based on services of the base protocol in order to support a specific type of AAA requests. While applications may reuse the Diameter base protocol accounting commands, the base protocol is always used in combination with a particular application that implements the actual authentication and authorization. The protocol is designed with the objective of simple extensions to be added on the top of the base protocol stack. All Diameter clients and servers must use the base protocol in conjunction with at least one diameter application e.g. diameter relay agents only need to implement the base protocol since it does not need authentication or authorization functionality.

The Diameter is a peer-to-peer protocol and any diameter node can initiate a request. Diameter has three kinds of network nodes: servers, clients and agents. A diameter server handles the authentication, accounting and authorization requests from the clients. Diameter clients are usually the end devices of the network that perform access control and originate AAA requests. The agent provides relay, proxy, redirect or translation services. Diameter messages are routed according to the network access identifier of a particular user. The flexibility to define new Diameter applications and vendor-specific attributes allows customization without threatening interoperability. This feature of Diameter is recognized by standardization bodies worldwide and 3GPP chose it as the AAA protocol in IMS.

2.3 Network Architecture

This section provides an overview of the IP-based network architecture; from access technologies to NGN core networks, up to service environments.

2.3. Network Architecture

2.3.1 Access Technologies

The idea of broadband access from anyplace at any-time is becoming a reality due to advances in broadband, fixed and mobile access networks.

2.3.1.1 Wired Network

For years the major barrier to broadband connectivity has been the access network. The inadequate network infrastructure and the huge cost of new installations formed the well-known *"last mile problem"*, which hindered broadband access at home. Connecting each house to broadband access networks however, represents an unprecedented opportunity to set the stage for a vast range of new multimedia applications and added value services to residential users, expanding the customer base beyond the corporate environment [3].

Digital Subscriber Line (DSL) technology is a modem-based access technology that leverages existing twisted-pair telephone lines to transport high bandwidth data, such as Internet traffic, IPTV or VoIP. There are a number of similar forms of DSL technologies which differ mainly in upstream and downstream bit rate. Currently the Very-High-Data-Rate Digital Subscriber Line (VDSL) defined in ITU G.993 series enables symmetrical delivery up to 100 Mbps with support of QoS. Future generations of VDSL2 will permit significantly higher data rates compared to current VDSL2, because data rates up to 0.5 Gbps were demonstrated in the lab using technology for line bonding and crosstalk cancellation for DSL, also known as vectoring.

To break down the bandwidth bottleneck of the access over twisted pair cables and to satisfy the requirements for high bandwidth services, Passive Optical Network (PON) was developed which is a point-to-multipoint access technology in which passive optical splitters are deployed to serve multiple premises. Gigabit Ethernet-PON (GEPON) enables symmetrical delivery up to 10 Gbps on a single fiber, in which the capacity can be shared among 32 subscribers.

2.3.1.2 Wireless Network

The incremental enhancement of wireless technologies results in the consideration of wireless access technologies for delivery of interactive multimedia applications. There are three types of wireless access networks:

3GPP-based Wireless Access Technologies : The 3GPP access technologies have evolved towards all IP-based infrastructures. The objective is to provide very high throughput with support of mobility and QoS. 3GPP access technologies support bidirectional unicast communication channels in which an individual mobile user can access a wide range of interactive multimedia applications. For instance, the Long Term Evolution (LTE) is supposed to increase throughput (up to 82 Mbps downlink and 18 Mbps uplink) and decrease end-to-end latencies. Although the cellular network was primarily voice centric following the point-to-point communication model, 3GPP has extended the core network and the radio interfaces in release 6 in order to support efficient broadcast and multicast IP packet delivery. The related subsystem is known as Multimedia Broadcast Multicast Services (MBMS) [26], which allows for two transmission modes: the broadcast mode and the multicast mode. In broadcast mode, transmissions take place regardless of user presence in a defined area (e.g. serving cell), whereas in multicast mode solely those areas are supplied where subscribers need to be served according to an initiated Join request. Concerning the radio interface point-to-multipoint transmissions in downlink direction are introduced in order to optimize radio resources. MBMS offers limited capacity - approximately three channels at 256kbits/s. In the core network, the MBMS makes use of application-based multicast instead of IP multicast. In comparison to previous 3GPP releases, the Broadcast/Multicast Service Centre (BM-SC) is introduced as a complete new functional entity serving as the central controlling unit. It is connected to the General Packet Radio Service (GPRS) Support Node (GGSN) over the interfaces Gmb and Gi. The former interface provides access to the control plane functions, the latter to the bearer plane.

IEEE-based access technologies : IEEE-based wireless access technologies cover various wireless technologies with different targeted applications. For instance, WLAN (IEEE 802.11) is targeted to provide wireless connectivity for home or business users with a coverage up to 100 m. WiMAX (IEEE 802.16) was initially developed to enable the delivery of last mile wireless broadband access as an alternative to cable and DSL and is enhanced with mobility and QoS features (IEEE 802.16e). However, WiMAX 802.16m can provide four times the data rate when compared to the performance of the previous standard.

Digital Video Broadcast : The DVB standard was designed to broadcast digital TV services and has been maintained by the DVB project since 1993 [27]. DVB systems transmit data using a variety of approaches: over satellite DVB-Satellite (DVB-S), cable DVB-Cable (DVB-C), terrestrial DVB-Terrestrial (DVB-T) and handheld DVB-Handheld (DVB-H). As DVB-T is mainly targeted at stationary receivers and is not suitable for mobile devices, the DVB-H standard was proposed, which enhanced the physical and link layers of DVB-T to reduce power consumption

2.3. Network Architecture

and improve performance in urban indoor environments. DVB-H can achieve a capacity of 5 to 11Mbits/s on an 8MHz channel. Depending on the configuration, 20 to 30 channels at 256kbits/s should be possible. While DVB was initially designed to support broadcast transmission, there are several standardized solutions such as DVB-RCS (Return Channel Satellite), DVB-RCT (Return Channel Terrestrial) or DVB-RCC (Return Channel Cable) or DOCSIS (Data Over Cable Service Interface Specification) that have been developed to facilitate bidirectional communication channels, thus supporting interactive applications (e.g. VoIP or VoD) [28]. The efforts of DVB-IPTV (DVB-IPTV), the collective name for a set of open, interoperable technical specifications developed by the DVB Project, in order to facilitate the delivery of digital TV using the Internet Protocol over bi-directional fixed broadband networks, is the DVB project's answer to current activities in the sphere of IPTV. In addition to DVB's interactive middleware specifications, DVB-Multimedia Home Platform (DVB-MHP) and Globally Executable DVB-MHP (GEM) [29], which also include IPTV profiles, give the DVB Project a good standing in the IPTV world.

2.3.2 Transport

The transport nodes are responsible for routing multimedia packets from source to access networks with specific QoS. Two technologies, namely the IP multicast and the 3GPP Evolved Packet Core, are presented in the next two subsections, from efficiency and mobility perspectives, respectively.

2.3.2.1 IP Multicast

In an IP-based network, a terminal that wants to receive information related to a particular multicast channel, "joins" one or several content channels (e.g. expresses interest to receive content associated with this channel identified by an IP multicast group address). This information is processed in the routing layer of the core network and is used for optimizing the data delivery path. "Optimizing" means that, over connections shared by receivers of the same multicast channels, data is transmitted just once, even if it needs to be delivered to a large number of receivers. Once the terminal wants to terminate the session, it sends a leave message to the edge router. The protocol used to join or leave a group is called the Internet Group Management Protocol (IGMP) which is defined by the IETF for IPv4 in three versions, namely v1 RFC1112, v2 RFC 2236 and v3 RFC 3376. IGMP Version 3 (IGMPv3) enables fast channel changes since a single message could contain both join and leave information. For IPv6, the Multicast Listener Discovery Version 2 (MLDv2) defined in RFC 3810 provides functionality equivalent to IGMPv3.

In IP multicast, the implementation of the multicast concept occurs at the IP routing level, where routers create optimal distribution paths for packets (mostly UDP packets) sent to a multicast destination address spanning tree in real-time. The IETF defined Protocol Independent Multicast (PIM) protocol is used to calculate the optimal multicast trees across the IP network based on the Interior Gateway Protocol (IGP) route calculations. The IGMP defines four messages which are:

JOIN : generated by user equipment to indicate interest to receive multicast packets from a dedicated multicast group

LEAVE : generated by user equipment to indicate interest in stopping the reception of packets from a multicast group

QUERY : generated by the edge router to ask a user equipment which multicast groups it is member of.

MEMBERSHIP REPORT : generated by user equipment to report on the multicast groups it belongs to.

Recently, IP multicast has garnered considerable interest due to the rapid deployment of the IPTV systems in telecom operators' networks.

2.3.2.2 Evolved Packet Core

Recognizing the need for integration into a converged wireless environment of 3GPP and non-3GPP access technologies, 3GPP initiated the standardization of the Evolved Packet Core (EPC) as an all-IP architecture [30] and [31]. The EPC is able to support access control, subscription based resource reservations, security and seamless mobility between different access networks. The EPC contains a clear delineation between the control and the data path through the core network. Its main components are classified based on their functionality as follows:

- Subscription data entities (e.g. HSS, AAA Server, etc.) - store, update and are able to transmit notifications on the subscription profile of users and perform authentication and authorization;

- Control Entities (e.g. PCRF and Mobility Management Entity) - based on various functional triggers, they make policy-based decisions regarding connectivity, access control and resources required by a UE.

2.3. Network Architecture

- Gateways (e.g. Serving GW, Packet Data Network-GW, etc.) - forward the data traffic of the UE and ensure access control, QoS and mobility management according to the decisions made by the control entities.

Together these entities enable the provisioning of connectivity and the allocation of resources according to the profile of the user and based on the requirements of each application. The applications are considered external to the EPC architecture and are generically named Application Functions (AFs). The role of the Application Function (AF) can be taken by IMS architecture, by a service broker, by an intermediary node of the operator on the application path or directly by the infrastructures of third party service providers.

2.3.3 Real-time Multimedia Content Control in NGN

The initial specification of the NGN core is based on the IP Multimedia Subsystem (IMS), initially defined in 3GPP release 5 and further enhanced in subsequent releases - release 10 is currently being defined [32]. The specifications include [33]:

1. The logical architecture - functionalities of logical elements, a description of the interfaces between the elements, selected protocols and procedures.

2. user authentication and authorization based on mobile identities,

3. definite rules at the user network interface for compressing SIP messages,

4. security and policy control mechanisms

5. charging framework,

6. service control and

7. interworking with legacy and IP-based networks.

Since the IMS specifications are based on the Internet Engineering Task Force (IETF) protocols, other standardization bodies targeting the realization of all-IP-based infrastructure have adapted the IMS according to their business and technical requirements. The 3rd Generation Partnership Project 2 (3GPP2) defines the IMS as part of the IP Multimedia Domain (IMD), which contains the Packet Data System as well. Although 3GPP2 IMS is based on 3GPP IMS specifications, there are still distinctions between both systems due to the different underlying packet and radio technology. The ITU-T and the ETSI TISPAN NGN architecture consider the IMS to be a central function that offers control capabilities for delivering multimedia services [2, 1]. Since ITU-T and ETSI TISPAN NGN architecture follow a subsystem-oriented architecture, IMS elements and related functions are distributed in different subsystems, namely the IMS core for session control, the Resource and Admission Control Subsystem (RACS) for QoS and the User Profile Server Function (UPSF) for user database management. Furthermore, PacketCable adopted in version 2.0 specifications many of the basic functional entities and reference points defined in the IMS of release 6 [28]. However, it has been decided that the concept of common IMS for unifying all IMS standards' efforts from all bodies (3GPP2, TISPAN, CableLabs) will be in 3GPP at 3GPP release 8 and beyond.

The IMS is considered today to be the control overlay for the delivery of IP-based multimedia services over fixed and mobile access technologies. It has become the global standard for unifying service provisioning and forms the base for generic service concepts such as Fixed Mobile Convergence (FMC), triple/quadruple play, NGNs and IPTV.

2.3.3.1 IMS Architecture

The IMS is defined as overlay control layer on IP-based network for multimedia session management following the client-server paradigm and provides media processing and interworking capabilities with other IP-based network or circuit switch technologies. Due to the fact that all IMS core related issues are defined by 3GPP, the following discussion will follow 3GPP specifications according to release 8 (finalized by 3GPP recently) which consider four parts:

1. **IP Multimedia Subsystem Core Network** that comprises all IMS core related elements for provisioning of multimedia services including application servers.

2. **IP Connectivity Access Network** (IP-CAN) that provides for the transport of multimedia signaling and traffic. IP-CAN will maintain the services while the terminal moves. An example of IP-CAN is the 2G/3G PS Core Network and UTRAN. IP-CAN may contain Policy and Charging Control (PCC) that has the capability to provide QoS, and apply packet classification and policies. PCC also provide charging control based on service data flow. PCC architecture includes Policy and Charging Rules Function (PCRF), and Policy and Charging Enforcement Function (PCEF). The PCC is equivalent to the ETSI TISPAN Resource and Admission Control Subsystem (RACS).

3. **User Equipment**, where the IMS stack and all IMS-based services of the client are installed and enable the user to communicate with the

2.3. Network Architecture

IMS network through the IP-CAN. For IMS connectivity, the UE uses IMS IMS Subscriber Identity Module (ISIM) which stores IMS Public User Identity (IMPU) and IMS Private User Identity (IMPI).

4. **IMS Interworking** that defines signaling and media interfaces to other IMS or IP-based network and legacy circuit switches technologies, such as Public Switched Telephone Network (PSTN) and Global System for Mobile Communications (GSM).

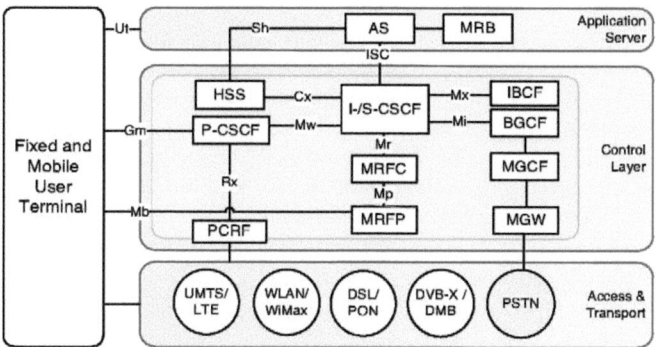

Figure 2.1: Overall IMS logical architecture

Figure 2.1 illustrates an overall IMS Core Network architecture; a detailed architecture that conforms to 3GPP Release 8 is depicted in Appendix A. The IMS core elements can be divided into five categories, as follows:

Call Session Control Function (CSCF) : There are four CSCF elements responsible for session switching in IMS network [32]. These are:

- Proxy CSCF (P-CSCF): The first contact point within the IMS Core Network. Its IP address is discovered by UEs during Packet Data Protocol (PDP) context activation or through the use the Dynamic Host Configuration Protocol (DHCP). The P-CSCF behaves like a proxy, accepting requests and servicing them internally or forwarding them. It performs functions like authorizing the bearer resources for the appropriate QoS level, emergency calls, monitoring, header (de)compression, resolving the IP address of the Interrogating CSCF (I-CSCF) and ensuring that SIP message contains Network Access Type

- I-CSCF: The first contact point of the IMS home network for all connections directed to a subscriber of that network operator, or a roaming subscriber currently located within that network operator's service area. There may be multiple I-CSCFs within an operator's network. I-CSCF performs functions like assigning an Serving CSCF (S-CSCF) to forward SIP messages and translates E164 addresses.

- S-CSCF: In charge of session control for the endpoint and maintains session state as needed by the IMS core network. The important functions performed by S-CSCF include user registration/de-registration and interaction with services platforms for user subscribed services on the Application Server (AS). The S-CSCF decides whether an AS is required to receive information related to an incoming SIP session request to ensure appropriate service handling. The decision at the S-CSCF is based on filter information downloaded from the Home Subscriber Server (HSS) during user registration. This filter information is stored and conveyed on a per application server basis for each user.

- Emergency CSCF (E-CSCF): Responsible for receiving emergency calls from P-CSCF and then routing the call to emergency call service after location validation (if connected to Location Retrieval Function).

Although 3GPP defines different interfaces between the CSCFs, all these interfaces use SIP as signaling protocol, but only with header modification according to element role. A detailed description of the IMS reference points and related specifications are provided in Appendix A.

User Profiles : HSS is the repository of user profiles and is equivalent to the ETSI TISPAN UPSF and the Home Location Register (HLR) in 2G systems. The HSS maintains user profiles of all IMS subscribers and service-related data of the IMS core network. The main data stored in the HSS covers user identities, security, registration information, and filter criteria. The DIAMETER Protocol is used in order to communicate with the HSS and the SLF and thus different interfaces are defined between both elements and the other IMS entities. Media Processing: The IMS includes two types of media-processing entities; namely the media gateways and the media server. Each type has an associated controller. A Master-Slave model is followed between the two, in which the controller is the master giving commands and the slave is the processing node performing actions (i.e. the gateway or the media server). The Media

2.3. Network Architecture

Gateway (MGW) or Trunking Gateway (trGW) provides transcoding and gateway capability between IP based streaming nodes (e.g. IMS UE or media server) and legacy Time-division multiplexing (TDM) nodes (e.g. PSTN or Public Land Mobile Network (PLMN)). One or a set of MGWs is controlled by the Media Gateway Control Function (MGCF) via the H.248 protocol. On the other hand, the MGCF interacts with the IMS core via the SIP. In case of deploying distributed MGWs in the IMS network, the Breakout Gateway Control Function (BGCF) is defined between the S-CSCF and the MGCFs in order to select the appropriate gateway for each call.

Resource Management : The IMS defines roles and policies that ensure the delivery of QoS-aware multimedia services based on user subscription. Therefore there are several functions distributed among several IMS elements which are:

- PCRF: Enables the communication between the IMS core (on the application layer) and the IP core (GGSN or packet data network gateway (PDN-GW)). Based on negotiated SIP messages between the two end IMS nodes and operator defined network policy, the PCRF provides policy decision and charging control functionalities to the PCEF. The P-CSCF sends session information (e.g. intended media traffic, destination IP addresses, ports, codec, etc.) over the Rx interface to the PCRF via the DIAMETER protocol. In turn, the PCRF provides the related policies and IMS Charging Identifier (ICID) to the PCEF over the Gx interface via the DIAMTER protocol [34].

- PCEF Provides policy enforcement of IP bearer resources, service data flow detection, QoS handling, and online/offline charging interactions. This functional entity is commonly located at GGSN in the 2G/3G PS case [34].

- Bearer Binding and Event Reporting Function (BBERF): Provides similar PCEF functions, which define the generic capabilities of PCEF for LTE and non-3GPP access network gateways.

- Media Policy Information: This information is stored as part of the service profile data, which is stored on the HSS. It contains an integer that identifies a subscribed media profile in the S-CSCF (e.g. allowed SDP parameters). This information allows IMS operators to differentiate between IMS subscribers. They may define different customer classes, such as gold, silver and bronze with various authorized media types (e.g. A gold user may use a HD video call, but a silver user only a standard video call). The S-CSCF is in charge of checking user requests against user authorized media profile stored in the user profile.

- Offline and Online Charging Functions: The IMS defines the architecture of online and offline charging systems that collect charging information from IMS nodes and transfer these data to the billing domain.

- TISPAN RACS: Contrary to the 3GPP PCRF, the RACS is defined by the TISPAN. RACS is responsible for elements of policy control, resource reservation and admission control. RACS also includes support for core Border Gateway Services (BGS) including Network Address Translator (NAT). RACS essentially provides policy based transport control services to applications. This enables applications to request and reserve transport resources from the transport networks including access and core network within the scope of RACS.

In spite of the fact that the RACS and the PCRF provide similar functions and use DIAMETER protocol, each has different protocol profile with various Attribute-Value Pairs (AVPs) supporting the same level of service. In the meantime, 3GPP has recently started an activity targeting the harmonization of the related reference points between AF and the PCRF and the RACS; namely the Rx and Gq', respectively.

IMS Interworking : There are two types of interworking interfaces with other network technologies, namely interconnecting with IP-based networks and TDM-based technologies. The Interconnection Border Control Function (IBCF) is used to interconnect with other IMS and IP-based networks. To interconnect IMS subscribers with circuit switch networks like PSTN or GSM, the BGCF, the MGCF and the MGW are defined as described in the previous subsection.

2.3.3.2 Media Processing

The Media Processing Function (MPF) is comprised of the Media Processing Function Processor (MRFP), which provides the processing capabilities and the Media Processing Function Controller (MRFC) that controls one, or a set of MRFPs. Media processing capabilities are defined to support telephony applications. These capabilities include streaming audio or video announcements, recording, transcoding and stream mixing (e.g. in a Conference Bridge). Application Servers can request these capabilities from the MRFC via SIP.

2.3. Network Architecture

In all cases of Application Server control, all session control requests that are passed between the Application Server and the MRFC are sent via the S-CSCF using the ISC interface and the interface of the Mr reference point using SIP protocol. Based on SIP messages the MRFC creates H.248 commands towards a dedicated MRFP. In addition to the session control requests, media control related commands and resources (e.g. audio message) may be passed between the Application Server and the MRFC using a new interface called Cr, which was defined in release 8.

On the other hand, the Media Resource Broker (MRB), which was defined recently in release 8, is a functional entity responsible for both the collection of appropriate published MRF information and the supplying of appropriate MRF information to the AS. The MRB supports the sharing of a pool of heterogeneous MRF resources by multiple heterogeneous applications. MRB assigns specific suitable MRF resources to calls as requested by the AS, based on MRF capability specified by the applications as well as other criteria. The Rc interface is used by the AS to request that media resources be assigned to a call when utilizing MRB. The details for how the AS uses the MRB for the media resource characteristics it wants for a particular call are not yet specified [35].

2.3.4 Service Environment

There are various alternatives to an NGN application server, which can be classified in two categories; namely, services hosted on one Application Server (e.g. SIP AS, JAIN, or OSA AS) or autonomous services built directly on top of IMS reference points (OMA enablers). The following subsections will focus on the technologies related to this research work.

2.3.4.1 Application Server Concept

According to the IMS specification, an Application Server (AS) provides the service logic and service creation environment for applications and services. The AS is intended to influence and maintain the various IMS SIP sessions on behalf of the services. It may act in five modes:

1. Terminating point for SIP signaling

2. Originating point of a SIP session

3. Redirecting or forwarding SIP requests acting as a SIP redirect server or a proxy server, respectively;

4. Third Party Call Control in which the AS interconnects two (or more) SIP UAs to a multimedia session whereas the AS invited the corresponding SIP UAs to a multimedia session by passing the SDP parameters among these SIP UAs (often without any modifications).

5. Back-to-Back SIP UA in which the AS acts as a termination point for SIP UA requests, but it initiates accordingly new SIP requests towards another SIP UA to get it involved in this session and thus it keeps controlling the entire SIP session. In this model, SIP UAs are not aware of each other (at least on SIP signaling level where SIP dialogs are built between the AS and the SIP UAs, but not among the SIP UA themselves).

Services in this instance refer to IMS services, which are based on the IMS reference points (e.g. instant messaging, presence, conferencing etc.). The advantage of the application server is that it enables IMS to operate in a more flexible and dynamic way, while the AS provides the system with more intelligence.

Native SIP services can be developed and deployed on a SIP application server. For this reason, there are several technologies for achieving this purpose: SIP servlets, Call Processing Language (CPL) script, Common Gateway Interface (CGI) and Java API for Integrated Networks (JAIN) APIs. Most of the current available AS solutions leverage the Java programming language and thus make use of all its provided mechanisms, like SIP servlets, JAIN SIP, JAIN Service Logic Execution Environment (SLEE) [36], etc. JAIN standardizes signaling protocols of the communication channels in Java application programming interfaces. In general, the SIP Application Server simplifies service development due to the availability of high-level as well as low level programming interfaces as depicted in Figure 2.2.

SIP Servlet API [37] was defined to simplify the development of SIP-enabled applications. By using the already existing servlet architecture, it is relatively easy for developers who are familiar with HTTP Servlets to create SIP enabled applications. Basically for each type of SIP message a method is defined to handle it. One example is a "doInvite" method that handles SIP INVITE messages. Currently there are many JSRs defined by the Java community as summarized in Table 2.4.

2.3.4.2 Open Mobile Alliance

In 2002 the Open Mobile Alliance (OMA) was established by many mobile networking players as a global organization for the standardization of mobile

2.3. Network Architecture

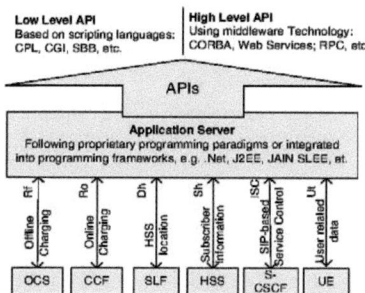

Figure 2.2: Application server interfaces

JSR #	Description	Comments
116	Initial specification of SIP Servlet as a high-level extension API for SIP servers to be deployed and managed based on the servlet model SIP generic APIs 289 Enhancement to JSR 116 to meet new industry requirements	SIP generic APIs
180	SIP API for J2ME defines a multipurpose SIP API for J2ME clients. It enables SIP applications to be executed in memory limited terminals, especially in targeting to mobile phones.	SIP generic APIs targeting J2ME
281	IMS services API provide a high-level API to access IMS core services (registration, QoS, media connection, etc.) by simplifying the API defined in JSR 180	Targeting general IMS core services but not specific applications
325	IMS Communication Enablers (ICE) define a high level API targeting Java ME based devices in order to access a set of dedicated IMS Enablers such as presence, messaging, PoC, etc.	Targeting dedicated applications

Table 2.4: SIP JSRs

services based on open global standards, protocols and interfaces and not dependent on proprietary technologies. Primarily, OMA stems from the Open Mobile Architecture initiative and the WAP forum. Currently OMA integrates many forums, such as the WAP Forum, Location Interoperability Forum (LIF), Wireless Village, Mobile Gaming Interoperability Forum (MGIF), etc. The design concept of the OMA can be considered as a step towards a Service Oriented Architecture (SOA). It enables the mapping of service elements onto the underlying network infrastructure and the integration with other enablers or applications with little effort. The modular elements used in OMA (enablers) have clear functional roles and a clear set of dependencies on one another. This means that a particular enabler may require some cooperation with other enablers. For instance, the Push-to-talk over Cellular (PoC) enabler makes use of the presence enabler and XML Document Management Server (XDMS) enabler.

OMA Presence Enabler OMA defines the architecture for the Presence Service Enabler, which includes a general network-agnostic model for mobile presence using the IETF SIMPLE specifications based on SIP and event framework introduced in the clause 2.2.3.1. The presence enabler is defined by the OMA in several documents, but overall architecture is defined in the architecture document [38]. The Presence Enabler manages user presence information that can be invoked from other enablers. Those enablers can assume one or more of the following roles:

- Presence Source: publishes Presence Information to the Presence Enabler;

- Watcher: subscribes to retrieve Presence Information from the Presence Enabler;

- Watcher Information Subscriber: subscribes to retrieve Watcher Information from the Presence Enabler; and

- XDMC: manages XML documents stored in the Presence XDMS, RLS XDMS (Resource List Server) and Presence Content XDMS.

The presence enabler is composed of the following functional entities:

Presence Server (PSE) is a network entity that is responsible for managing presence information on behalf of a presence entity. Aggregates information related with a presentity (i.e. Presence Entity) for watchers.

- Accepts and stores Presence Information published to it.
- Distributes Presence Information and Watcher Information.
- Retrieves Presence Information from Presence Sources.
- Regulates the distribution of Presence Information and Watcher Information in the manner requested by Watchers.

Presence Source (PSO) provides Presence Information to a Presence Service. The Presence Source can be located in a user's terminal with or within a network entity, which we refer to as Presence User Agent (PUA) or Presence Network Agent (PNA), respectively.

2.3. Network Architecture

Watcher requests Presence Information about a Presentity or multiple Presentities from the Presence Service. The Watcher can be located in a user's terminal or within a network entity.

Watcher Information Subscriber (WIS) requests Watcher Information about a Presentity from the Presence Service. It provides a mechanism for a user agent to find out what subscriptions are in place for the presence event package. The related subscription event package is known as winfo. The Watcher Information Subscriber can be located in a user's terminal or within a network entity.

Resource List Server (RLS) is a network entity that accepts and manages subscriptions to:

- Presence Lists and Request-contained Presence Lists, which enables a Watcher to subscribe to the Presence information of multiple Presentities using a single subscription transaction; and
- Request-contained Watcher Information Lists, which enables a Watcher Information Subscriber to subscribe to the Watcher Information of multiple Presentities using a single subscription transaction.

Table 2.5 provides a summary of the functional entities of the presence enabler and the related mapping to the IMS architecture. In the case that the Presence Source (PS) is located in the network, it may interact with S-CSCF and HSS for collecting subscriptions and registering information. It can retrieve information from S-CSCF from the 3rd party register and with subscription to the reg-event package. Furthermore, the presence enabler makes use of the XDMS to store different type of XML documents, as follows:

- Presence XDMS which manages presence subscription rules and permanent presence state. It supports subscription to and notification of changes to stored documents.

- Resource XDMS which manages presence lists. A resource list is identified by a URI, and it represents a list of zero or more URIs. Each of these URIs is an identifier for an individual resource for which the subscriber wants to receive information.

Presence Content XDMS which is capable of managing media files for the Presence Service. The Presence Source can store a media file (e.g. icon) in the Presence Content XDMS and include a static URI pointing to that media file as part of Presence Information. The Watcher can use the URI to obtain the media file using XML Document Management Client (XDMC) procedures.

Presence Function	IMS
Presence Server	Application Sever (Presentity)
Presence Source	User Equipment & AS (Presentity)
Watcher	UE & AS (Watcher)
Watcher Information Subscriber	UE & AS (Watcher)
Resource List Server	AS (Watcher)

Table 2.5: Relationship of the presence enabler and the NGN core

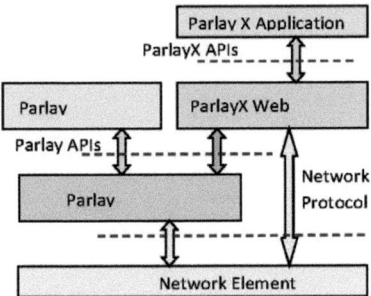

Figure 2.3: Parlay and Parlay-X architecture

The presence enabler is defined to be deployed on the top of any SIP-based network, but should be realized in an IMS-based network in order to utilize the IMS capabilities like SIP messages routing, user authentication, maintenance of the registration state and charging.

2.3.4.3 Service Openness

For opening network functions and capabilities, the Open Service Access and Parlay Group specifies a set of open Application Programming Interfaces (API) based initially on CORBA and later on Web services technologies [39]. The target is enabling application developers to conceive network protocol details and particular network sophistications by abstracting these functions through open standardized APIs. The design of Open Service Access (OSA)/Parlay APIs has evolved from the idea of mapping network functions into a set of standardized programming interfaces, called Service Capability Features (SCF) in OSA/Parlay terminology. Compared to Parlay, Parlay-X interfaces present more abstract and simplified interfaces than those of Parlay.

Figure 2.3 shows the relationship between the CORBA-based Parlay and the web-services-based Parlay X APIs over a network element. The parlay

2.3. Network Architecture

Gateway maps CORBA Interfaces to the network element functions with the corresponding protocol (SIP, SS7, INAP, etc.). Above that, Parlay applications can get access to these SCFs implemented on the Parlay Gateway through the CORBA APIs using any kind of programming languages.

The SCFs present the network functionality and provide the mechanism through which applications can access underlying network capabilities by invoking certain interfaces. SCFs can be run on Service Capability Servers (SCSs), which are the logical entities that implement the OSA APIs and interact directly with the core networks. Therefore the SCSs can be considered to be black boxes like the SIP AS. In contrast, the OSA/Parlay approach has the advantage of opening the network services towards the 3rd party providers and hiding network technologies and their protocols.

Furthermore, OSA/Parlay interfaces are not bound to any underlying network technology. As an example, the SIP AS is tightly coupled with SIP protocol whereas OSA is protocol independent from a developer perspective.

2.3.4.4 IMS-based IPTV

ETSI TISPAN and the ITU-T (among other standardization bodies, such as ATIS [4]) have been working on the specification of an IMS-based IPTV framework. In this section, we are going to introduce the ETSI TISPAN IMS-based IPTV architecture, which is still under definition in release 3 (which was proposed to be finalized at the end of 2010). Figure 2.4 illustrates the functional architecture based on the IMS core and other TISPAN transport and control functional elements; namely the NASS and RACS. The other functional components are as follows:

Application and IPTV Service Functions : This layer defines a set of ITV functions based on the IMS core and interacts with the UE either via the ISC, Ut or Xa interfaces. These functions are:

- IPTVService Control Functions (SCF): The SCF node is in charge of managing the IPTV session, triggering media functions and providing IPTV services. Session management includes session handling, user authorization, and checking user credit limit and credit control. Based on user capabilities and media delivery functions, the SCF select the relevant TV media functions provided by the MDF. The SCF behaves as an IMS application server thus it relies on the ISC interface and uses the UPSF to store user related IPTV service profile. There are multiple IPTV services specified, such as linear/broadcast TV (with or without supporting trick functions), time shifted TV, content on demand (CoD), network/client

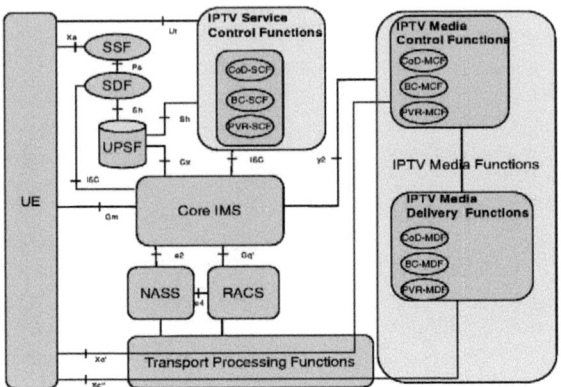

Figure 2.4: TISPAN IMS-based IPTV Architecture

Personal Video Recorder (PVR), interactivity, etc. For more information, we refer to the related standard [40].

- Service Discovery Function (SDF) and Service Selection Functions (SSF): The SDF and the SSF provide information to the IPTV subscriber about IPTV services. The SDF is in charge of generating and providing service attachment information to the customer according to his subscription and preferences (e.g. device capabilities or personalized setting). The subscriber can obtain such configurations after the performance of the IMS registration based on pull or push mode. The SSF provides a list of available services that the user can browse and select. For each IPTV service, the SSF delivers three types of information: (1) a service identifier that is used by the SCF and the media delivery function to serve user initiated requests; (2) network parameters needed for use during session initiation and (3) service description of each IPTV service.

IPTV Media Control Functions (MCF) and Media Delivery Function (MDF)
: IPTV Media Functions are responsible for controlling and delivering media flows to the user. The Media Control Functions (MCF) is in charge of controlling media delivery functions provided by one or a set of media servers (i.e. MDF). Within this context, it keeps tracking the status of the available media processing functions provided by the MDFs, and content distribution. Based on this information, it delegates media

2.4. Related Work

processing requests to a selected MDF. It enables the SCF to trigger the media processing functions via SIP and through the IMS core. On the other hand, the MDF is in charge of media flows delivery by applying the required media processing functions (such as encoding, transcoding, content ingestion, etc.), if required. Further, the MDF is responsible for content storage and may apply required protection.

User Profile Server Function (UPSF): The UPSF is the main data repository in the ETSI TISPAN NGN architecture and thus the IPTV services use the UPSF to store all user related data. The IPTV control elements (SCF, SSF, SDF and the IMS core) interacts with the UPSF via the Cx and Sh reference points via Diameter protocol.

IMS-based Session Control : IPTV services are IMS-based applications that use IMS protocols to initiate, modify and update session parameters. With this regard, UE has to host (e.g. the set-top-box or home gateway) shall install IMS protocol stacks in order to communicate with the IMS core and make use of IMS services (e.g. presence, messaging and telephony), as well as IPTV services.

Transport Control and Processing Function : The IPTV makes use of the NASS and RACS to control transport and access nodes for the delivery of video content with QoS to users.

In spite of the fact that the IMS-based IPTV specifications are in the final stages, there are no implementations available currently in the market. However, there are several IMS deployments around the world.

2.4 Related Work

Various research efforts tackle the problems of multimedia delivery over IP networks. As there were only limited research works in the IMS-based content delivery area available at the beginning of this dissertation, the essential requirements of the corresponding framework were published in [41]. The following subsections will present several research works related to this thesis.

2.4.1 IMS-based Streaming Platforms

An IMS-based architecture for delivering TV services has been introduced in [42]. Although the authors comprehensively discussed the interfaces between the user equipment (IPTV Terminal Function) and the network side, the paper does not explain how the IPTV service controls the media delivery components (media servers) for content delivery and media processing (if this is required). Furthermore, it is not clear how the content provider, the service provider and the network operator could be smoothly integrated in the value chain of the content delivery.

The authors of [43, 44] outline motivations, benefits and the feasible technical challenges in the IMS-based IPTV framework. The authors of [43] present an architecture to provide IMS based IPTV according to the ETSI-TISPAN deployed in the ScaleNet project [44] consisting of functional elements and the description of basic call flows to provide IMS based IPTV according to ETSI TISPAN. Their work describes an IPTV service called "*Click to Multimedia Service*".

2.4.2 IMS and Peer-to-Peer Integrated Architecture

Within the Ambient Networks project [45] service specific overlay networking for adapting multimedia content has been designed, which is based on a peer-to-peer communication model for service discovery and service path management for media delivery [46]. The authors introduce the integration of the overlay-networking for media processing into the IMS session, while assuming that the end-terminals are part of the overlay network and the IMS network. Since the overlay network - called Service-Specific Overlay Networks (SSONs) - already provides end-to-end session management, the integration of the IMS session will introduce an additional delay into the session setup between session participants. Unfortunately the paper does not provide any evaluation result for this concept.

2.4.3 Session Establishment

There have been several research efforts analyzing the signaling delay for the establishment of an IMS-based session depending on the type of access technology used: Munir [47] analyzed the end-to-end delay when the source is UMTS and the destination is WiMAX and vice versa. The signaling delay is analyzed separately for transmission delay, processing delay and queuing delay. Fathi et al. [48] studied the optimization of SIP session setup delay for voice over IP (VoIP) service in 3G wireless networks. Analysis of SIP-based mobility management in 4G wireless networka is introduced with some delay issues in [49]. Ulvan et al. [50] analyzed the end-to-end delay including the IMS core and terminals where the originating equipment and the terminating equipment connected either to UMTS or WiMAX access networks. In spite of these efforts, the evaluation of different SIP interactions models and the corresponding impact on the network is still missing. However, changing the

2.4. Related Work

interactions model of an application can have more impact on performance and efficiency than the signaling delay of the communication protocol used for that interaction.

In most VoIP network deployments, SIP is implemented over User Datagram Protocol (UDP) protocol. While the UDP is useful when carrying a small message size of signaling traffic, it is inappropriate for large message size (larger than the Maximum Transmission Unit (MTU)). However, new XML-based session description formats like presence information can increase this average size dramatically. For significant signaling loads, the fast retransmit algorithms and their congestion control mechanisms make Transmission Control Protocol (TCP) and Stream Control Transmission Protocol (SCTP) much better choices than UDP. Gonzalo C. et al. [51] evaluated the SIP protocol over the TCP, UDP and SCTP on a network simulator and compared the three transport protocols under different network conditions. They concluded that SCTP is somewhat better suited to signaling transport than TCP, providing a slight increase in performance from the end user's perspective.

Vingarzan et al. [52] conducted end-to-end performance measurements of the IMS signaling plane using the FOKUS open IMS core [53]. The test cases focused on voice call sessions in which the IMS clients communicated over different wireless technologies such as wireless LAN 802.11b and 802.11g, 3G Universal Mobile Telecommunications System (UMTS) and GPRS. The objective of the work was to determine whether or not each of these wireless technologies was a suitable access technology for supporting IMS-based services. While the performance measurements conducted in this work were based on two SIP methods, namely the SIP Register and SIP Invite methods, the evaluation of different SIP transactions in respect to different types of multimedia applications was not considered.

2.4.4 Multimedia Content Delivery

In a managed network multimedia, content can be transmitted in either unicast or multicast delivery modes using RTP (over UDP), as discussed in 2.2.1. However, due to some limitations in the use of IP multicast in the Public Internet (which is an unmanaged delivery network as discussed in 1.3.1), Application Layer Multicast (ALM) [54] techniques have been proposed where the ALM is implemented by network endpoints as discussed in 2.2.1.2. ALM has been further refined with different approaches being proposed that optimize the routing of packets within the overlay network and also by combining IP multicast with overlay multicast in a hybrid approach [55].

In contrast to content provided over a managed network, the OTT providers' content delivery is based on the best-effort model and thus the OTT service providers do not have any way to allocate network resources for guaranteed service delivery. The lack of end-to-end QoS allocation and in particular on network access has led to the use of adaptive streaming protocols that are mainly based on HTTP (over TCP), such as the HTTP Live Streaming Protocol which is still an IETF draft at the time of writing this dissertation [56]. However, some proprietary implementations are already available such as Microsoft Smooth Streaming [57] and Adobe HTTP Dynamic Streaming [58].

2.5 Discussion

This chapter has introduced the fundamentals of multimedia content delivery together with the related network architectures in NGN and service environments. The benefits and drawbacks of the broadcast, multicast and unicast multimedia content delivery modes were discussed for a better understanding of the scenarios in which they can be applied. While the broadcast and multicast delivery modes have inherent scalability and efficiency, the unicast mode is more suited to personalized and interactive multimedia content delivery, such as VoD services or personalized advertisement. Therefore the content delivery platform needs to make use of all these transmission modes according to the situation/environment of a user.

Common control models for content delivery in IP-based network are classified in three classes; (1) centralized control model such as the client-server and master-slave model, (2) decentralized control model like P2P overlay and (3) session-based control model like state-full applications (e.g. VoIP service). Each of the control models has benefits and drawbacks, but the most efficient model for content delivery is the session-based control model, as it enables efficient and fair utilization of network resources (e.g. QoS and content adaptation).

Multimedia delivery protocols are classified into three categories: (1) Signaling protocols that manage the entire session between content source and recipients and trigger the required network resources for content adaptation, such as SIP and H.248; (2) Transmission Protocols that are used to transfer multimedia content stream or data like RTP or HTTP protocols and (3) Resource Management protocols are used to carry authentication, authorization and accounting messages like Diameter. In an NGN environment, a multimedia session may involve more than one protocol; therefore the selection of a specific interaction model associated with the chosen protocol(s) is significant for resource usage efficiency and performance in content delivery. However, the SIP (with 3GPP specific extensions) is the main signaling protocol in the

2.5. Discussion

NGN. It enables session establishment, modification and termination. A session can be any network connection a user initiates that lasts for a certain time e.g. voice call, VoD session, gaming and so on.

The idea of broadband access from anyplace at any-time over any access medium still presents a challenge. While the broadband fixed access technologies (such as DSL and PON) support the unicast and multicast delivery models, the wireless technologies still face problems. First, although the 3GPP MBMS extends the radio and core with multicast and broadcast capabilities, there is no MBMS deployment available in the market today. Second, it is expected that all IEEE wireless technologies support unicast and multicast transmission modes, but we still experienced many problems with multicast over WLAN in our lab experiments (these problems were, however, traced to deficiencies in the WLAN manufacturer's protocol stack implementation). Third, while the DVB-MHP and GEM extend the DBV with interactive middleware specifications, the DVB is still considered to be broadcast technology. Thus, operators will probably never take DVB into account when it comes to personalized interactive scenarios where AAA (Authentication Authorization and Accounting) and QoS features are to be taken into consideration.

Various IP-based converged wired and wireless network architectures for delivering multimedia content have been presented. The main focus has been on the control and application layers, as they are responsible for session management and content adaptation in an NGN environment. Recently, the IP Multimedia Subsystem (IMS) has gained global acceptance by telecommunication and cable operators as an access agnostic control layer for delivering multimedia services and thus several deployments of the IMS are running over fixed and mobile networks in different countries worldwide. The market forecast of global revenue from IMS components is that it will grow from USD 1612.6 million in 2008 to USD 7964.3 million in 2012 at a CAGR (Compound Annual Growth Rate) of 49.1% and the user equipment market will grow from USD 3.88 billion in 2008 to USD 34.86 billion in 2012 at a CAGR of 73%, according to a Bharat Book Bureau report [33]. On the other hand, the analysts forecast that the number of global IPTV subscribers will grow from 41.2 million at the end of 2010 to 101.7 million in 2014, a compound annual growth rate of 25.3% [59].

Three categories of multimedia services are currently offered by the telecommunication operators through different service delivery platforms. The first category includes audio and video telephony services. The second category covers messaging, presence, gaming and file sharing. The third category covers the delivery of TV services (e.g. LiveTV, VoD with and without trick modes, local or remote Personal Video Recorder). In fact, there is a strong market demand for more sophisticated integration levels that will enable the "blending" of the capability of these services into innovative service packages offered to the end user with personalized and context-aware services providing users with an enhanced multimedia experience.

Extending IMS to support a set of generic service capabilities that collectively build basic service delivery functionalities will easy enable the development of new innovative services. The result of such integration is rapid cost-effective deployment and reduction in CAPEX and OPEX. Furthermore, multicast-aware content delivery through an IMS-based infrastructure will enable the delivery of new multimedia services like community services and E-learning applications on a huge scale.

Although the integration of generic multimedia service capabilities over the IMS will enable cross fertilization of multimedia services seamlessly, it will further introduce new requirements for the IMS infrastructure. These requirements will include multicast-aware multimedia session control, content management, content provisioning and efficient content delivery.

Developing IMS-based applications will lead to inherent complexity of the IMS in addition to the complexity in multimedia applications that may be composed of different communication channels to end users or to other network entities through multiple interfaces and various protocols. Furthermore, in a multimedia application, more than one party may be involved in the service delivery through multiple network domains including content provider, service provider and network operator.

At the time this dissertation was begun, there was only limited research work in the IMS-based content delivery area available, as discussed in 2.4. To differentiate from concurrent research efforts, this work:

- Provides an in-depth analysis of content delivery in general, in which the content provider, service provider and consumer are involved, rather than focusing exclusively on the delivery of TV services [60]

- Extends IMS session for content delivery over multicast and broadcast bearers [61, 62]

- Introduces service openness towards third parties and the enabling of interactivity and personalization.

CHAPTER 3
Media Delivery Core Requirements

3.1 Introduction

This chapter deals with the definition of the requirements and identifies potential functional requirements by ensuring efficient content delivery in an NGN-based network. Multimedia content delivery in an IMS-based control network is addressed by several standardization bodies, but they focus mainly on communication services. Although ETSI TISPAN, and recently the Open IPTV Forum, specify an IMS-based IPTV delivery subsystem, this effort is still ongoing and thus requires further study and investigation.

First, content delivery properties of key interest are discussed by identifying the real-time transmission and signaling properties, as well as the architectural properties for designing NGN-based multimedia applications properly. Then, the requirements of core functionalities are grouped and defined in three categories: multimedia content management, session management and content delivery.

3.2 Content Delivery Properties of Key Interest

3.2.1 Real-time Delivery Properties

Despite the continued evolution of access and transport technologies there are a set of common properties that will be considered for the delivery of multimedia content efficiently and with high quality. These properties are defined as following:

3.2.1.1 Audio Properties

For the evaluating of network performance for delivering real-time audio content, the following properties will be considered:

1. **Delay**: This parameter defines the elapsed time (delay) for transferring a packet from the source to the end user. So, if the delay is great enough

to be perceptible, then we have latency problems. For instance, most people begin to notice deterioration in conversational quality when the delay of voice is higher than 150 ms; and thus when it exceeds 200ms, they find it disturbing and describe the voice quality as poor. The one way delay of media stream is usually composed of four components:

- Propagation delay: the time to travel end-to-end across the network.
- Transport delay: the time to get through the network devices along the path.
- Encoding/Decoding & Packetization/De-Packetization delay: the time taken for the codec to digitize the analog signal and to construct packets/frames - and for the decoder to reproduce the original signal at the other end.
- Jitter buffer delay: the delay introduced by the receiver or network elements (e.g. wireless access point) to hold one or more packets, to damp variations in arrival times.

Furthermore, signaling delay adds to the total latency that has an impact on user-perceived quality, so that the performance of an action is measured in terms of its impact on the user of an application rather than the rate at which the network moves information. The primary measures for user-perceived performance are latency and completion time [6].

2. **Jitter**: Jitter is a variation in packet transit delay caused by queuing, contention and serialization effects on the delivery path through the network. In general, higher levels of jitter are more likely to occur on either slow or heavily congested links. The sending side sends packets at a regular periodic rate, say every 20 or 30 ms in a voice session. Ideally, the receiving side would receive the packets at the same rate, in which case there's no jitter. However, due to different factors, few packets arrive quickly while others arrive more slowly. If slow packets arrive too late, they are discarded to make way for the packet that follows them. There are different types of jitter that can take place in the network:

    - Constant Jitter: roughly constant level of packet to packet delay variation.
    - Transient Jitter: characterized by a substantial incremental delay that may be incurred by a single packet.

3.2. Content Delivery Properties of Key Interest 51

- Short Term Delay Variation: characterized by an increase in delay that persists for some number of packets, and may be accompanied by an increase in packet to packet delay variation.

3. Packet Loss: This parameter refers to packets that were not successfully delivered between two points. Lost packets appear as a momentary gap in the session, but some tiny gaps are acceptable according to traffic type. For instance, underneath the defined threshold of 0.1% a human listener wouldn't readily notice the gap in speech, however small packet losses can have large impacts if compression is used. Packet loss can be caused by a number of factors, including signal degradation over the network medium, congested network links, etc. The quality of service degrades most significantly when the loss is "*bursty*". A burst is generally considered a loss of a set of consecutive packets. Moreover, discarded packets at the receiver end, due to late arrival (i.e. missing the play out time of the jitter buffer), also contribute to packet loss even though the packets were successfully delivered to the destination.

3.2.1.2 Video Properties

The characteristic of video signal differs from audio signal radically, as the data rate created by a video signal is highly variable due to different compression techniques, image position, motion activity or selected resolution. All these factors have significant impacts on determining the required bandwidth for content transmission. Therefore, even for a network that can manage to allocate bandwidth for a dedicated stream, the amount of the allocated bandwidth either has to be the peak bandwidth required during the whole session or has to be changed over time to reflect the variability of video traffic. The first choice results in waste of bandwidth because the allocated peak bandwidth is not utilized all the time. The second choice is better in bandwidth utilization but is also more complex to implement, as network nodes should be aware of the state of content stream and the available bandwidth along the communication path. In general there are two types of video traffic:

1. **Linear streaming** where content is streamed without applying any buffering or caching mechanisms, as in the case of broadcast TV, live captured event or inter-active video conferencing. The requirements of QoS parameters (delay, jitter and packet loss) for both audio and video tracks can be considered equivalent.

2. **On-Demand streaming** where content is streamed by enabling buffering, caching and support of trick functions such as pause, stop, fast-forward and back-forward. On-Demand streaming has less stringent

QoS requirements since it is not delay and jitter sensitive (due to application buffering). However, On-Demand streaming might be used for important applications such as e-learning, e-health applications or webcast, in which case it requires a certain level of QoS.

3.2.1.3 Signaling Properties

It is also important to take into account the signaling traffic and related QoS parameters. Although signaling traffic is much less than media traffic, packet dropping of signaling traffic may result in a perceptible delay in session setup or channel zapping delay, which will be translated into a bad user experience. For instance, the ITU-T recommendation E.721 defines the mean values for IAM (Initial Address Message) end-to-end delay for session setup of an international voice session at less than 4 seconds. Unfortunately, the ITU-T has not defined the requirements of the session setup or channel zapping time yet, as discussed in G.1080 [63]. However, the channel zapping time should be less than two seconds in order to order to satisfy the user's QoE, as proposed to be standardized by the ITU-T in [64].

3.2.1.4 QoS Properties

As already stated, delay, Jitter, and packet loss represent the simplest evaluation approaches that could estimate the quality of the transmission path over various access technologies, network topologies, different routing mechanisms, and with variable QoS settings. In addition to these metrics, Peak Signal to Noise Ratio (PSNR) and Mean Square Error (MSEr) are the most common arithmetic metrics usually employed for the objective evaluation of audio or video signals [65]. These approaches are commonly applied in combination with subjective tests, which are based on Mean Opinion Scores (MOS) statistics in order to fully incorporate perceptual attributes of the audio or the video signal. MOS statistics are obtained by conducting live tests with human listeners in a highly controlled lab environment and collecting their feedback through a questionnaire for conducting audience surveys. Furthermore, subjective tests are very useful in cases where the impact of various parameters is not predetermined, often due to the characteristics of the content itself.

Therefore access and transport technologies have to define and maintain a set of traffic characteristic parameters to ensure the efficient delivery of signaling and media traffic. Most of these variables are defined by different access and network technologies such as in ATM (Asynchronous transfer mode), Ethernet IEEE 802.1p, or 3GPP TS23.207 [66]:

Resource Type Classifier : A scalar value which refers to a set of parame-

3.2. Content Delivery Properties of Key Interest 53

ters which determine packet forwarding characteristics on the access as well as across the routing path. Network nodes could make use of this parameter in order to distinguish different type of data flows and thus implement related policies. In general, flows are classified in two categories: (1) Guaranteed Bit Rate (GBR), (2) non-Guaranteed Bit Rate (non-GBR).

Upstream Maximum Bit Rate (UL MBR): indicates the authorized maximum bit-rate for the uplink traffic originating from the UE towards the network. UL MBR can be maintained for each data flow or for total traffic. Downstream Maximum Bit Rate (DL MBR): It indicates the authorized maximum bit-rate for the downlink traffic towards the UE. DL MBR could be maintained for each data flow or for total traffic.

Upstream Guaranteed Bit Rate (UL GBR): indicates the authorized guaranteed bit-rate for the uplink traffic originating from the UE towards the network. UL GMBR can be maintained for each data flow (e.g. voice traffic) or for total traffic.

Downstream Guaranteed Bit Rate (DL MBR): indicates the authorized guaranteed bit-rate for the downlink traffic originating from the network towards the UE. DL GBR can be maintained for each data flow or for total traffic.

3.2.2 NGN Architectural Properties

One of the goals of this dissertation is to provide design guidance for the task of selecting or creating the most appropriate architecture for delivering multimedia content in IMS-based networks, keeping in mind that an architecture is the realization of an architectural design and not the design itself. An architecture can be evaluated by its run-time characteristics, but we would obviously prefer an evaluation mechanism that could be applied to the candidate architectural designs before implementation. Unfortunately, architectural designs are notoriously hard to evaluate and compare in an objective manner. Like most artifacts of creative design, architectures are normally presented as a completed work, as if the design simply sprung fully-formed from the architect's mind [6]. In order to evaluate an architectural design, we need to examine the design rationale behind the requirements it places on a system, and compare the functions derived from those requirements to the target of efficient multimedia content delivery.

The first level of evaluation is set by the application's functional requirements, which will be discussed in more detail in the next subsection. However, in practice, other properties shall be taken into consideration, such as the efficiency of interaction models and the delivery properties of multimedia sessions, discussed above.

Fielding [6] defines a set of properties used to differentiate and classify architectural styles. I have included only those properties that are clearly related to our subject in the following subsection. In general, *efficiency is defined in 1.4 as the ability to delivery multimedia content with minimum usage of network resources*. However, in order to determine the efficient content delivery methods and interaction models the real-time properties defined in the previous section as well as the architectural properties introduced in the following clauses will be considered in this thesis.

3.2.2.1 Performance

The performance of a multimedia application is bound first by the application requirements, then by the chosen communication model (e.g. push method, pull method, client-server, peer-to-peer, master-slave, etc.), followed by the realized architecture, and finally by the implementation of each component [6]. The performance can cover:

Network performance measures the efficiency of network resource usage, such that the solution can effectively minimize use of the network when it is possible to do so. Network performance can be described through a set of communication attributes such as throughput, overhead, bandwidth, etc. A style (solution) impact network performance by their influence on the number of user transactions and the granularity of data elements. For instance, a protocol that encourages small interactions will be efficient in an application involving small data transfers among known components.

User-perceived performance QoS measures the impact of a transaction on the user of an application. The primary measures for user-perceived performance are latency and completion time. Latency is the time period between sending a request and receiving the response. The difference between an action's completion time and its latency represents the degree to which the application is incrementally processing the data being received.

3.2.2.2 Scalability

The scalability refers to the ability of the solution to support large numbers of entities, or transactions among system entities. Scalability can be improved

3.2. Content Delivery Properties of Key Interest

by simplifying entities, or by distributing functions across scalable network entities. The type of communication influences these factors by determining the location of application state, the extent of distribution, and the coupling between entities.

3.2.2.3 Mobility Support

The mobility refers to the ability of the architecture to enable its entities (e.g. user) to move across different networks while performing transactions with other entities. The SIP is an example where a SIP UA may change the physical location - accordingly IP connectivity - and still be able to interact with SIP network.

3.2.2.4 Reliability

Reliability, with respect to communication styles, can be considered the ability of a protocol to transfer data among protocol entities consistently. Furthermore, it can be viewed as the degree to which architecture is vulnerable to failure at the system level in the presence of partial failures within its entities. A proposed protocol, for example, can improve reliability by avoiding packet loss and single points of failure, enabling redundancy, allowing monitoring, or reducing the scope of failure to a recoverable action.

3.2.2.5 Visibility

Delivery styles or protocol can also influence the visibility of interactions within an IMS-based application by restricting interfaces via generality or providing access to monitoring. Visibility in this case refers to the ability of a component to monitor or mediate the interaction between two other components. Visibility can enable improved performance via the shared caching of interactions, scalability through layered services, reliability through reflective monitoring, and security by allowing the interactions to be inspected by mediators (e.g., network firewalls). The peer-to-peer communication model is an example where the lack of visibility may lead to security concerns.

3.2.2.6 Simplicity

The primary means by which delivery style or protocol induces simplicity is through the application of the principle of separation of concerns to the allocation of functionality within components. If functionality can be allocated such that the individual components are substantially less complex, then they will be easier to understand and implement. Likewise, such separation eases the task of reasoning about the overall architecture. Applying the principle of generality to architectural elements also improves simplicity, since it decreases variation within an architecture.

3.3 Core Functionalities

The continued innovations in Web technologies has enabled today's Internet to deliver multimedia streaming services ranging from classical video telephony to interactive TV services as well as other media rich services. The fact is that service providers, who operate over the top of the telecommunication domain, exploit the availability of broadband networks for delivering multimedia services with high quality, as explained in chapter 2. This leads to a global competition for customer ownership among service providers, network operators and access providers. On the other hand, value added telecommunication services and related service delivery platforms have not fulfilled their promises to establish an open services market in the past.

The standardization of the IMS represents the natural consequence in face of this dilemma by combining traditional telecommunications concepts and Internet service technologies. The IMS can be considered an overlay control subsystem over heterogeneous access networks that enable fixed and mobile convergence and the support of service mobility across various access and operator networks. Furthermore, as it defines standardized interfaces towards the application layer, the deployment cycle of IMS-based applications is expected to be reduced compared to existing approaches.

Building multimedia streaming services based on the IMS shall utilize the NGN basic capabilities such as user authentication, media authorization, access agnosticism, and user availability through different devices due to registration management, session handling, and negotiation of device capabilities. Common scenarios for IP-based streaming services already available in the market are IPTV and web-based (HTTP-based) content streaming such as YouTube, as described in chapter 2. Although IPTV is based on a managed end-to-end delivery model in order to enhanced user perceived quality of service, the IMS-based content streaming framework shall support both models; namely managed and un-managed content delivery.

Since content streaming is real-time critical, the efficiency for content delivery shall consider three types of traffic; signaling, resource management and media. Signaling traffic (e.g. SIP messages) shall be sent when it is required with the right protocol and suitable method. Resource management messages should be minimized and network nodes should possibly have self-management mechanisms (i.e. autonomic control of resources decision-making-elements and

3.3. Core Functionalities

mechanisms that can be incorporated into the device architectures and overall network architecture). Media traffic shall use the available and suitable transport channel using either unicast, multicast or broadcast mode and according to defined policies or criteria. Further the access and transport core networks shall achieve media quality metrics as defined in subsection 3.2.1.

As recent application development is based on service openness and follows a SOA architecture, the proposed delivery framework shall provide basic delivery services for multimedia content with defined open interfaces accessible from any 3rd party application.

As the IMS core provides functions that support SIP session management, but with limited scope of application logic, the application layer shall be in charge of session handling and management among several players ranging from content provider, to service provider and up to consumers.

In this context, the next subsections will define the detailed requirements for the application layer functions that are classified into three categories, namely; multimedia session management, multimedia content management and content delivery functions.

Figure 1.4 illustrates the relational diagram showing the inter-relations of the above system functional entities with each other and with other components (i.e. content providers, users, IMS core, etc.). The requirements derived in this section can then be mapped to these relationships. In this regards, the next subsections address the detailed requirements for specific functional entities.

3.3.1 Multimedia Content Management

A multimedia application may be composed of several content components (e.g. video, audio, image, text, etc.) provided by several content providers. Therefore, each content component shall have a unique identifier that identifies the content component within the service provider domain.

There are different delivery use cases of multimedia content originating from the content provider, as follows:

1. Content provider delivering multimedia content to one or a set of targeted end users like the push to talk application, which end user can select a set of users from his address book to send them a multimedia message.

2. Content provider publishing or uploading multimedia content to a web-portal like YouTube

3. Content provider broadcasting multimedia content like TV or radio channels

4. Service provider requesting multimedia content form a dedicated content provider.

Service provider may have business relationships with several content providers. Therefore the framework shall support dynamic mechanisms for content publishing and discovery, so the content provider can announce the status of any multimedia content in production or available for acquisition and the service provider can find this content.

Service Providers shall be able to control the delivery of multimedia content originating from one or a set of content providers. Multimedia content available in the service provider domain or in the media delivery network (either stored or live) must be managed in order to be sent to the consumer. As content capturing is a task related to the content provider domain, it does not need to be considered here.

3.3.2 Multimedia Session Management

Delivering any type of multimedia content to a set of end users in different contexts and with various business relationships with the service provider requires session handling and management. With regards to content delivery, user context may include the capability of user equipment (supported audio/video codecs, network devices, display resolution, etc.), user location, available access networks and user presence status. However, other physical or environmental context information can be considerable as well. Therefore the framework shall make use of context information in order to adapt the content and network resources To attract user interest in any multimedia application or content stream, announcement and discovery are essential steps before starting with the content delivery process. Therefore the framework shall provide mechanisms in order to allow the user to discover, search and indicate his interest in any published multimedia content, whether it is via the public Internet or within a closed community or service provider domain.

Multimedia content may be delivered to the end users based on either the pull or push model:

- The pull model shall enable the end users who are interested in any multimedia content (live or stored) to acquire the content from the network by sending a message request.

- The push model shall enable an application to request the session manager to send multimedia content to one or a set of users.

A large number of end users may be interested in a particular multimedia content. For instance, a live event such as a world cup football match, music

3.3. Core Functionalities

concert or any other event in which a considerable sized audience accesses the event. Therefore the system must be able to handle the associated signaling traffic and allocate required media delivery resources and processing functions.

As users are in different contexts, the session manger need to provide tools to adapt multimedia content in order to satisfy user perceived quality of experience. Multimedia content might be generated with best quality (e.g. HD video) and encoded with uncompressed codec. Therefore the session manager shall trigger the media processing element in order to transcode or reduce video stream resolution. In a media delivery session involving a large audience, multi-mode communication channels shall be used in order to reduce the impact of media streams on transport and access networks.

Due to the continuous deployment of new broadband access technologies, in the near future a significant growth of the heterogeneous wireless environments is expected, in which mobile devices will have interfaces to different radio technologies simultaneously and thus have the choice of deciding the access method used to retrieve multimedia content. Therefore, personal and session mobility are essential features the support of which should be considered in advanced multimedia applications. The SIP protocol provides the required methods to support both features; namely via the SIP REGISTER and SIP REFER methods [67], respectively. Regarding session mobility the SIP REFER method is the primary tool used for session transfer in SIP network, however session state should be maintained by the corresponding user agents (e.g. the IMS application server).

The session manager shall provide open interfaces in order to support a multi-service provider model. Each supported basic function (e.g. push multimedia content) shall be exposed with an open interface. Furthermore, the session manager shall maintain awareness about current user multimedia activity (e.g. current watched TV channel or movie) and enable a third party application to obtain such information while maintaining user privacy.

This framework shall be responsible for the entire session handling and management during the whole process of the content delivery from content provider to the end user; however it shall support the multi-service provider model in order to enrich domain-oriented applications (e.g. e-health, e-learning or e-government) with multimedia content.

3.3.3 Content Delivery

The demand of multimedia services has resulted in the evolution of various communication technologies and frameworks, in both mobile and fixed domains. These technologies, still in their infancy, have their own benefits and shortcomings based on different deployment environments and service scenarios. For instance, existing IPTV or mobile TV solutions provide their services only within the operator domain. Further, Internet streaming portals like YouTube offer multimedia content without any adaptations to the capabilities of user devices.

In general, a key objective of the technology evolution is to offer end users adaptable and context-aware communication services that have an impact on how we communicate and how we find the right content at any place and any time. The exponential increase of end-users who consume or produce multimedia content with various terminals and through different access networks leads to the need for flexible processing capabilities that support efficient content delivery to heterogeneous devices.

Two classes of media delivery functions are required during content transmission between content provider and end users. The first class covers the transfer functions of multimedia content from content provider to end users with or without changing content quality. This class shall support the following functions:

1. Fetching stored multimedia content from the content provider through either pull or push mode

2. Storing the multimedia stream received from the content provider

3. Streaming stored multimedia content to end users with or without trick function support (e.g. play, pause, fast-forward and fast-backward)

4. Relaying the received multimedia stream from content provider to a set of recipients over multi-transport modes (i.e. relaying content from a unicast channel to a multicast channel).

The second class covers the media processing capabilities that could be applied while delivering multimedia content to end users. These capabilities refer to a set of functions such as:

1. Transcoding function that converts the content from one format into other format (e.g. from H.264 into H.263)

2. Adapting content by scaling down the resolution or data rate without changing the codec

3. Content recording of content stream which is based on user (content provider) or application request.

There are several services that require flexible and efficient media processing capabilities such as:

1. TV services (live and VoD) that are transmitted over the Internet Protocol (IPTV),

2. Content casting services that offer multimedia content (e.g. news, sport, weather, etc.) to a set of subscribers as a regularly scheduled service,

3. Personalized streaming services (e.g. personalized advertisement),

4. Location-based streaming services (e.g. tourist guide), etc.

Therefore an application server shall be able to trigger these functions with an appropriate signaling protocol. One key issue is the performance of such a node in which media processing consumes a lot of processing resources whether hardware or software. Therefore load distribution and deployment aspects shall be considered during the design of the control protocol as well of the media processing node.

3.4 Summary

Telecommunication infrastructures are built as multi-layer architectures for the delivery of a large range of services. This dissertation examines the highest level of abstraction in the telecommunication architecture, where the interactions among multimedia content delivery components are capable of being realized within an IMS-based network. However, this dissertation aims to define a set of generalized content delivery functions in a multi-domain environment. These functionalities will enable the delivery of personalized and community-aware multimedia services efficiently and with low-cost.

In this chapter, the content delivery properties of key interest are initially discussed by identifying the real-time transmission and signaling properties found in the literatures as well as the architectural properties for the evaluation of different interaction models in the NGN environment. With this regard, a set of properties used to differentiate and classify interaction models and architectural styles are applied for benchmarking the developed solution. These are: performance, scalability, mobility, reliability, visibility and simplicity. However, it is not intended to be a comprehensive list, but only those properties are included that are clearly influenced by the set of technologies taken into consideration. Note that not necessarily all criteria will be applied to every evaluation. The list of criteria extends the criteria for classifying network-based application architectures defined in [6]. In this thesis, the real-time and architectural properties are both going to be considered in order to determine the efficient content delivery methods and interaction models for NGN-based multimedia applications.

62   Chapter 3. Media Delivery Core Requirements

Thereafter, the requirements of multimedia content delivery functionalities are grouped and identified in four categories: First, the NGN core is composed of session control (e.g. IMS) and IP transport supporting unicast and multicast packet forwarding, QoS and mobility functions. The identified requirements are:

1. The framework shall rely on the NGN core in order to utilize NGN basic functions.

2. The framework shall be accessible from and to both managed and unmanaged networks.

3. Signaling messages shall be sent with the specific protocol only when required and using a suitable protocol method.

4. The media path shall use the available and suitable transport channel (unicast, multicast or/and broadcast) in order to utilize network resources.

5. The access and transport core network shall support the delivery of real-time multimedia content streaming.

6. The framework shall expose delivery capabilities through defined open interfaces following the SOA paradigm.

Second, content management defines functional requirements that enable the service provider to obtain or receive multimedia content from multiple sources including professional and/or amateur Content Providers. The identified requirements are:

1. The content component shall have an identifier that is unique within the service provider and media delivery network.

2. The framework shall be able to manage different types of multimedia content delivery from the content provider to the end users or to the service provider domain.

3. The framework shall support content discovery and announcement mechanisms between the service provider and content provider.

Third, session management functional requirements include management and control functions for content delivery from multi-sources to multi-users over the NGN core. This entails the need of efficient and scalable control techniques in terms of session signaling procedure and utilization of various

3.4. Summary

transmission modes. In this regards, the IMS will play an important role for session negotiation and content delivery; however the current IMS specification does not consider the multicast capability for content delivery. On the other hand ETSI TISPAN has defined control and delivery functions for TV services only [40]. The identified requirements are:

1. User context shall be considered during session management in order to adapt content stream and optimize network resources.

2. Session manager functionality shall enable end users to request multimedia content based on pull model.

3. Session manager functionality shall enable the application to push multimedia content to a set of end users.

4. Session manager functionality shall be able to handle the large number of users interested in receiving multimedia content (live or store).

5. Session manager functionality shall be able to trigger media processing nodes to adapt the content according to user context.

6. Session manger functionality shall utilize the available transmission modes (unicast, multicast and broadcast) to optimize network resource usage.

7. Session manager functionality shall expose supported basic functions through open programming interfaces to enable the support of a multi-service provider model.

8. Session manager functionality shall maintain user multimedia activity and provide such information to other application.

Finally, content delivery and processing functional requirements are specified for the transmission and adaptation of multimedia content based on the capabilities of the consumer environment (e.g. device used, available access network and so on). The identified requirements are:

1. Media delivery node shall be capable of conveying multimedia content from content provider to end users with or without modifying content quality.

2. Media delivery node shall support media processing functions in order to satisfy user requirements and optimized transport resources.

3. Media delivery node shall enable the application to trigger media delivery and processing functions via an appropriate signaling protocol.

These requirements and challenges are published in [41]. From here onwards, the *term framework collectively refers to those set of multimedia content delivery core functionalities, unless noted otherwise*. The next chapter will discuss several interaction models and analyze these requirements in more detail in order to provide guidelines for the design of more efficient multimedia content delivery functionalities in the NGN environment.

CHAPTER 4

Major Design Aspects for Session-based Multimedia Content Delivery

4.1 Introduction

In the previous chapter several requirements for multimedia content delivery were introduced. In this chapter, these requirements will be further discussed and analyzed. Accordingly a conceptual model for media delivery is introduced and, based on the requirements defined in the previous chapter, several IMS-based signaling patterns and interaction models are analyzed in order to determine the optimal and most efficient methods for content delivery.

4.2 Overall Architecture

The requirements defined in the previous chapter introduce the properties of the targeted architecture with its functional and non-functional properties. Since the system includes several distributed players/actors in various domains, we refer to such an architecture as a domain-based system architecture. Each of these players is identified by specific roles and with a set of constraints. Each of these players can be defined as follows, as depicted in Figure 1.4:

1. The *Consumer* is the domain where multimedia content and related services are consumed

2. The *Content Provider (CP)* is an entity that creates, owns or is licensed to sell content.

3. The *Service Provider (SP)* is the entity that provides a service to the consumer. The service provider is the mediator between the content provider and consumer. It makes use of media control and delivery functions to provide the consumer with multimedia services.

4. The *Network Operator* is in charge of content delivery from the source (content provider) to the consumer and responsible for the required control and processing functions.

These players are defined - among other entities - by the Open IPTV Forum [5] and ETSI TISPAN [68]. Our definitions are general, rather than limited to only IPTV systems and related services. As the architecture embodies several players with different properties and behaviors, the communication (interactions) between these players (components) may follow various communication styles (model); such as client-server, peer-to-peer, event-based model, etc. A detailed classification of various architectural styles is described and evaluated in Fielding's dissertation [6]. He evaluates each of these styles for a given property depending on the type of system interaction being studied. To differentiate and classify architecture styles, the architectural properties defined in the previous chapter are used 3.2.2.

4.2.1 Multimedia Content Delivery Life-Cycle

In spite of all network-related delivery aspects, the delivery of multimedia content may undergo different phases, which are depicted in Figure 4.1:

1. **Advertisement phase**: this phase will allow the user (service provider or consumer) to get multimedia content information, which is referred to as metadata. This phase can be done during content production or after content creation. It provides content or service description and possibly facilitates discovering scheduled delivery time.

2. **Subscription phase**: this phase allows the user to purchase or subscribe to a particular multimedia content.

3. **Announcement phase**: In this phase, subscribed users get information about the available multimedia content/service and receive the scheduled content delivery plan. Note that the subscription phase should be completed before this phase. Also this phase may happen at the same time as the advertisement phase.

4. **Session Establishment phase**: In this phase, system entities negotiate media delivery parameters and setup required processing and delivery resources. Content delivery can be started directly after session setup or later.

5. **Resource Reservation phase**: During or after session setup, the required delivery resources are allocated in order to ensure a certain level

4.2. Overall Architecture

of quality of service according to user subscription and operator defined policy. Note that this phase might not be present in un-managed service delivery fashion (i.e. best-effort).

6. **Content Delivery phase**: In this phase, multimedia content is transmitted from the CP to the SP or from the SP to the consumer over the dedicated transmission model. However, media processing might be applied along the delivery path according to the session parameters negotiated during the session setup.

7. **Updating Network context phase**: During content delivery, the network context may change. For example, changing network context may be handover or switching between different resources (e.g. multicast addresses) within the same service. In the former case, horizontal or vertical handover occurs due to mobility or degradation over the delivery path. However, in zapping between several IP bearers (e.g. multicast address), for example, multimedia content is transmitted over several bearers with different quality (e.g. different codecs or resolutions/rate).

8. **End-to-End session update**: Whenever the network context changes and in order to facilitate content adaptation, session parameters have to be re-negotiated between the consumer and the service provider.

9. **Termination phase**: this phase will make system entities aware of the termination of the session or content delivery.

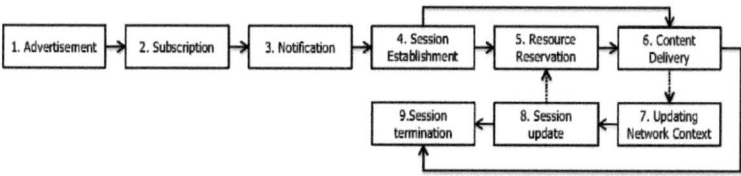

Figure 4.1: Network delivery phases

The next subsections discuss the functional requirements and analyze corresponding possible solutions by taking into account all the requirements defined in the previous chapter. As a result of the analysis, we suggest recommendations for the architectural framework and then provide an analytical evaluation of the resultant impact on network performance.

4.2.2 Evaluating the Interaction Models of Content Delivery

The evaluation of each solution will be based on its impact upon functional and architectural requirements. However, design evaluation is frequently a question of choosing between trade-offs. One of the possible evaluation methods is placing a numeric weight against each architectural property to indicate its relative importance to the architecture, thus providing a normalized metric for comparing candidate solutions. But, in order to be a meaningful metric, each weight would have to be carefully chosen using an objective scale consistent across all properties. Therefore, we follow Fielding's [6] evaluation method in which all of the information concerning the possible solutions is presented in a readily viewable form, and then the solution is intuitively guided by the visual pattern. This will be demonstrated in the following subsections.

A table of solution versus architectural properties is used as the primary visualization for the analysis. The table values indicate the relative influence that the solution (e.g. protocol or communication model) for a given row has on a column's property. Minus (-) symbols accumulate for negative influences and plus (+) symbols for positive, with plus-minus ± indicating that it depends on some aspect of the specific application. Although this is a gross simplification of the details presented in each corresponding subsection, it does indicate the degree to which a solution has addressed (or ignored) an overall architectural property.

4.2.3 IMS core Functions

According to the NGN core requirement defined in the previous chapter 3.4, the IMS core supports the following functions on the application servers:

1. User authentication and media authorization based on the subscription information stored in a user profile which is maintained by the HSS and downloaded during user registration by the S-CSCF and application servers. Therefore the application server does not need to re-authenticate the user again.

2. SIP messages routing among IMS nodes so that requests addressed to IMS users are routed to the destination locations (IP addresses) according to various criteria: first, registered IP addresses; second, user agent capabilities published during IMS registration, OPTIONS responses, and requests and responses that create dialogs (such as INVITE) [69]; third, caller preferences that indicate the type of targeted SIP user agent

4.2. Overall Architecture 69

(e.g. video support) [70]. However, forwarding requests to the application servers is derived from the filter criteria stored in the user profile or the Public Service Identifier (PSI) of the corresponding service.

3. Media delivery resources allocation such that the application server can request the required resources on the transmission path, and trigger content adaptation according to the end user subscription and device capabilities. To ensure user-perceived QoS, the IMS conveys session parameters to the corresponding transport and access nodes through the PCRF/RACS, and enables the application server to trigger media processing functions in order to adapt the content stream, as discussed in subsection 2.3.2.

It is important to note that the use of the concept of filter criteria invokes service logic in a peer-to-peer session, in which the application server acts either as a proxy or redirect server. The PSI, to the contrary, is applied for addressing services that act either as terminating or originating user agent or both, as discussed in subsection 2.3.2, which are sufficient for most of multimedia applications. From a network performance perspective, routing based on PSI requires less transactions among IMS nodes, when compared to processing filter criteria. Routing mechanisms of PSIs in IMS network are defined in detail in [71].

According to the NGN core requirement defined in the previous chapter [71], the IMS core may allow the subscribers to access IMS services from the public Internet, but the related media traffic will be delivered with best-effort without guaranteed QoS.

The IMS network uses several signaling and transport protocols, each of which has several functions and related methods. If we understand the functions supported by each protocol, then its behaviors and corresponding impact on the network performance give us an understanding of the overall design's architectural properties. The specific needs of a multimedia application can then be matched against the properties of the design. Comparison becomes a relatively simple matter of identifying which architectural design satisfies the most desired requirements for that multimedia application. With this regard, we need to first understand the functional requirements of the components needed for content delivery and the associated content and session management functions.

4.2.4 Content Information Provisioning Function

It is important to point out that the purpose of building multimedia applications is not to create a specific topology of interactions or use of a particular control protocol. It is rather to deliver multimedia information that meets user interest and satisfaction. With regard to this, as defined in the requirements of content management functionality in subsection 3.4, the targeted architecture shall support mechanisms to attract user interest to multimedia content that matches his preferences, needs and current context. On the other hand, production of multimedia content involves several phases, ranging from planning up to production. Therefore, *multimedia content information* is content-related information, which contains content related metadata such as content description, production status, content possessor and license, and shall be shared among the CP, the SP and the consumer. The content provider is in charge of providing such information. The related delivery mechanisms from the content provider to the service provider are discussed in the next subsection.

In this context, mechanisms like announcement and discovery functions, as defined in subsection 3.4, are initial key features of any multimedia delivery system. Therefore, a dedicated functional entity shall be in charge of managing multimedia content information among all system entities in order to support the nine phases defined above. We refer to the corresponding functionalities with the term Content Information Provisioning Functions (CIPF). Note that we limit our discussion to delivery mechanisms of metadata, excluding creation, processing, classification and interpretation. H. Kosch et al. [72] describe the life cycle of multimedia metadata and introduce different search and retrieval mechanisms for multimedia content based on stored metadata resulting from the production process. However, the related delivery mechanism is not considered.

From service provider perspective, multimedia content information is essential information that can facilitate:

- the discovery of multimedia contents in production, test, trial, or ready for delivery,

- the development of multimedia applications that compose or rely on such multimedia content components (e.g. combining two or more multimedia content in one service package or integrating an interactive component, like shopping, based on content information)

- the personalization of multimedia content information according to consumer preferences and context

- announcing associated multimedia applications to customers.

If the service provider does not create (or integrate different multimedia content components in) new or personalized multimedia service, multimedia content information provided by the content provider can be forwarded

4.2. Overall Architecture

to the consumers as is. Otherwise, it constructs for each multimedia service dedicated metadata that we refer to as *multimedia service information*, which comprises service-related information including service description, delivery information (e.g. sources like Internet Protocol (IP) or Public Service Identifier (PSI)), status, etc. The associated mechanisms for delivery to the consumer are discussed in the next subsection.

Likewise, multimedia service information, with its associated multimedia content, will enable the consumer to register interest in specific:

- multimedia content (e.g. content ID or based on classification)
- multimedia service (e.g. sport news, live orchestra, etc.) or
- content provider (e.g. CNN, person)

Sharing multimedia content information among system entities will allow, for instance, the SP to plan and possibly to develop multimedia applications, while the multimedia content matter is still (stored or not-yet-captured) in the content provider premises. This leads to the improvement of network performance and system scalability.

From the CIPF point of view, the following system entities will have different roles, as depicted in Figure 4.2. These are:

Content Information Publisher (CIP) is the entity that publishes multimedia content information to a set of interested entities (e.g. the SP or the consumer directly). The content provider is in charge of this functional entity.

Service Information Publisher (SeIP) is the entity that publishes multimedia service information to a set of interested consumers. The service provider or 3rd party application is in charge of this functional entity.

Content Information Watcher (CIW) is the entity interested in multimedia content information. The service provider or the consumer can act as CIW in order to retrieve multimedia content information.

Service Information Watcher (SIW) is the entity interested in multimedia service information. The consumer or other application can act as SIW in order to retrieve multimedia service information.

The CIPF is the rendezvous point that manages multimedia content information and multimedia service information among the above functional entities. The next subsection discusses the CIPF functions and the interaction models between the CIPF and these functional entities.

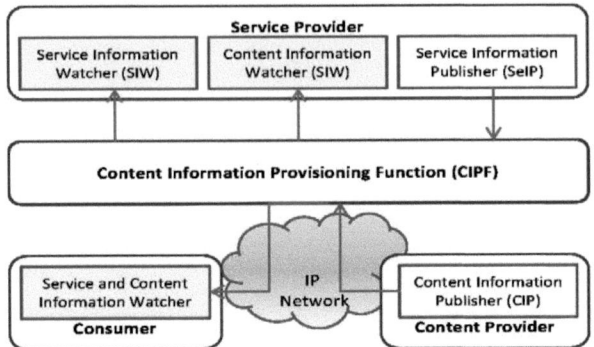

Figure 4.2: Content Information Provisioning functional entities

4.2.4.1 Functional Requirements

As stated above, two functions must to be supported:

1. Announcement function facilitates the content provider in the publishing of multimedia content information to one or more service providers. Further, it enables the SP to announce multimedia content information and multimedia service information to potential users whose context and/or preferences match such content.

2. Discovery function allows the SP or end users to find out the information related to any particular multimedia content or multimedia service, which are available, scheduled for transmission or not yet in production.

Both functions can assist the entire life-cycle of multimedia content delivery by sharing multimedia content information among system entities. Multimedia sessions with a live streaming content component (or linear delivery, as defined in 3.2.1.2) can take advantage of all provisioning functions during all nine phases of life-cycle of content delivery, defined in 4.2.1, by enabling watchers interested in the live stream, to monitor the delivery state and possibly the remaining transmission time of simultaneous multimedia content streaming. In contrast, an on-demand (unicast) streaming or download session cannot be facilitated from the provisioning functions during session establishment and the delivery phases among a set of watcher because multimedia content is typically stored content and thus each user can acquire it over unicast transmission modes at any time, whereas live or linear streaming is always set to a defined schedule and for a terminated time interval.

4.2. Overall Architecture

The communication between the CIPF and the four entities, namely the CIP, the SeIP, the CIW and the SIW can be classified in two categories: Information publishing/announcement and discovery. As the CIP and SeIP are responsible for any change to or update of their multimedia content and service information, the push method is the best communication style for publishing multimedia content and service watchers, namely CIWs and SIWs. There are several communication models that can be applied to assist the realization of the interaction between the CIWs, the SIWs and the CIPF. These models are described below and summarized in Table 4.1:

1. **Push method**, in which the CIPF pushes the multimedia content or service information to the content watcher or service watcher, respectively. The push method is inefficient because the CIPF must maintain a permanent connection to each CIW and SIW or establish a new connection to each CIW/SIW for every information update. In order to improve the efficiency of this method, a broadcast transmission mode can be used, but the support of personalization is complex.

2. **Pull method** differs from the push method in that the content and the service information watcher each sends periodic requests to the CIPF in order to be informed about new update. Since there is no need for a permanent connection to be maintained in the CIPF for notifying the watchers about any update, the performance of these components is improved. However, the disadvantage of this model is that it may decrease network performance by increasing the repetitive, unnecessary pulling request in the case that content information has not been changed. Further watchers might receive outdated or untimely updated information, which will lead to a decrease in user-perceived QoS.

3. **Event-model** allows watchers to register an interest in content and/or service information updates, and when update is announced, the CIPF accordingly notifies all registered watchers. This model can improve network efficiency by removing the need for pulling or pushing interactions. In case that events are broadcasted (e.g. event bus) or distributed through a central controller (e.g. IMS core), this immediately leads to scalability issues with regard to the number of notifications. Other disadvantages of the notification model is that it is not suitable for exchanging large-grain data [73].

4. **Event-Pull-model** is a hybrid model composed of the event and pull models in which the watchers register their interest in particular content or service information with the CIPF, and when the information

is announced or changed, the CIPF itself notifies the registered watchers about state change, delta or a complete state representation. As a result, the watcher can retrieve the updated content information from the CIPF. This hybrid model can improve the network efficiency, user-perceived performance and reliability. Network efficiency is improved because unnecessarily polling requests are removed. User-perceived performance is improved since new updates are received just in time. Reliability is improved because the updated data can use a consistent transmission path.

Therefore, it is recommended that the Content Information Provisioning function should implement the event-pull-method between content watcher and service watcher.

Method	Net. Perform.	UP Perform.	Scalability	Reliability	Visibility	Simplicity
Push	-	+	-	+	+	+
Pull	-	-	+	++	+	+
Event	-	++	-	-	-	-
Event-Pull	+	++	+	+	+	-

Table 4.1: Evaluation of provisioning methods

The realization of such a framework can follow the SIP event framework with a new defined event package, as described in 2.2.3.1, and combined with HTTP-based methods (e.g. POST or GET) for pulling requests. On the other hand, the discovery process can be achieved via an HTTP POST method [74]. With regard to this, a detailed analysis of the SIP event package and HTTP is discussed in sections 4.4.1 and subsection 4.5.

4.2.5 Content Management

The service provider may have several relationships with a set of content providers between Professional Content Producer (PCP) or User Generated Content (UGC). However, the service provider may allow its own subscribers to store their private content (e.g. network PVR) in the network, rather than in their private premises equipment's (e.g. local PC or mobile device). Furthermore, the SP may store multimedia content in central or distributed media servers. For these reason, it is important to manage relationships to all content providers and the available content in the service provider domain.

4.2. Overall Architecture

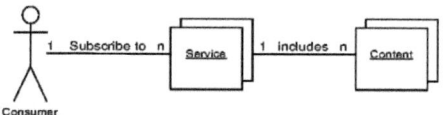

Figure 4.3: Consumer, service and content relationship

Furthermore, an individual content component shall have a unique identifier that may have reference to key words of the content description, possessor, location, etc. or an integer number (refer to requirements defined in subsections 2.5 and 3.4). Alternatively, the SP may bundle several content components in a single application offer (e.g. broadcast channels, e-learning service, movies, etc.). Figure 4.3 illustrates the relationship between the service, content and the consumer, where the consumer subscribes to n services each of which may include one or n content components.

From the content management point of view, another restriction to the scope of this dissertation is that we limit our discussion to multimedia content delivery from the content provider to the service provider, excluding content production, capturing, aggregation or versioning.

4.2.5.1 Content Identification

In order to be aligned with the IMS specification and to fulfill the requirements defined in subsection 2.5, there are two approaches to content identification:

1. Content identification by the SIP Uniform Resource Identifier (URI)

2. Content identification by SDP session or media attribute

The first approach implies content identification in two ways:

- Either every content identifier gets its own SIP URI. For example: *sip:CID=mymovie123@domain.com*

- Or it follows the RFC 3261 [75], which proposes the use of a header parameter - Content Identifier (CID), which identifies the required content. Headers fields in the SIP request can be specified with the "?" mechanism within a URI. The header names and values are encoded in ampersand separated hname = hvalue pairs. For example: *sip:user@domain.com?hCID=mymov*

Both approaches have a significant constraint. For instance, when using SIP re-INVITE message to switch among several content streams, including the CID as a header parameter would result in non-compliance with the RFC

3261 [75]. That is because it is required that the To, From, Call-ID, CSeq, and Request-URI headers of a re-INVITE message must be set according to the same rules as for regular requests within an existing dialog. This means in case of re-INVITE, the SIP URI must not change.

Contrary to SIP URL, the SDP body does not conflict with re- INVITE. The definition of a session or media attribute within the SDP body that identifies the requested content is an alternative approach, as described in the subsection 2.2.3.2, for example: *a=CID:mymovie123*

According to RFC 4566 [17], a media description may have any number of attributes ("a=" fields) that are media specific; e.g. the content ID of the audio track of a movie with a specific language. Such attributes are referred to as "media-level" attributes. Attribute fields can also be added before the first media field, which are referred to as "session-level" attributes to convey additional information that applies to the session as a whole, rather than to individual media.

4.2.5.2 Functional Requirements

According to the requirements defined in subsection 2.5 and the nine life-cycle phases of multimedia content delivery discussed in 4.2.1, Content Management Functions (CMF) are applied to session establishment, media delivery and session termination between the content provider and service provider. With regard to session establishment, interactions between a service provider and a content provider can be classified into two categories:

1. **Push method**, in which the content provider requests the service provider to upload or to stream content. This method is typically used for storing multimedia content in the service provider domain or relaying multimedia content to a set of users.

2. **Pull method**, in which the service provider requests the content provider to stream or upload/download content stream or stored file. This type of session setup can be applied when it is desired that multimedia content remains in the content provider domain upon receiving consumer request or a dedicated application controls the session setup among different users (e.g. e-learning application).

During session setup the delivery mechanism with the related transmission protocol and session parameters are determined. Straightforward, media delivery can be followed by one of the following functions:

1. Uploading multimedia content to the service provider domain, like UGC, YouTube, etc.

4.2. Overall Architecture

2. Streaming of live or available audio and/or video streams, like live public events, online courses, broadcast TV, etc.

3. Relaying of multimedia content to a set of end users, like PoC or video surveillance applications

The communication between the SP and the CP shall follow a session-based client server model, in which a session is first established between the client and the server then followed with content transmission. In this regard, the client initiates a session to the server and then invokes a series of services on the server, finally terminating the session. The application state is kept entirely on the server. In the case of the push method, the CP acts as a client and the SP as a server, while in the pull method the SP behaves as a client and the CP as a server.

Multimedia content information (metadata) published by the content providers can be useful for the content management function, because information like content status and location can help the CMF to optimize network delivery resources (i.e. if it is still in the content provider domain).

Content delivery of stored content can be transmitted through the HTTP POST method as specified in the RFC 1867 [74], or through FTP, while content streaming, particularly live content, shall use the RTP protocol, as introduced in section 2.2.3.4. However, section 4.4.2 gives a brief comparison between streaming either over UDP or TCP. On the other hand, session establishment requires a dedicated protocol like SIP or HTTP, which both follow the client server model. There are, however, advantages and disadvantages to each protocol and these will be further discussed in section 4.4.1.

4.2.6 Multimedia Session Management

Session management provides the necessary signaling to deliver a specific multimedia content to its consumers according to consumer, application or content provider request. It handles session establishment, session renegotiation, session termination and session mobility. The enrichment of the session management with network and user context makes it possible to have a session that may respond to context changes in order to adapt and satisfy user-perceived QoS.

A multimedia application usually provides the consumer with specific added-value features in certain business domains (e.g. e-health, smart-city, e-learning, etc.). In this context, multimedia applications can have four type of interactions associated with any multimedia content:

1. **Multimedia Content** which the application includes as integral component of its offer.

2. **Consumer** who is interested in receiving multimedia content according to his context or previous subscription. In addition to receiving the content, he simultaneously may interact with the application in an integrated interactive event associated with the multimedia content (e.g. interactive voting, shopping, web-link, etc.).

3. **Network resources** that provide media processing and content delivery so that the application (i.e. session manager) triggers (and possibly allocate) the required resources on network nodes like media servers or routers.

4. **Application Enablers** that provide their functions on the application level or make use of other enabler functions, such as user-related context information, content information, user profile data (e.g. HSS or XDMS), etc.

From the session management point of view, multimedia content information can be retrieved from the content manager, interact with the IMS subscribers and network resources through the IMS core, and communicate with other enablers or applications through open programming interfaces (e.g. web-services).

4.2.6.1 Service Identification

As stated in the previous subsection, each user might subscribe to a set of multimedia applications, as depicted in Figure 4.3. Therefore, each IMS-based application shall have a unique identifier which the user and the IMS core both use to trigger the corresponding application server. This identifier shall follow the syntax of the IMS PSI, as defined in [32]. With this context, each session manager function shall have a unique PSI to be reachable within the IMS network from either a SIP-based or a web-based node.

4.2.6.2 Functional Requirements

Although the Content Information Provisioning functions are not part of the Session Management Functions (SMF), the selected mechanisms will obviously influence the interaction style between the session manager and the end users. Providing the end user with most content properties (such as description, current production status, scheduling time, subscription method, etc.) will certainly guide the user to show interest in such content prior to session establishment or bearer activation for content delivery. Consequently, the session manager will be able to allocate the required processing and delivery resources in the network.

4.2. Overall Architecture

Therefore the session manager shall interact with the CIPF in order to obtain user subscriptions to certain multimedia content, because that information can be useful to predict or allocate required media processing and delivery resources. Consequently, it should interact with the corresponding nodes on the delivery network and thus will lead to optimizing the efficiency of delivery, as discussed in subsection 3.4.

According to the requirements defined in subsection 3.4 and the nine lifecycle phases of multimedia content delivery, discussed in 4.2.1, the session management functions can support session establishment, media delivery and session termination. Session setup deals with the negotiation of capabilities and media parameters for the activation of the required media delivery functions between the service provider, the media delivery nodes and the consumer. The related functions can be classified in three categories:

1. **Pull method**, in which the user initiates a request to the application for inquiring certain multimedia content. The request may indicate linear streaming delivery or on-demand streaming (stored content). In this model, the session manager shall check user authorization for requesting multimedia content. The pull model is suitable for session setup of stored multimedia content because each consumer initiates session setup at any time and thus the load is distributed over the time. However it is inefficient for session setup of live multimedia content that starts in a defined time, because if users are not continuously informed about content-related information (metadata) and current delivery state, consumers may behave unpredictably; some of them might forget the event completely, others miss part of it or other initiate requests even before the delivery time.

2. **Push method**, in which the session manager setups a session to one or n recipients for multimedia content delivery. In this model, session establishment is typically initiated due to application request (according to for example change on user(s) context or previous subscription) or content provider request (e.g. the CP push of multimedia content to a set of users). If the session manager and the transport nodes are not dimensioned well, sessions with quite a lot of participants might lead to a heavy load that effects network performance, and a decrease in user-perceived performance due to a large session setup delay. Furthermore, the consumer might receive the session setup request during an unsuitable situation (e.g. busy, meeting, etc.).

3. **Event-Induced Session Setup**, in which the session establishment is induced by the notifications sent by the CIPF due to any update

Chapter 4. Major Design Aspects for Session-based Multimedia Content Delivery

Method	Net. Perform.	UP Perform.	Scalability	Reliability	Visibility	Simplicity
Push	-	-	+	-	-	-
Pull	-	+	+	+	+	+
Event-Induced Session Setup	++	++	++	+	+	+

Table 4.2: Evaluation of session setup methods

on multimedia content information that the user is interested in or has subscribed to. With regards to this, each user can initiate requests whenever he wants to join a live session or receive a stored stream. On the other hand, during the subscription process, information about a particular multimedia content can assist the session manager (or application) to decide the appropriate delivery time by allocating the required resources. As a result, this model improves network performance and user-perceived performance. Network performance is improved because, first the required resources can be predicted, and second the associated signaling and media load is distributed over time. User-perceived performance (QoS) is improved because the application can determine user context and content subscription, by communicating to presence server (context server) and Content Information Provisioning function, respectively.

The event-induced session setup matches the requirements defined in subsection 3.4 such that applying this model leads to the minimizing of signaling traffic among the system components, as summarized in Table 4.2.

The interaction between the consumer and the SMF shall a follow session-based client server model, in which a session is established between the client and the server then followed by content transmission. In case of the push method, the session manager (or the application) acts as a client and the consumer as a server, while in the pull method the session manager behaves as a server and the consumer as a client. As the entire system operates in an IMS-based network, the SIP matches perfectly with the requirements of the session management and thus it will be selected to establish and maintain the multimedia session between the service provider and consumers.

Multimedia content may be available in the service provider domain, meaning that content is stored in media delivery nodes, available as a live stream directly from the content provider or received from the satellite. As multimedia content locators are managed by the CMF, the Multimedia Session Management function shall interact with the CMF to retrieve content iden-

4.2. Overall Architecture

tification before interacting with media delivery nodes for triggering content delivery.

Content delivery to the end consumer can be transmitted over a unicast, a multicast or a broadcast transmission mode. Bearer selection is based on several criteria such as:

1. Service package subscription,
2. Number of content recipients,
3. Capabilities of user equipment,
4. Network capabilities (e.g. support for UE codecs, video resolution, supported bearer)
5. Contemporary network condition (e.g. load, congestion, etc.)

In general, content can be downloaded or streamed in linear or on-demand mode, i.e. with or without support of trick functions. In a managed network, content streaming is mostly transmitted via RTP over UDP protocol. Multicast mode is used for transmitting broadcast TV, whereas unicast for VoD content. However, a broadcast bearer, like MBMS or DVB-H introduced in 2.3.1.2, can be used to serve mobile users. The deployment of multicast and broadcast modes for delivering multimedia content to group of end users, who are in same context will improve network performance and scalability, thus satisfying the requirement defined in subsection 3.4, in which the session manager is supposed to serve a large number of users and utilize the available transmission modes (unicast, multicast and broadcast) to optimize network resource usage. RFC3170 [76] provides an informative description for the challenges involved with designing and implementing multicast applications, but without any solution, in particular to session management functions.

On the contrary to UDP, the TCP is most frequently used over a unicast bearer for content streaming in an unmanaged network (web-based streaming in the Internet). Section 4.4.2 provides a brief comparison between streaming over either UDP or TCP. With regard to media delivery, the session manager needs to know the available media delivery and processing entities and their capabilities. Therefore the session manager shall interact with the media delivery controller (e.g. MDF Controller (MDFC)), by using for example the SIP Option method by which the media delivery controller includes the supported capabilities in the 200 OK response message. Accordingly, the session manager triggers the media delivery function and, if required the processing functions by including the capabilities of the termination points (either recipient device capabilities or multicast capabilities) and the multimedia content Identifier.

According to IMS specifications, SIP is used between the application server and the media delivery controller, as discussed in clause 2.2.3.3.

4.2.7 Media Delivery Function

In order to meet all the proposed innovative features defined in the previous chapter, the media delivery service architecture should be content aware and have knowledge of the access technologies, as well as of the utilized end-user device capabilities and characteristics. Therefore, Media delivery functions can be classified into two categories:

1. Multimedia content delivery functions which provide transmission capabilities from one input channel (in-port) to a set of output channels (out-ports).

2. Media processing functions which support media adaptation according to out-port (output channel) characteristics.

In order to enable the application server within an IMS-network to trigger these functions the SIP protocol is selected because it provides a general session setup for the multimedia session by including in the body of the SIP message any type of text messages (e.g. XML, SDP, plain text, etc.) that contains the required parameters of the media processing function.

Various research efforts have proposed solutions for the support of the delivery of multimedia streaming in heterogeneous networks. Tariq et al. [77] propose a proxy-based dynamic configurable multimedia processing entity, but the integration of such a proxy within an IMS-based network has not been considered. Niebert N. et al. [45] introduce service specific overlay networking for adapting multimedia content within the ambient networks project. Such overlay is based on the peer-to-peer communication model for service discovery and service path management for media delivery. Although this solution has been evaluated in terms of simulation, there has not been any realization yet. Overlay networking could be an alternative to the current network platforms, but it is still in an infancy stage and the integration with the current standardized system such as IMS or TISPAN requires further investigation. However, the integration of media processing based on the overlay-networking paradigm was introduced in [46, 78], in which such a concept could be applied within a SIP-based session in IMS environment is described. This approach implies that session participants or the IMS core are registered with the overlay network, which is in charge of media processing as well as the required QoS. Conversely QoS and media processing are key features supported by the IMS.

4.2. Overall Architecture

One of the goals of this dissertation is to provide design guide-lines for the task of integrating media delivery and processing functions within IMS-based multimedia application frameworks rather than studying how such architecture should be modulated or distributed. The next subsections discuss the functional requirements for media delivery, processing and control functions supported by the MDF.

4.2.7.1 Media Delivery Functions

According to the requirements defined in subsection 2.5, delivery functions can be classified into two classes:

File-based content delivery : In which multimedia content is considered as a file during the delivery session. When the MDF acts as the receptacle for multimedia content we refer to the input channel as input-port, when it is the source, we refer to the output channel with out-port, as depicted in Figure 4.4:

1. **Fetching function**, in which multimedia content is downloaded from any host in the network following the client server model, where the MDF behaves as a client and the content provider as a server. The File Transfer Protocol (FTP) or HTTP protocol can be used for content transmission over a unicast bearer. This function is typically used to obtain multimedia content as input from professional content providers.

2. **Upload function**, in which a content provider (e.g. IMS user) uploads generated content to the MDF. Likewise, the FTP or HTTP protocol can be used for content transmission over unicast bearer and following client-server model. This function is frequently used as input from users who generate or want to store multimedia content in the MDF.

3. **Download function**, in which consumers can download multimedia content to be stored locally. This model is similar to the fetching function in which the consumer acquires the content for transmission via FTP or HTTP over a unicast bearer. From the MDF point of view, this channel is regarded as an output channel. However, the fetching function is performed by the MDF to obtain multimedia content from the content provider and thus it is considered as *input* rather than *output* channel.

4. **Unidirectional content delivery function**, in which multimedia content is transmitted over (unreliable) multicast bearer. This

Figure 4.4: Media Delivery Functions

kind of delivery is typically used for massively scalable multicast distribution. FLUTE [79] is suitable transport protocol for unidirectional multicast delivery mode. In this case, the MDF is the source of the file and thus the multicast channel is considered as output channel.

Streaming functions : In which multimedia content is transferred in the network by taking all aspects of real-time properties into account, as discussed in 3.2. The typical protocol used is the RTP over the UDP. This class comprises the following delivery functions:

1. **Receiving function**, in which content provider offers multimedia content as input stream to the MDF. The received stream can be stored or be considered as source for further delivery.

2. **Linear-streaming function**, in which the received stream or stored content is transferred via RTP over UDP and without a track function mode. Unicast or multicast mode can be used to carry the multimedia stream.

3. **On-Demand streaming function**, in which multimedia content is streamed with a unicast bearer with support of trick functions.

It is important to point out that the MDF shall relay multimedia content (stored or received on a dedicated input-port) to a set of output-ports among unicast and broadcast channels. Note that the distribution of such MDF nodes in the network and related locations is out of the scope of this dissertation.

4.2.7.2 Media Processing Functions

According to the requirements defined in subsection 3.4, the intention of the proposed media processing is only to enhance media delivery with a set of adaptation functions, in order to optimize network resources and satisfy user-perceived quality of experience. Therefore, further media processing functions such as image processing, video streams aggregation, object detection, etc. are intentionally excluded.

4.2. Overall Architecture

As users have different device capabilities and are attached to the network with various access technologies with diverse attributes and capabilities, multimedia content shall be adapted accordingly. The following two functions shall be supported:

1. **Bit-Rate or spatial adaptation function** in which stream rate or resolution (packet-rate) is adapted according to user and network condition. An audio stream can be encoded for example with the AMR (Adaptive Multi-rate) or AMR-WB (AMR-WideBand) codec which support adaptive rate ranging from 4.75 up to 12.2 or 6.6 up to 23.85 kbps, as defined in TS 26.090 and TS 26.190 [80, 81], respectively. The video stream can be encoded for example with the Scalable Video Coding (SVC), which represents an extension of the H.264/MPEG4 AVC video compression standard.

2. **Transcoding function**, in which original audio or video streams are decoded, then encoded with a lower rate (quality) codec according to the output channel characteristics (e.g. UE capabilities). For instance, the audio stream is transcoded from G.711 codec (64kbps) to AMR codec or video stream is transcoded from H.264 codec to H.263. Multimedia applications may request to record live stream in the MDF. The associated container format (e.g. wav, mp3, mp4, mov, etc.) can be terminated by the application or by the MDF.

4.2.7.3 Delivery and Processing Control Functions

According to the requirements defined in subsection 3.4 the application shall be able to trigger media delivery and processing functions. As the MDF and the application server are deployed within an IMS-based network, the appropriate singling protocol is SIP following 3GPP specifications discussed in 2.2.3.3.

As the media delivery and processing functions discussed above, do not create mid-session interactions, in any IVR-based applications (e.g. prompt and collect, conferences, etc.), SIP Invite-based session is sufficient to invoke any delivery and processing functions, such that the SIP URL indicates the required function and the media-related parameters are added in the SDP body. With this regard, the implementation shall follow the RFC 4240, introduced in 2.2.3.3. Therefore each delivery functions shall have a unique name for the user part of the SIP URI. For instance in order to store live stream the following SIP URL can be defined as follows: *sip:record@ims-domain.com*

Furthermore, the SDP body shall include all media-related parameters such as content provider IP address, port, protocol, codec and content ID.

Declaration of session parameters in the SDP body shall follow the IETF specifications. For instance, for the description of a unidirectional content delivery session using the FLUTE protocol, the SDP Descriptors for the FLUTE IETF draft is considered [79].

4.3 Analysis of Efficient IMS-based Content Delivery Network

According to the requirements defined in subsection 3.4, an NGN-based multimedia delivery network shall be able to serve a very large number of users who interact with the system using different applications such as TV, VoD, audio/video telephony, presence and messaging. Therefore the architecture shall gracefully and economically scale from a small number of users to millions of users. In this regard, several SIP message models associated with different multimedia scenarios will be analyzed. This will enable us to understand the impact on the IMS core and the transport network. Another goal is to provide a guideline for selecting the appropriate SIP method while developing multimedia applications for a carrier grade network that can serve thousands of multimedia session simultaneously and more efficiently.

It is assumed that the IMS core will control several applications such as telephony, messaging, presence and IPTV. Although the analysis will consider mainly the communication between the IMS subscribers and the IMS application servers, we will also address a few scenarios in which the content provider acts as an IMS subscriber in order to push multimedia content to a set of IMS subscribers.

Initially, basic dimensioning parameters and service profiles will be defined. Unfortunately currently there are not many IMS deployments done worldwide and thus there are insufficient traces available that could be considered input for such an evaluation. Then, quantification of message flows of different SIP applications that fulfill the requirements defined in the previous chapter will be conducted. All session related control flows shall be accounted for. Other control flows shall be accounted for, e.g. (re-, de-)registration traffic, etc. Although the charging records are generated by most of the IMS nodes, the associated elements are equally loaded and thus we will not consider such flows during this analysis.

4.3.1 Basic Service Profiles

IMS-based Multimedia applications are deployed on the top of the IMS core. With regard to this, most of the basic IMS traffic profiles (service profiles)

4.3. Analysis of Efficient IMS-based Content Delivery Network

Network attachment & IMS registration parameters	Typical values
Number of attachments per day	1
Number of terminals for a single subscription (Nt) (Note 1)	2
Registered users during the busy hour ($RegUBH$)	95%
Registrations with authentication? (Note 2)	Yes or No
Validity of registration in the IMS Core network (hours) (Note 3) ($RegTime$)	0.50
New registrations during the busy hour (Note 4) ($NewReg$)	0.30
De-registrations during the busy hour (Note 3) ($DeReg$)	0.25

Table 4.3: IMS registration profile

and related message flows are analyzed in the following clauses. It is assumed that the IMS core will serve a certain number of IMS Subscribers, which we denote in the following clauses with the notation $SubN$.

4.3.1.1 Registration Profile

As application servers could subscribe registration and de-registration messages for the subscriber automatically, following the third party registration procedure defined by 3GPP [32], it is important to include the IMS registration profile as defined in Table 4.3.

Note that all access related issues, such as lawful interception or emergency call are not considered in this analysis. Furthermore, we assume that a common IMS core serves subscribers connected via fixed and mobile access networks (e.g. 50% fixed and 50% mobile).

Note 1 : This parameter is for information only and not used for dimensioning. Dimensioning happens when the number of users is equal to the number of terminals. The number of subscriptions will be smaller if Nt>1. Terminals might be connected with the IMS core through fixed or mobile access networks (e.g. 50% fixed and 50% mobile).

Note 2 : A given terminal will be either authenticated at the IMS level using the AKA Authentication (=Yes) or based on the authentication during the connectivity (=No) following NASS Bundled Authentication or Early IMS Registration defined by the TISPAN and the 3GPP specification, respectively. A mix of both may coexist in the network.

Note 3 : With a validity of e.g. 1/2 hour two re-registrations per hour are required. To be divided by 3600 for the number of Re-registrations Per Second (RPS). The RPS is much higher (e.g. 1 message each $30 seconds$ results in RPS rate of 1/30) in case the IMS client/application is behind a NAT. Therefore the RPS between the user and the access node (P-CSCF or Session Boarder Controller) is different than the RPS between the access and the IMS core (e.g. 2 messages per hour out of 120). Two registration schemes are considered:

1. New registrations, re-registrations and de-registrations involving the core IMS network and the access part between UE and access control node (e.g. 2 out of 120 re-registrations + new-reg + de-reg).

2. Re-registrations in the access part only for keep alive of NAT bindings (e.g. 118 out of 120 re-registrations). However, NAT problem can be partially avoided the appropriate design.

Note 4 : It is assumed that during the busy hour, 25% of terminals are starting a new registration but this is compensated by almost the same amount of users quitting the service (25%) yielding the same number of registered users.

Total number of SIP REGISTER messages per hour:

$$REGISTER = \frac{SubN \times NregU \times Nt \times (NewReg + DeReg)}{RegTime} \quad (4.1)$$

4.3.1.2 Session Profile

IMS-based multimedia applications follow the four types of SIP communication models defined in subsection 2.3.4.1. The session model is mainly used in telephony sessions, but it is defined as well in the IPTV standard for initiating e.g. the TV and the VoD service. Moreover, multimedia applications such as gaming or multimedia push (PoC/PTT) may be based on the same model. Therefore we are going to consider only two profile types as follows:

1. Pull model in which a user requests to start a live TV or VoD (stored content) session as defined in TISPAN IPTV standard [40].

2. Push model in which a multimedia content is delivered to a set of users. This model could be applied to either an application or an IMS subscriber (acting as content provider) requesting the application server to convey multimedia content to a set of users.

Table 4.4 defines the service profile of the multicast and unicast streaming session in which a sub set of IMS subscribers (e.g. 30%) can acquire multimedia content from the IMS-based delivery network over multicast or unicast transmission mode. However, it does not include the telephony service profile. The multicast and unicast modes are considered for content delivery.

4.3. Analysis of Efficient IMS-based Content Delivery Network

IMS Session Parameters	Typical values		Comments
	Multicast streaming (e.g. TV)	Unicast streaming (e.g. VoD)	
Percentage of Application usage (AU)	30%	30%	Assumption
Percentage of Active Service Usage (ASU) (Note 1)	50%	30%	
Number of Active Users (AUe)	$SubN \times AU \times ASU$		
Number of Sessions per Active User per day ($SPAU$) (Note 2)	2	5	Assumption
Percentage of Session during Busy Hour ($SDBH$) (Note 3)	70%	30%	G. Yu el at. [82] & Assumption
Number of Sessions per Active User per BH ($SPUBH$)	1.4	1.5	$SPAU \times SDBH$
Number of Sessions per BH (SPBH) or Busy Hour Session Attempts ($BHSA$)	$AUe \times SPUBH$		
Session Holding Time (SHT) per seconds (Note 4)	1800	600	G. Yu el at. [82] & Assumption
Number of Concurrent Session during BH (CSBH) (Note 5)	$SPBH \times SHT/3600$		
Session Attempts Per Second (SAPS)	$SPBH/3600 (BHSA/3600)$		

Table 4.4: Multicast and unicast session profile

Requests are generated by the subscribers or applications following the pull or push model, respectively. While application request may include a bulk of end recipients, user requests are distributed across the network and over time. Session parameters of multicast session are defined according to live measurements conducted by G. Yu el at. [82], which are performed in a Swedish municipal network with 350 residential IPTV users.

Note 1 : The multicast mode is mainly used nowadays for transferring TV channels in an IPTV infrastructure, while the unicast mode is used for VoD, stored (or available) TV programs offered directly on a provided portal or user generated content (e.g. Youtube). Therefore the percentage of the service usage of the unicast mode will overtake the usage of the multicast mode.

Note 2 : According to IPTV specification, the user will issue only one SIP request (Invite message) to start the multicast delivery session, which includes several channels, but he or she will generate a SIP request for each unicast session (e.g. VoD). Switching among several multicast streams (e.g. TV channels) within an active session is defined in Table

Chapter 4. Major Design Aspects for Session-based Multimedia Content Delivery

IMS Session Parameters	Typical values	comments
Number of Switching requests per Active User per minute ($SwPUPM$) during BH	0.3	G. Yu el at. [82]
Number of Switching requests per Active User per hour ($SwPUPH$) during BH (Note 1)	7	G. Yu el at. [82]
Number of Switchings during BH ($SwPBH$) or Busy Hour Switching Attempts ($BHSwA$)	$AUe \times SwPUPH$	
Session Holding Time (SHT) per second	60	G. Yu el at. [82]
Number of Concurrent Switching requests during $BH(CSBH)$	$SwPBH \times SHT/3600$	
Switching Attempts per Second (SwAPS) (Note 3)	$SwPUPM/60$	

Table 4.5: Multicast switching profile

4.4.

Note 3 : According to G. Yu el at. [82] the average peak number of active users during the busy hour is around 68

Note 4 : According to G. Yu el at. [82] most of the sessions are very short (65% < 1 minute) while only 4% are longer than one hour.

Note 5 : The term Busy Hour Session/Call Attempts is equivalent to the term Number of Concurrent Session generated during Busy Hour.

According to Table 4.4, Session Attempts Per Second or number of INVITE requests per seconds can be calculated by applying the following equation:

$$Invite = \frac{SubN \times AU \times ASU \times SPUA \times SDBH}{3600} \quad (4.2)$$

Table 4.5: Multicast Switching Profile defines channel zapping profile during a multicast delivery session. After the session setup of the multicast delivery, the user may switch among available multicast channels using the IGMP protocol messages, as defined in 2.3.2.1, without modifying the SIP session. Session parameters are defined according to G. Yu el at. [82]. As the first three columns in the previous table define the subscription profile, they are not repeated in Table 4.5.

Note 1 : According to G. Yu el at. [82] the average numbers of switching (zapping) per minute per active user are between 0.1 and 0.2, while the peaks are around 0.35. Therefore we assumed the value shall be 0.3.

Note 2 : According to G. Yu el at. [82] measurements, the peaks always occur at the beginning of every half hour and thus the average of zapping

4.3. Analysis of Efficient IMS-based Content Delivery Network 91

requests become smaller. For this reason, average of the zapping requests per hour is small; 7 instead of 18(0.3 × 60).

Note 3 : Switching attempts per second shall be calculated according to the number of switching requests per Active User per minute instead of per hour, for the reason mentioned in note 2.

The term switching attempts per second identifies the number of switching requests generated via the IGMP protocol from all the users distributed across the IMS network. Accordingly the number of generated SIP messages notifying the application server per second can be calculated as follows:

$$Message = \frac{SubN \times AU \times ASU \times SwPUPM}{60} \quad (4.3)$$

The type of the SIP messages issued by the subscribers is evaluation- and possibly implementation-dependent.

4.3.1.3 Event Framework Profile

The SIP event framework defined in subsection 2.2.3.1 is implemented in various IMS services either as the basis of the service logic, such as the presence service enabler, introduced in the subsection 2.3.4.2, or as part of the application logic, such as in the OMA XDMS or the IPTV SDF, introduced in 2.3.4.4. In both, the subscription/notification messages are exchanged between corresponding service entities with a defined event package. As the presence enabler implements most of the major event framework specifications that are equivalent with the CIPF specification, as discussed in 4.2.6 and 4.2.6, the analysis and the resultant equations are applied for both. However, the CIPF shall support the RLS and presence management functions, such that the RLS shall interact with the storage server (e.g. XDMS) to obtain the user multimedia content list, referred to as buddy list (Nw) in Table 4.6. In addition, we include the IPTV as well, as presented in Table 4.6. According to the ETSI TS 183 063 [68], the IPTV UE makes use of the event framework in the following procedures:

1. Publishing current user IPTV activity (e.g. current activated broadcast channel) to the Presence Server,

2. Subscribing to retrieve the service attachment information from the SDF and

3. Subscribing to changes in the IPTV service profile.

Chapter 4. Major Design Aspects for Session-based Multimedia Content Delivery

The IPTV client sends the SIP PUBLISH messages with the "presence" event package to the presence server, which accordingly notifies the watchers about state change or IPTV user activity.

Event Framework Parameters	Presence	CIPF	IPTV
Percentage of Application usage (AU) (Note 1)	50%	30%	30%
Percentage of service usage (Nau)	90%	50%	50%
Number of Active Users ($Npau$)	$SubN \times Au \times Nau$		
Presentity parameters			
Number of PUA (Presence User Agent) per user (Note 2)	2	2	1
Number of PNA (Presence Network Agent) per user (Note 3)	0.5	0.5	0
Updates (state change) per hour per $PUA/PNA(Pu)$ (Note 4)	4	1	0.005
SIP PUBLISH per hour (refresh) (Pr)	1	3	Na
WATCHER parameters			
Average number of buddy lists/multimedia service group per user (Ng)	2	3	Na
Average number of buddies (watchers) per list (Nw)	10	10	Na
Percentage of active buddies (watchers) (Aul)	70%	70%	Na
SUBSCRIBE (any) refresh per hour and per user (Sr) (Note 5)	1	2	12
New SIP SUBSCRIBE (RLS/IPTV) per hour and per group ($RLSn$) per IPTV user ($IPTVn$)	1	1	0.2
New SIP SUBSCRIBE (WINFO) per hour (WINFOn) (Note 6)	0.5	0.5	0
SIP un-SUBSCRIBE (RLS/IPTV) per hour and per group ($RLSu$) per IPTV user ($IPTVu$)	0.1	0.1	0.2
SIP un-SUBSCRIBE (WINFO) per hour (WINFOu)	0.005	0.005	0

Table 4.6: Event framework profile

Note 1 : The numbers of the IMS users who are subscribed to the presence and IPTV services are part of IMS subscribers.

Note 2 : Presence source can be an IMS subscriber or an application, denoted as PUA (Presence User Agent) and PNA (Presence Network Agent), respectively. PUA can be an IMS client or IMS-based set-top-box.

4.3. Analysis of Efficient IMS-based Content Delivery Network 93

Note 3 : PNA can be any application that acts as a presentity (e.g. web-based application).

Note 4 : PNA/PUA can be an IMS client, IPTV client or any authorized application that modifies user state or activity. Due to frequent changes in IPTV activity, this value is almost equal to the switching rate described in Table 4.5. Furthermore, the percentage of the change to the state of the IPTV service profile or the service attachment information is considered to be small.

Note 5 : As stated above the IPTV UE sends two types of subscription messages to the SDF and to the SCF. According to ETSI standards [68], the IPTV UE shall automatically refresh the subscription, either 600 seconds before the expiration time if the initial subscription was for greater than 1200 seconds, or when half of the time has expired if the initial subscription was for 1200 seconds or less. For this reason, we assume that the expiration time is greater than 1200, so that the IPTV UE sends 6 SUBSCRIBE messages to the SDP and the SCF.

Note 6 : A user subscribes to Watcher Information Event Package (WINFO) to receive notification from the system (e.g. presence server) about the watchers, who are interested in particular event package information that is updated by this user (e.g. about user presence information).

$Number of active presence users = Npau = SubN \times Au \times Nau$; where: $SubN$ is total IMS users, Au is Presence usage (%) and Nau is the percentage of registered IMS users.

$Number of active IPTV users = Ntau = SubN \times Au \times Nau$; where: $Ntau$ is the number of active IPTV users using an event package, $SubN$ is total IMS users, Au is IPTV service usage (%) and Nau is the percentage of active IPTV users.

$Number of presence publishers (= presentities) = PUA + PNA$ Publish frequency = largest (Max) of Pu and Pr (note that this may be different for PUA and PNA, nevertheless we consider for both as equal).

Number of SIP PUBLISH methods :

Number of SIP PUBLISH transactions[1] per hour by presentities =

$$PUBLISH = Npau \times (PUA + PNA) \times Max(Pu, Pr) \quad (4.4)$$

---
[1]SIP transaction is defined in 2.2.3.1

SIP message issued by the UA or the PNA when presence information (e.g. availability or activity) is updated or when the validity of the registration has expired. Assumption: PUBLISH is combined for update and registration refresh, in other words, an update restarts the registration validity timer (Pr). In addition to the PUBLISH message, the presence server can be notified about further changes in user registration status by the IMS core (S-CSCF) either through a third party registration procedure, or through the subscription to the registration-event package. In the case the third party registration procedure is implemented, the number of registration messages generated by the S-CSCF towards the application server (e.g. presence server or IPTV SDF) can be calculated by applying Equation 4.1. In the case the reg-event procedure is implemented, the traffic impact can be calculated following the methodology described in the next subsection.

Number of SIP SUBSCRIBE methods:

SIP SUBSCRIBE methods are generated towards the presence server in three contexts:

1. Subscription, subscription refresh and un-subscription of watchers to list servers (RLS).

2. Subscription, subscription refresh and un-subscription of RLS to individual presentities.

3. Subscription, subscription refresh and un-subscription of watchers to presence server for Watcher Information Event Package.

SIP SUBSCRIBE messages issued by UA Watchers to subscribe to a list of presentities on the list server (RLS) are defined as follows: Number of SIP SUBSCRIBE(UA to RLS) transactions per hour =

$$SUBSCRIBE(UA \to RLS) = Npau \times Ng \times (PUA+PNA) \times (Sr+RLSn+RLSu) \quad (4.5)$$

Once the watcher issued a SUBSRIBE message for his groups (buddies) to the RLS, the RLS will subscribe individually to the presence information of each buddy in the list. Note that all these subscriptions need to be regularly refreshed. Accordingly, the number of the associated SIP SUBSCRIBE transactions is calculated as follows: Number of SIP SUBSCRIBE(RLS to PS) transactions by RLS per hour =

$$SUBSCRIBE(RLS \to PS) = SUBSCRIBE(UA \to RLS) \times Nw \quad (4.6)$$

4.3. Analysis of Efficient IMS-based Content Delivery Network 95

SIP SUBSCRIBE(WINFO) transactions issued by UA watchers to subscribe to watcher information event packages can be calculated as follows:
Number of SIP SUBSCRIBE(WINFO) transactions by watcher per hour =

$$SUBSCRIBE(WINFO) = Npau \times (PUA+PNA) \times (Sr+WINFOn+WINFOu)$$
(4.7)

SIP SUBSCRIBE methods are generated towards the IPTV server in two contexts:

1. Subscription, subscription refresh and un-subscription of watchers to SDF.

2. Subscription, subscription refresh and un-subscription of watchers to SCF.

SIP SUBSCRIBE messages issued by an IPTV UA watcher to subscribe to any changes of service attachment information are defined as follows: Number of SIP SUBSCRIBE to SDF and SCF transactions per hour =

$$SUBSCRIBE(IPTV) = Ntau \times (PUA+PNA) \times (Sr+IPTVn+IPTVu)$$
(4.8)

In the case that the IPTV framework enables any application or network node modifying user profile or service attached information, the PNA is greater than 0.

Number of SIP NOTIFY Methods:

The SIP NOTIFY methods are used to acknowledge a SIP SUBSCRIBE or to inform about a state change during the validity of the subscription. SIP NOTIFY generated by the presence server appears in the three contexts listed above. SIP NOTIFY (RLS to UA) messages are issued to acknowledge a subscription to watchers of a group and for each update of a presence status within the group.

Number of SIP NOTIFY (RLS to UA) transactions per hour =

$$\begin{aligned}NOTIFY(RLS \to UA) &= SUBSCRIBE(UA \to RLS) \\ &+ Npau \times (PUA+PNA) \times Ng \times Nw \times Pr \times Aul\end{aligned}$$
(4.9)

SIP NOTIFY (PS to RLS) messages are issued as a direct result of a SIP SUBSCRIBE (RLS to PS) to a RLS. State changes in the watched presentities by RLS are also notified.

Number of SIP NOTIFY (PS to RLS) transactions per hour =

$$\begin{aligned}NOTIFY(PS \to RLS) &= SUBSCRIBE(RLS \to PS) \\ &+ Npau \times (PUA + NPA) \times Pr \times Ng\end{aligned}$$

(4.10)

SIP NOTIFY (WINFO) is issued as a direct result of a SIP SUBSCRIBE (WINFO) to a single presentity by presence server. Each new subscription or any change to watcher information event package is notified to the watcher. The number of the corresponding SIP NOTIFY can be calculated as follows:

Number of SIP NOTIFY (WINFO) transactions per hour =

$$\begin{aligned}NOTIFY(WINFO) &= \\ SUBSCRIBE&(WINFO) \\ + Npau \times (PUA &+ PNA + RSLn + RSLu) \times Ng \times Nw \times Aul\end{aligned}$$

(4.11)

SIP NOTIFY (IPTV) is issued as a direct result of a SIP SUBSCRIBE (IPTV) to a single presentity by a watcher. State changes in the watched presentities (IPTV service profile or service attachment information) by individual watchers are also notified. Accordingly the total number of SIP NOTIFY messages can be calculated as follows:

Number of SIP NOTIFY (IPTV) transactions per hour =

$$NOTIFY(IPTV) = SUBSCRIBE(IPTV) + Ntau \times (PUA + PNA) \times Pu$$

(4.12)

As the SIP SUBSCRIBE/NOTIFY event framework is very demanding on network resources and NOTIFY messages generated by the subscription refreshes do not indicate any change in the event state messages, it is important to implement the optimization mechanisms defined in the RFC 5839, as described in 2.2.3.1. As a consequence, the total number of Notification messages is reduced, as only new subscriptions are considered for notification. Considering Equation (4.9),

$$\begin{aligned}NOTIFY_{opt} &= SUBSCRIBE(RLSn) \\ &+ Ntau \times (PUA + PNA) \times Ng \times Nw \times Pr \times Aul \\ &= Ntau \times Ng \times (PAU + PNA) \times [RLSn + (Nw \times Pr \times Aul)]\end{aligned}$$

(4.13)

The total notification is reduced by the total message of $Ntau \times (PAU + PNA)(RLSn+RLSu)$. When followed, NOTIFY equations (Equation (4.10), Equation (4.11) and Equation (4.12)) shall substitute the total number of new subscription messages for the total number of subscription messages.

4.3. Analysis of Efficient IMS-based Content Delivery Network

4.3.2 Message Flows

In this subsection, several message flows are introduced with regard to the evaluation of the load of SIP-based traffic on the application server side, but it is not intended to evaluate the IMS core itself and not to include all types of SIP message flows. Note that in the following flows, only the generated SIP messages (denoted as Nb_SIP_Msg) for the IMS core and the application server are accounted for. Furthermore, load by received messages will be calculated using the number of SIP transactions, denoted as Nb_SIP_Transactions.

The IMS specifications consider the QoS reservation as part of the session establishment, so that the IMS subscriber requests the required resources from the network (during bearer activation regarding 3GPP wireless network) and negotiates allocation status with the corresponding IMS node. In practice, the QoS allocation is the responsibility of the transport network (on behalf of the application request, e.g. P-CSCF) and does not require subscriber involvement. As a result of such constraints, we exclude the subsequent QoS SIP transactions (SIP Prack and Update messages) from the Invite session setup flows.

4.3.2.1 Registration

As the application server can subscribe to the IMS registration messages, it is essential to consider the related load of the forwarded messages to the application server.

The IMS registration includes three types of registration messages: New registration, Re-registration (refresh) and De-registration.

Each registration can happen with or without authentication, but the authentication process does not impact the application server. Each registration is notified to an application server only when the user is subscribed to one or more additional services (e.g. presence, IPTV, telephony supplementary services, etc.) that are configured for third party registration messages.

	IMS core	Application Server
Nb_SIP_Msg	6	3
Nb_SIP_transactions	3	3

Table 4.7: SIP transactions of registration flow

It is important to note that the re-registration messages may include the IMS registration validity and NAT (Network Address Translation) binding validity. As the objective of the latter registration messages, which are more frequent than the former, is only the the preservation of the NAT binding,

Chapter 4. Major Design Aspects for Session-based Multimedia Content Delivery

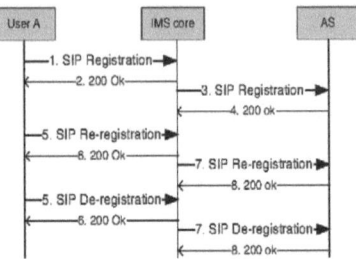

Figure 4.5: SIP registration flow

allowing terminals behind NAT to be reachable, the IMS registration validity messages are only forwarded to the application server. As each registration message is composed of a single transaction (in spite of authentication messages), the total SIP transactions are three, as illustrated in Figure 4.5 and Table 4.7.

In an IMS network, we consider a set of application servers Nas denoted as $A = \{1, 2, \ldots, Nas\}$, that are configured for the 3rd party registration. The percentage of application usage is denoted as Au:

$$Au = \{au_i | \exists i \in A : 0 \leq au_i \leq 1\}$$

Furthermore, the percentage of Active Service Usage of each AS is denoted as Asu:

$$Asu = \{su_i | \exists i \in A : 0 \leq su_i \leq 1\}$$

According to Equation (4.1) the total registration messages arrive the application server i is as follows:

$$AsRegMsg(i) = REGISTER \times au(i) \times su(i)$$

The consequence of the total impact on the IMS core; namely on the S-CSCF; is as follows (however, our main objective is to study the impact on the AS rather than the IMS core):

$$CoreREGISTER = REGISTER + \sum_{i=1}^{Nas} AsRegMsg(i)$$

4.3. Analysis of Efficient IMS-based Content Delivery Network

4.3.2.2 User Initiated Invite-based Session

IMS user can enquire about a multimedia content, uploading or stream content following the pull style by initiating a SIP Invite message that includes the targeted public service identifier and related session parameters in the SDP body. Accordingly the application server might decide to select a unicast or a multicast mode in the case of streaming or downloading content, however uploading content uses a unicast bearer. The next two subsections consider both use cases and the resultant impact on the application server. Note, with the intention of simplifying the diagram, messages interactions between the AS and the MDF do not pass the IMS core. Although this is not complaint with IMS specifications, the related impact on the IMS core will be accounted for in the corresponding table in brackets.

Unicast Delivery Session:

This use case can cover all types of delivery functions discussed in 4.2.7.1, including content consumer or IMS-based content provider (e.g. UGC). For each unicast bearer the AS, shall trigger the MDF for content delivery upon each received consumer invite request, as depicted in Figure 4.6 and Table 4.8.

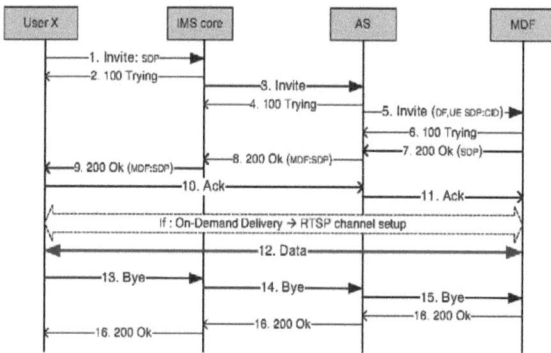

Figure 4.6: User-initiated invite request for unicast delivery mode

	IMS core	Application Server
Nb_SIP_Msg	6(+6)	6
Nb_SIP_transactions	2(+2)	4

Table 4.8: SIP transactions of user-initiated Invite unicast mode

The number of arrival SIP Invite messages at the application server can be calculated according to Equation (4.2) and the number of generated SIP Invite messages towards the MDF is equal to the arrival Invite messages. Note, when the IMS core mediates the signaling between the AS and the MDF (which is not illustrated in Figure 4.6), the related Nb_SIP_Msg and Nb_SIP_transaction become double; namely 12 and 6, respectively.

Multicast Delivery Session:

Multicast bearer is used to stream or download multimedia content. The IMS subscriber initiates a SIP Invite request either for each multicast bearer or a single invite request for a set of multicast bearers (e.g. broadcast TV service as defined in the IMS-based IPTV specification discussed in 2.3.4.4).

In the case that the session manager offers the user a set of multicast IP addresses (e.g. in line with a service subscription to a set of broadcast TV channels) during session setup or service provisioning, there are three options for the realization of channel zapping among these multicast IP addresses. Therefore we distinguish in the next flows between multicast session setup and multicast switching (zapping).

	IMS core	Application Server
Nb_SIP_Msg	6(+6)	6
Nb_SIP_transactions	2(+2)	2 + 2 (MDF transaction)

Table 4.9: SIP transactions of user-initiated invite request for multicast delivery mode

Multicast Session Setup : Figure 4.7 shows the session establishment of a multicast service where two IMS subscribers (can be more) having similar context properties acquire identical multimedia content. Once the application server determines the usage of a multicast bearer for delivering multimedia content upon receiving the first invite request, the AS invokes the relay function on the MDF following the back2back SIP user agent by issuing a SIP Invite message which includes the SIP URI of the relay function (as discussed in 4.2.7.3), the IP multicast address and media properties. As a consequence, the AS does not require triggering the MDF for successive user initiated Invite requests with identical delivery properties (e.g. content ID, codec, attached access network, etc.). Note, that the AS terminates the relay (or download) session by issuing the SIP Bye message (step 32) after receiving the last leave request from the multicast session .

4.3. Analysis of Efficient IMS-based Content Delivery Network

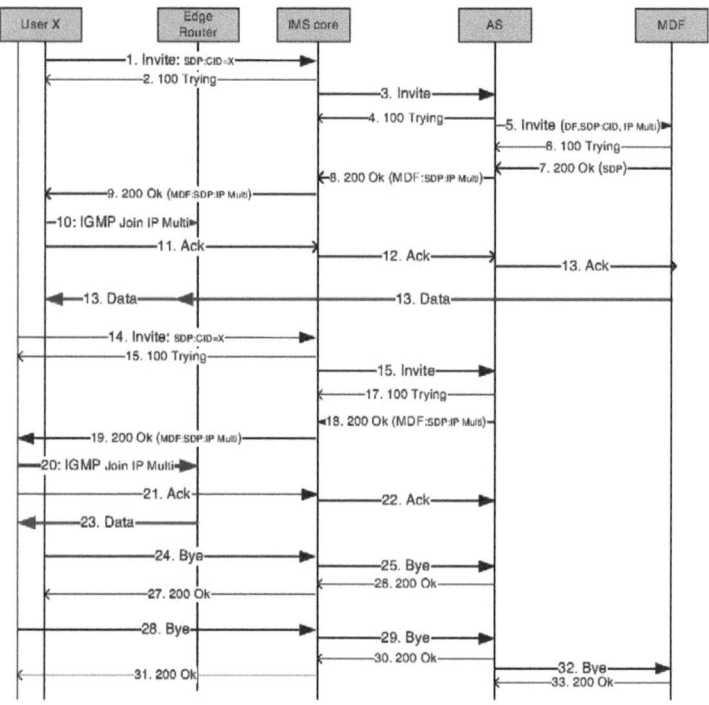

Figure 4.7: User-initiated invite request for multicast delivery mode

The number of arrival SIP Invite messages by the application server can be calculated according to Equation (4.2). However, the number of generated SIP Invite messages from the AS to the MDF is equal with the number of required multicast bearers to be used for delivering multimedia content, as shown in Table 4.9.

	IMS core	Application Server
Nb_SIP_Msg	3	1
Nb_SIP_transactions	1	1

Table 4.10: SIP transactions of user-initiated multicast switching request via SIP Re-Invite

Note when the IMS core mediates the signaling messages between the AS and the MDF (which is not illustrated in Figure (4.2)), the related

Chapter 4. Major Design Aspects for Session-based Multimedia Content Delivery

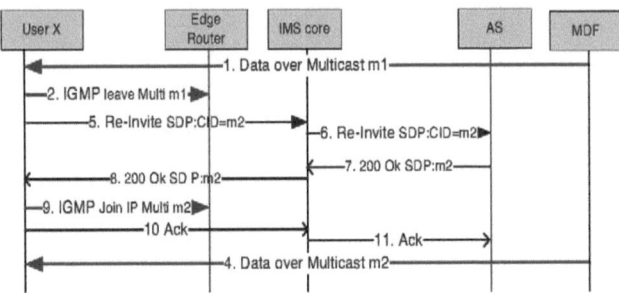

Figure 4.8: User-initiated multicast switching request via SIP Re-Invite

Nb_SIP_Msg and Nb_SIP_transaction increase according to the number of the used multicast bearers.

Multicast Switching : There three options for the realization of multicast switching within a set of multicast channels. These are Re-Invite-based, Info-based and Event-based switching, as follows:

1. **Re-Invite-based switching**: In which the IMS subscriber issues a SIP Re-Invite message indicating channel ID and possibly delivery parameters, as depicted in Figure 4.8 and 4.10. As consequence, the AS responds with the associate bearer parameters. The advantage of this model is twofold. First, the user can declare any change in his delivery parameters (e.g. codec, local IP address, etc.) upon individual channel switch. Second, the AS can decide upon receiving the re-invite request whether to select a multicast or a unicast bearer. However, the disadvantages are that it may decrease network and user-perceived performance. The network performance is decreased due to the additional SIP transactions produced by the Invite-message. The user-perceived performance is decreased because the re-invite request adds delay to the total signaling latency - IGMP leave and join requests (in addition to the local media processing, in the case of RTP streaming).

   The number of arrival SIP Re-Invite messages by the application server can be calculated according to Equation (4.3) aligned with the associated service profile.

2. **Info-based switching**: In which the AS announce all multicast addresses (within a subscribed service package) during multicast session establishment or session provisioning. Consequently, the

4.3. Analysis of Efficient IMS-based Content Delivery Network

IMS subscriber informs the AS via a SIP Info message after channel zapping. Figure 4.9 illustrates the related message flows in which the user issues the SIP info message with the same call ID of the session setup (as specified in RFC3261) and Table 4.11 shows the related SIP transactions. This leads to improved user-perceived QoS and network performance. It is more network efficient because SIP Info requests are composed of only two messages (request and confirmation) covering concerned switching channel information. User-perceived performance is improved because the signaling delay (due to SIP Info message) does not contribute to the total latency. The primary disadvantage is that the AS shall maintain all received SIP Info messages, and that rate is certainly much larger than the multicast session setup (rate of Invite requests), as introduced in Table 4.4 and Table 4.5.

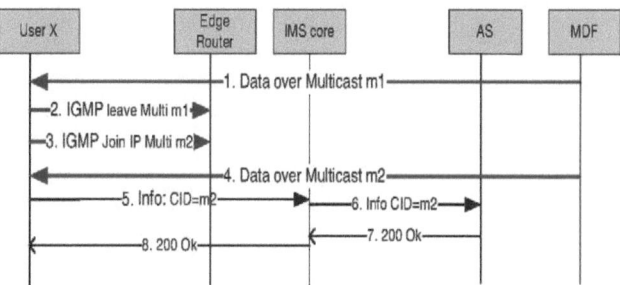

Figure 4.9: User-initiated multicast switching request assisted with SIP Info

	IMS core	Application Server
Nb_SIP_Msg	2	1
Nb_SIP_transactions	1	1

Table 4.11: SIP transactions of user-initiated multicast switching request assisted with SIP Info

The number of arrival SIP Info messages to the application server can be calculated according to Equation (4.3) aligned with the associated service profile.

3. **Event-based switching**: likewise the previous model, the IMS subscriber is aware of all multicast addresses and thus switches between these channels by issuing the corresponding IGM leave

and join messages. Thereafter the subscriber announces the recent channel zapping activity by sending a SIP Notification message to the AS (e.g. the session manager) or a SIP Publish message to the presence server. In the latter use case, the AS can subscribe for user channel zapping activity with the presence server in order to be informed about the recent zapping state. The advantage of the notification-based announcement is that the AS does not need to interact with additional components to obtain zapping activity. However the Notification-based announcement model introduces an additional load on the IMS core as well as on the AS, due to subscription messages generated by the AS to zapping activity upon multicast session setup and maintenance of the related timer, as depicted in Figure 4.10 and Table 4.12. In the latter model (referred to as Presence-based announcement), although the scalability is improved because the load is distributed among several application servers, the rate of SIP Publish messages will introduce an additional load on the presence server and between the AS and the presence server. Note that interaction messages between the AS and the presence server are not depicted in Figure 4.11 and Table 4.13.

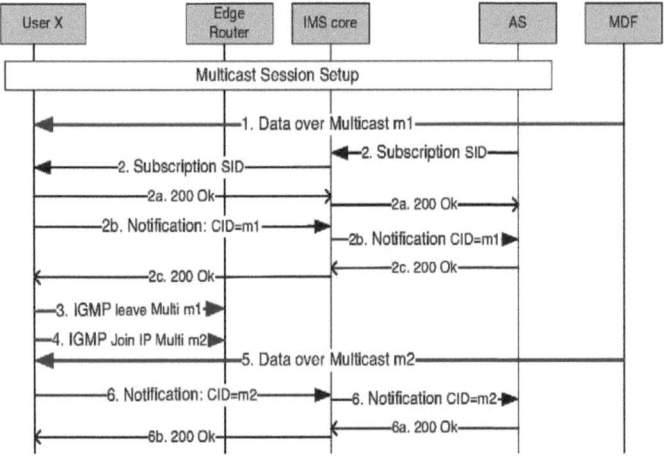

Figure 4.10: User-initiated multicast switching request assisted with Subscription-Notification

4.3. Analysis of Efficient IMS-based Content Delivery Network

	IMS core	Application Server
Nb_SIP_Msg	2+(4)	1+(2)
Nb_SIP_transactions	1+(2)	1+(2)

Table 4.12: SIP transactions of user-initiated multicast switching request assisted with Subscription-Notification

The number of arrival SIP Notification messages on the application server can be calculated according to Equation (4.12) aligned with the associated service profile, where Pu is equal to switching rate (e.g. as defined in Table 4.5). Furthermore, the number of the associated subscription messages (per hour) issued by the AS can be calculated as follows:

$$ZappingSubscription = MulticastSessions \times (1 + Sr) \times 3600 \tag{4.14}$$

Whereas MulticastSessions can be calculated according to Equation (4.1). The AS shall refresh the subscription with the rate Sr during the entire multicast session.

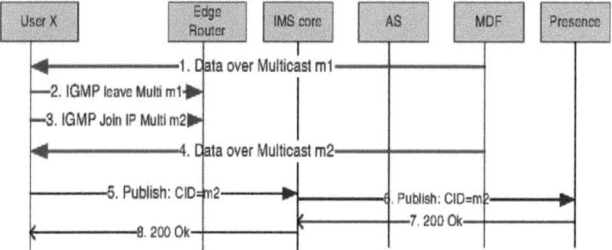

Figure 4.11: User-initiated multicast switching request assisted with presence server

	IMS core	Application Server
Nb_SIP_Msg	2	1
Nb_SIP_transactions	1	1

Table 4.13: SIP transactions of user-initiated multicast switching request assisted with presence server

On the contrary, the number of arrival SIP Publish messages by the presence server can be calculated according to Equation (4.3), where $Max(Pu, Pr)$ is equal to the switching rate as well.

4.3.2.3 Application Initiated Invite-based Session

In line with the requirements defined in subsection 3.4 the session manager shall enable third party applications to trigger the delivery of multimedia content to a set of IMS subscribers. In this regard, the session manger (referred to in the following with the term AS) may use a unicast or multicast transmission mode for content delivery. Application initiated invite-based session setup follows push style with regard to multimedia content delivery method.

Unicast Delivery Session:

Upon receiving an application request (through defined programming interface e.g. WS) including content ID or source and targeted IMS subscribers, the application server sends, for each subscribers, a dedicated SIP Invite request with its public service identity, but without any SDP offer. Upon receiving user 200 OK message covering the SDP offer, the AS initiates for each user request a dedicated SIP Invite message addressed to the MDF to relay the requested multimedia content with certain delivery parameters indicated in the SDP offer. Consequently, the MDF responds with an SDP answer that is then forwarded to the user. In the case of content streaming, the delivery can be linear or on-demand (as described in 3.2.1.2). In the latter use case, the SDP answer shall include a link to an RTSP resource for controlling media delivery. Figure 4.12 illustrates the detailed interactions between all IMS network nodes and Table 4.14 shows the related SIP transactions.

	IMS core	Application Server
Nb_SIP_Msg	$7(+6) \times N$	$6 \times N$
Nb_SIP_transactions	$3(+2) \times N$	$5 \times N$

Table 4.14: SIP transactions of application-initiated unicast session

The number of issued SIP Invite messages sent to the consumers as well as to the MDF is equal to the number of invited users assigned in the application request. The number of the associated SIP transactions is shown the table above. The primary disadvantage of this model is that the session setup may exceed a few seconds due to local notification in UE upon reception of the Invite request (step 4 to 8). Furthermore, if the content is a live captured stream, a large number of invited users may introduce long session setup (due the previous reason in addition to network delay) that shall be managed by the AS carefully.

Multicast Delivery Session :

4.3. Analysis of Efficient IMS-based Content Delivery Network

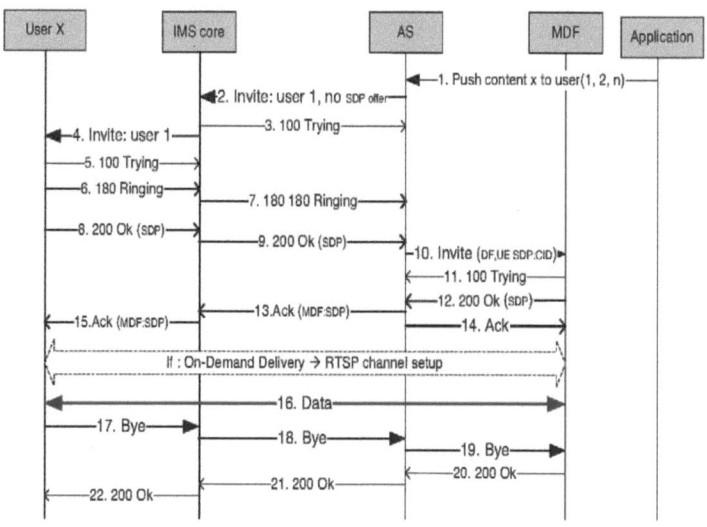

Figure 4.12: Application-initiated unicast session

Similar to the previous unicast delivery session, the application requires the AS to push multimedia content to a set of N IMS subscribers. Accordingly, the AS issues a SIP Invite request for each IMS subscriber without SDP offer. Figure 4.13 shows the corresponding message flows for just 3 users, however the session may comprise more than that. Table 4.15 shows the related SIP transactions. Upon receiving the first set of 200 ok respond messages, the AS determines bearer parameters (e.g. codec, IP multicast address, etc.) and then triggers the MDF to relay the content over IP multicast bearer. According to Figure 4.13, the AS waits until all IMS subscribers respond to the initiated AS Invite message (up to step 3c), however this case might not occur in practice, because the ringing phase may take a few seconds. Therefore, after receiving the first 200 ok message by the AS, the processing time for the following transactions will be less than 500 ms; otherwise the IMS subscriber will assume packet loss and thus re-sends the 200 ok message again. For this reason,phase may take the AS shall trigger the MDF as soon as possible and send the SIP Ack message back to the user. As a consequence, this model can work fine, with a few users, but with large numbers of users, the AS shall measure for each Invite request the corresponding delay in order to avoid packet retransmission. As alternative to this solution, the AS may finalize session setup of each responded Invite request and then send a Re-Invite message for any further session parameter update; however this may introduce additional load on the network, but simplify the processing on the AS.

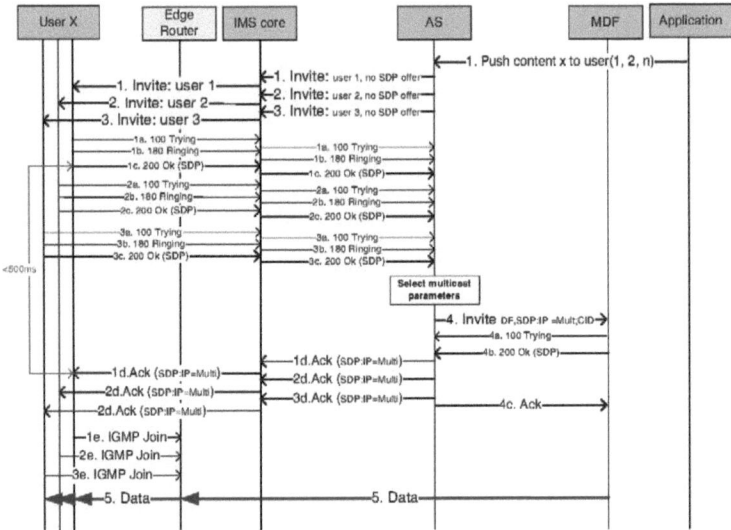

Figure 4.13: Application-initiated multicast session

	IMS core	Application Server
Nb_SIP_Msg	$7 \times N(+6)$	$3 \times N + 3$
Nb_SIP_transactions	$3 \times N(+2)$	$3 \times N + 2$

Table 4.15: SIP transactions of application-initiated multicast session

The primary disadvantage of this model is that the session setup may exceed few seconds due to various waiting time ringing in user device. Furthermore, users that joined late will not receive the multimedia content from the beginning. The number of issued SIP Invite messages equals the number of invited users passed in the application request. The number of the associated SIP transactions is shown the table above. The number of SIP INVITE messages issued by the AS to the MDF is equal to the number of required IP multicast bearers (one IP multicast is illustrated in 4.13). Note, Figure 4.13 does not show the SIP Bye transactions, but we consider them in the table. If

4.3. Analysis of Efficient IMS-based Content Delivery Network 109

the IMS core intermediates AS and MDF interactions, the associated number of SIP messages and transactions are in brackets.

4.3.2.4 Event-Induced Session

To avoid unexpected user or network behavior in the push delivery style, as discussed in the previous subsection 4.3.1.1, we propose the event-induced session setup as an alternative, as introduced in 4.2.6.

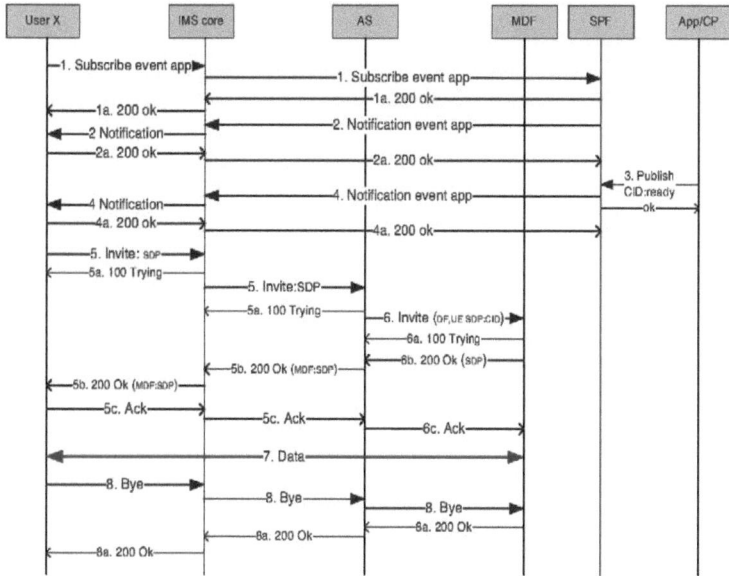

Figure 4.14: Event-induced session flow

	IMS core	Application Server
Subscription and Notification		
Nb_SIP_Msg	4	2
Nb_SIP_transactions	2	2
Session setup (Invite-based)		
Nb_SIP_Msg	6(+6)	6
Nb_SIP_transactions	2(+2)	2

Table 4.16: SIP transactions of event-induced session flow

In this style, the SM (session manager) collaborates with the CIPF (Content Information Provisioning function) for multimedia content delivery following the pull style. Initially, the IMS subscriber shows interest in multimedia service/content information by issuing a SIP Subscribe message with the related event package and addressed to the CIPF as public service identifier. When changes occur (e.g. certain content is available for download or streaming), the CIPF informs all associated subscribers by issuing SIP Notification messages with the related session parameters (e.g. content ID, SIP or IP multicast resource, supported codec, etc.). As a consequence, each IMS subscriber, who is interested in the content, issues a SIP Invite request to the associated SIP resource. If the resource is an IP multicasts address and the related multicast session has been established, the subscriber just needs to join the multicast group following one of the procedures introduced in 4.3.2.2.

The number of SIP transactions of Subscribe and Notification messages can be calculated according to Equation (4.5) and Equation (4.13), respectively, where:

- Subscription and notification messages are negotiated between the IMS subscriber and the CIPF through the IMS core, because the CIPF shall support the RLS functions

- Ng: s (service package) per user; e.g. $Ng = 3$, comprise multimedia service, multimedia content or content provider, as defined in 4.2.4.

- Nw:Average number of multimedia content (channel) per service package or Average number of content provider; e.g. $Nw = 10$

The generated SIP Invite requests depend on the publish rate of multimedia content information induced by the application or the content provider through API or SIP Publish message, respectively. Therefore the number of SIP Invite transactions can be calculated according to Equation (4.2), where:

$$SPUA \times SDBH = Max(Pu, Pr)$$

Pu and Pr are defined in Table 4.6 Event Framework Profile.

4.4 Protocols Evaluation

This subsection explores the differences between the SIP and the HTTP as well as streaming over UDP or TCP.

4.4. Protocols Evaluation

4.4.1 SIP vs. HTTP

Referring to session setup and multimedia content delivery, the SIP and the HTTP will play an important role, but the question remains of to what extent each of both protocols can be used efficiently. In general, the best protocol performance is obtained by minimizing interactions. Before answering such questions, we want to understand first the main distinctions of both protocols.

Feature	SIP	HTTP
Communication style	Nodes can simultaneously act as client and server (peer-to-peer), due to registration	Either client or sever, as server address is known (URL) but client can be anonym
Supported methods	Session support (Invite, Ack, Bye, Cancel, Option Prack, update, and register) Messaging support (Info and Message) Event-package (Subscription, Notification and Publish)	Support only data modification methods (Get, Post, Put, Delete and connect)
State	Stateful and stateless	Stateless
Reliability	Reliable due to confirmation request for each transaction	Unreliable and thus depends on reliable transport protocol
Mobility	Support personal mobility due to steady updating of the binding of SIP URI and IP address	No support
Transport protocol	UDP is most frequently used, but TCP or SCTP [83] can be used as well	TCP due to unreliability on the IP protocol

Table 4.17: SIP vs. HTTP Features

Although SIP follows the syntax and the semantics of HTTP, the primary distinctions between both protocols are the communication style between protocol components, supported methods, state maintenance, reliability, mobility support and the transport protocol. Table 4.17 shows these differences. SIP is on the way to becoming the dominant session-based control protocol for fixed and mobile all IP networks. However, due to the continued interest in HTTP in the Internet and web-based traffic, there needs to be an acknowledgment that no single protocol holds all the answers to fulfill all requirements of multimedia applications.

Protocol	Net. Perform.	UP Perform.	Scalability	Mobility sup.	Reliability	Visibility
UDP	++	++	++	-	-	+
TCP	+	+	+	+	++	-

Table 4.18: Evaluation of streaming via UDP vs. TCP

4.4.2 Streaming over UDP vs. TCP

Most of the available web-based streaming services (e.g. YouTube) transfer content streams over the HTTP protocol, which mainly relies on the HTTP over the TCP protocol, as discussed in 2.4.4. Indeed, TCP is conventionally regarded as inappropriate for multimedia streaming, because of its back-off policies implicit in the TCP due to packet loss and retransmission mechanisms that may lead to long delays which violate the real-time requirements of multimedia streaming. B. Wang et al. [84] provides an analytic performance study of single-path TCP streaming and found that its performance is generally satisfactory when the achievable TCP throughput is roughly twice the media bit-rate, with a few seconds of startup delay. This result partly explains why TCP streaming can be considered as an alternative in practice, such that bandwidth requirements can be satisfied for broadband connections (e.g. VDSL or FTTH). Although TCP supports reliable end-to-end content delivery, it is not network efficient.

On the contrary, streaming via RTP over UDP is most efficient and can have a very positive impact on user perceived performance, because it supports unicast and multicast delivery modes. Streaming over UDP improves visibility, as media proxies can mediate the stream for further processing (e.g. transcoding). However, the only downside to UDP is that many network administrators close their firewalls to UDP traffic, limiting the potential audience for UDP-based streams.

In general, the advantage of streaming over UDP is the improved efficiency that can meet user-perceived QoS, while steaming over TCP can be used only for content streaming in one direction (e.g. a server streams stored content to a web-browser). On the other hand, streaming over TCP enables the utilization of existing infrastructures, because the web-based approach uses only the standard web server and the Internet browser. As a consequence of this, streaming over UDP will be available in a managed service offering, while streaming over TCP will remain dominant for web-based traffic in the public Internet.

4.5 Discussion

This chapter analyzed the requirements defined in chapter 3 and mapped these requirements to capabilities provided by dedicated functional components. First, a state model of session-based content delivery in the NGN environment was introduced. Based on this model and along with architecture properties defined in the previous chapter subsection 3.2.2, different interaction models of multimedia content delivery are evaluated. The result of this evaluation is provided as a recommendation for a given interaction model for a specific delivery function. The design recommendations are matched to five functional components, as follows:

IMS core : Routing SIP requests between IMS subscribers and the Application Server (AS) should be based on the PSI (Public Service Identifier) rather than the evaluation of defined user filter criteria.

Content Information Provisioning Function : The CIPF shall implement the event-based pull model between system entities for handling multimedia content and service information.

Content Management Function :

- The content identifier may be covered in SIP headers or in the SDP session or media attributes.
- The content manager shall make use of multimedia content information (metadata) managed by the CIPF in order to resolve content location and delivery status.
- The communication between the SP and the CP shall follow a session-based client server model.

Multimedia Session Management :

- Each session management function shall have a unique IMS PSI reachable within the IMS network either from a SIP-based or a web-based node.
- The session manager shall make use of subscription information to multimedia content managed by the CIPF in order to optimize required delivery resource usages.
- Multimedia Session Management function shall implement the event-induced session setup model for session establishment towards the subscribers

- SIP shall be used for session management between the service provider and the consumer
- Multimedia Session Management function shall interact with the CMF to retrieve content identifiers with the service provider domain
- Session manager shall select the appropriate transmission mode unicast, multicast or broadcast for multimedia content delivery to the end users.
- The SIP protocol shall be used for triggering media delivery and processing functions.
- For discovering media delivery and processing capabilities the SIP INFO message can be used.

Media delivery function :The SIP Invite-based session shall be used to control the media delivery and processing functions provided by the MDF according to the RFC4240. One of the significant requirements of an NGN-based multimedia delivery network is to serve a very large number of users who interact with multiple applications such as live streaming, VoD, audio/video telephony, presence, messaging, etc.. Therefore, the architecture shall gracefully and economically scale from a small number of users to millions of users. In this chapter, several IMS-based service profiles and dimension parameters are proposed. Afterwards, quantification of the related message flows that fulfill the requirements defined in chapter 3 were conducted. Along with the analysis guidelines defined in clause 4.2.4, the mathematical formulation of several IMS interaction models are developed in clause 4.3.1 and comprehensive study concerning message flows in several delivery use cases, the functional requirements introduced in this chapter were discussed. As a consequence of this discussion, recommendations for suggested protocol or protocol combinations for several multimedia delivery use cases were made from the perspective of content-to-service provider and service-provider-to-consumer.

Content Provider to Service Provider : Based on the discussion of the interaction model between the content provider and service provider, as well as the corresponding functional requirements introduced in sections 4.2.4, 4.2.5 and 4.2.7, Table 4.19 gives a summary of the proposed use cases and suggested protocols. The service provider is in charge of the CMF (Content Management Function), the application and the delivery functions.

4.5. Discussion

Use case	Function	Protocol	Comment
Push live content	Session setup	SIP+SDP	
	Streaming	RTP via UDP	Refer to 4.4.2
Push stored content	Session setup	SIP or HTTP	Depend on CP device capabilities; SIP following RFC 4483 [85]
	Upload	FTP or HTTP	
Pull live content	Session setup	SIP+SDP or RTSP+SDP	Depends on CP device capabilities;
	Streaming	RTP via UDP	
Pull stored content	Provisioning or Session setup	SIP or HTTP	CP provides multimedia content information to CIPF, refer to 4.2.6
	Download	FTP or HTTP	

Table 4.19: Content and Service Provider use case relationship

Service Provider to Consumer : Based on the discussion of the interaction model between the service provider and the consumer, as well as the corresponding functional requirements introduced in sections 4.2.4, 4.2.6 and 4.2.7, this section provide a summary of the required use cases and suggested protocols. The service provider is in charge of providing the application logic, the CIPF, the SMF and the required delivery functions.

Since multimedia service offerings usually cover large number of IMS subscribers, the analysis will primarily follow the discussion of the requirements for large IMS-based content delivery networks introduced in section 4.3. However, two use cases could further impact network performance and user-perceived performance and thus both require further investigation. These use cases are the multicast switching problem and application-initiated push sessions. As stated in subsection 4.3.2.2, there are four options for multicast channel switching after session establishment, summarized in the first column in Table 4.20. However, in order to evaluate the corresponding impact on the IMS core as well as on the AS, Equations (4.3), (4.12), (4.13), (4.14) and service flows of (4.14) are put into practice exercise. Appendix B.1 includes further details on the service profile and related parameters. The results show that the first three options (Re-Invite, Info and Publish) produce an equal number of SIP transactions, while the Subscription-Notification option produces 15 times SIP transactions compared with the other three options. Although we consider the optimization technique for reducing notification messages, according to RFC 5839 and reflected in Equation (4.13), the generated load is still 8 times more than the other three options. However the refresh rate of Subscription messages is defined to be half of that suggested by the IPTV specifications [40].

Method	Net. Perform.	UP Perform.	Scalability	Mobility sup.	Reliability	Visibility	Simplicity
Re-Invite-based	-	-	+	+	+	+	+
Info issued to AS	+	+	+	-	+	++	++
Event-based: Publish	+	++	++	-	-	-	+
Event-based: Sub/Notify	-	+	-	-	+	-	-

Table 4.20: Evaluation of multicast switching options

In spite of the fact that the total numbers of SIP transactions of the first three options are equal, each option has different pros and cons, as discussed in-depth in clause 4.3.2.2 and summarized in Table 4.20. From an implementation point of view, the Info-based message notification is simple and exhibits good network and user performance. However, if the presence server is deployed with the intention of enabling IMS subscribers to share their multimedia experience with each other, as discussed in different scenarios in [62], the SIP Publish message covering channel zapping information is more efficient and leads to a more scalable infrastructure, as the AS (multimedia session function) does not need to process a high rate of SIP Info messages and only service to service interaction within the network infrastructure (where application servers can be deployed in different service provider domains).

On the other hand, subsections 4.3.2.3 and 4.3.2.4 describe the multimedia push scenario, where in the former case, the application triggers the SMF to invite a set of IMS subscribers, while in the latter case, each IMS subscriber initiates the session by himself after being notified by the CIPF content availability (i.e. CP or application updating multimedia content information status). Similar to the previous use case, Equations (4.2), (4.5), (4.9) and (4.13) as well as service flows of subsections 4.3.2.3 and 4.3.2.4 are put into practice, as included in Appendix B.2. It is clear that the event-induced session setup leads to decreased network performance, because it produces additional traffic due to the generated subscription and notification transactions when compared with the application initiated session setup; furthermore, the results show that the event transactions are 2.4 times the number of the SIP Invite transactions of the application initiated session. However

4.5. Discussion

event transactions can be reduced to 32% by optimizing the number of generated SIP Notification messages, following Equation B.

Use case	Function	Protocol	Comment
Push or Pull live content	Session setup	SIP+SDP	
	Streaming	RTP via UDP	see to 4.4.2 unicast or multicast
Push stored content	Session setup	SIP+SDP	
	Media control	RTSP	In case of on-demand delivery
	streaming	RTP via UDP	Delivery in managed domain
Push stored content	Session setup	SIP+SDP	Content indirection following RFC 4483 [20] or [86]
	Download	FTP or FLUTE	Unicast or multicast
Pull stored content	Session setup	HTTP	Web-based access
	Streaming	TCP	
Pull stored content	Session setup	SIP+SDP or HTTP	SIP content indirection following RFC 4483 [85] or HTTP
	Download	FTP or FLUTE	multicast only in managed domain
Multimedia service provisioning	Subscription and notification	SIP event package	HTTP to be considered

Table 4.21: Service Provider and consumer use case relationships

In spite of the load, the event-induced session noticeably improves the user-perceived performance, scalability, system visibility and simplicity, as shown in Table 4.2. The user-perceived performance is improved because the user can decide to inquire or join the multimedia content delivery at his leisure and with the preferred end device. Scalability is improved because signaling load is distributed among several nodes, namely the SMF and the CIPF. Furthermore, the SMF needs to manage only terminated sessions with fewer numbers of transactions, as the Invite transactions of the event-induced session are reduced by 40% compared to those produced in the application-initiated session, refer to Figure 4.12, Figure 4.14 and Appendix 4.14. The reliability is improved because of the load and function distribution among the SMF and the CIPF. The visibility and simplicity are improved because the SMF does not need to establish many connections in parallel.

Table 4.21 summarizes the SP use cases, related functions and protocols.

As a consequence, the incorporation between the CIPF and the SMF facilitates efficient multimedia content delivery and satisfies user-expectation.

However, multimedia applications may require the push functions, such as the PoC service. For this reason, Table 4.21 includes the corresponding functions with the related protocols.

This chapter examined the scope of the dissertation by analyzing the requirements defined in the previous chapter and discusses a corresponding conceptual functional model covering mainly the functional elements, namely the CIPF, the CMF, the SME and the MDF. Furthermore, several communication styles and how they can be used are evaluated in order to guide the architecture design in the next chapter.

The next chapter uses the insight garnered from this analysis and classification to propose guidelines to effectuate improvements in the design the IMS-based multimedia delivery network.

CHAPTER 5
Design and Specification of COSMIC

5.1 Introduction

In chapter 3 the system requirements for IMS-based efficient content delivery were identified, discussed, and analyzed these requirements with the aid of a conceptual model and mathematical analysis in chapter 4, which together provide guidelines for architectural design and efficient communications methods between the functional entities. In this chapter the design principles and consequent framework are introduced. Furthermore, the design of all system components and related interfaces are comprehensively explained.

5.2 Content Delivery Core Components

The overall research framework and the NGN environment introduced in Figure 1.4 and discussed in section 1.4 and in section 4.2 are used to define a detailed architecture of the proposed framework that enables efficient delivery of multimedia content in an NGN environment. Therefore, the framework will use all 3GPP and TISPAN IMS interface notation and follows the recommendations defined in chapter 4. Figure 5.1 illustrates the architecture of a generic framework in line with NGN layering approach defined by the ETSI TISPAN and ITU-T NGN architecture [1]. The proposed framework is composed of two planes (*the content provider and the consumer*) and four layers as follows:

Access and Transport Layer : The access and transport layer shall cover various access technologies, IP core and media delivery functions.

- The access layer should be capable of supporting bidirectional communication over fixed (e.g. DSL/FTTH and Cable TV) and wireless (e.g. 3GPP, WLAN and possibly DVB-T/H) technologies and at the same time, enable the delivery of IP packets via unicast, multicast or broadcast transmission mode.

Chapter 5. Design and Specification of COSMIC

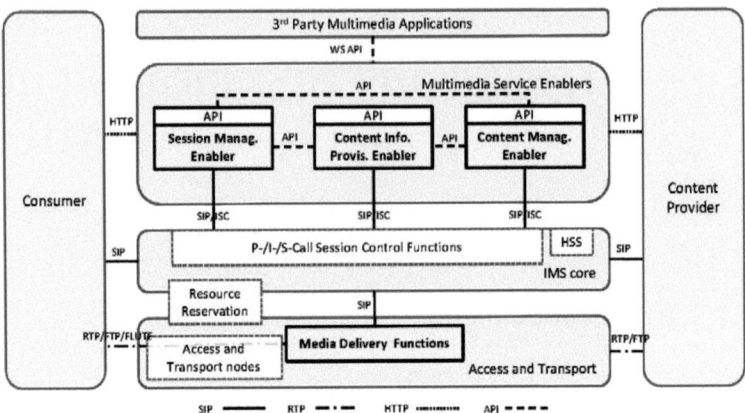

Figure 5.1: Generic framework for multimedia content delivery in NGN environment

- The transport layer is responsible for the management of the IP addresses and routing IP packets, along with resource reservation functionality that controls the required resources on the access, as well as on the IP core. The Media Delivery Functions (MDF) is realized through a set of distributed media servers denoted as Content Delivery and Processor Function (CDPF) that provides media processing and content delivery from the content provider to the consumers that will be defined in detail in subsection 5.2.4.

IMS Core : It is responsible for SIP session control as discussed in section 2.3.3.1. It consists of all IMS functions such as the CSCFs, the BGCF/MGCF, the MRFC and the HSS. Most of IMS nodes are not depicted in Figure 5.1. It is in charge of the following functions:

- Routes the SIP signaling between the IMS users, IMS application servers and the interworking with other IMS networks;
- Provides discovery and address resolution services;
- Supports SIP compression/decompression;
- Performs authentication and authorization of the IMS functional entities;
- Maintains the registration state; and
- Provides charging information.

5.2. Content Delivery Core Components 121

Multimedia Service Enablers Layer : Is represented through a set of service functional blocks each of which provides an internal functionality used by the end-user, other multimedia service enabler or third party application. Although there are several IMS enablers defined by different standard organizations such as the OMA, this dissertation identifies the following three enablers that pertain to aspects of multimedia content delivery:

1. Content Information Provisioning Enabler Content Information Provisioning Enabler (CIPE)
2. Content Management Enabler Content Management Enabler (CME)
3. Session Management Enabler Session Management Enabler (SME)

For efficient content delivery, these three enablers are used during the entire life-cycle of multimedia content delivery defined in 4.2.1. The architectural design of these enablers satisfies the most desired properties and recommendations defined in previous chapter. The enablers, by design, try to be aligned with most of standardization bodies like OMA, IETF, 3GPP and ETSI TISPAN.

Note that in fact there are additional functions, such as - among others - authorization, charging, accounting and digital rights management, that are essential for any commercial deployment of a multimedia content delivery framework, this work limits the scope to propose new design for delivering multimedia content with an emphasis on efficiency and supporting interactivity and personalization, as well as service openness, rather than focusing on BSS (Business Supported System) and Operating Support System (OSS) aspects. Therefore, the next subsections describe the architecture of the proposed enablers; however, functions and the interfaces between enabler functional components have been moved to Appendix C.

5.2.1 Content Information Provisioning Enabler

The CIPE manages subscription and notification events between the source of content and service information and the consumers in an IMS networks. However, it shall support multi-IMS domain networks as well through which the IMS core interworks with other IMS domains.

Referring to the discussion conducted in subsection 4.2.4 and 4.5, the CIPE follows the event communication style and thus mainly uses the SIP Subscription, Notification and Publish methods. From an architectural perspective,

122 Chapter 5. Design and Specification of COSMIC

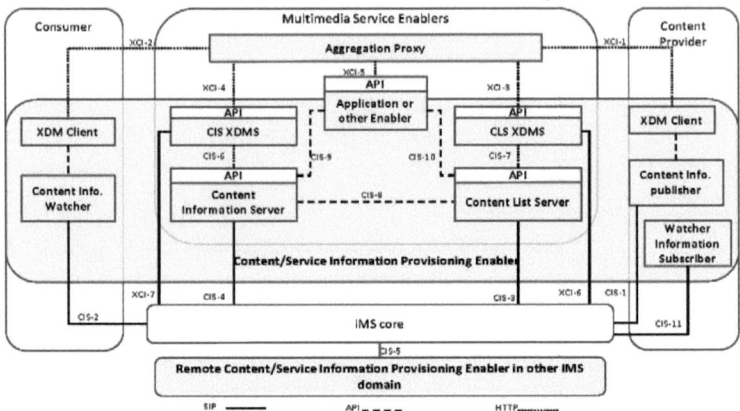

Figure 5.2: Content Information Provisioning Enabler architecture

CIPE functions are similar to the presence server function introduced in subsection 2.3.4.2. However, the CIPE manages multimedia content information while the presence server manages the presence information of IMS subscribers. Figure 5.2 illustrates the architecture of the CIPE, which leverages the OMA XDMS functions and the notation of the OMA presence enablers. The CIPE functional entities are described in the next subsection, while external entities and the related reference points are described in C.1. The CIPE may interact with other subsystems such as charging subsystem, user profile, BSS and OSS, but the related interfaces are not considered in the depicted logical architecture.

5.2.1.1 Functional Entities

Content Information Server (CIS) : The CIS is in charge of the following functions:

- Authorizes publications from counter information sources
- Accept and store multimedia content information published by the content source/provider.
- Authorizes Watchers' subscriptions and distributes content information according to RFC3265 and RFC3856 [14, 9] with a new event package.

5.2. Content Delivery Core Components

- Regulates the distribution of multimedia content information and watcher information in the manner requested by Watchers and Watcher Information Subscribers;
- Subscribes to changes in documents stored in the CIS XDMS;

Content Information Publisher (CIP): The CIP is an entity that provides multimedia content information to a Content Information Server via a SIP Publish method. It can be located in a user's terminal or within a network entity. It may interact with the CIS via HTTP or APIs (Application Programming Interface). It supports the following functions:

- Publishes Multimedia Content Information according to RFC3903;
- Monitors extended Watcher Information via a Watcher Information Subscriber for optimized publication decision;
- Publishes Multimedia Content Information based on the notification messages from the Content Information Server;
- Compresses/decompresses the presence-related SIP messages when the Multimedia Content Source resides in the terminal;
- Publishes Multimedia Content Information;
- Fetches the XML document with the lists of multimedia content for each content source;
- Manages permanent Multimedia Content Information according to RFC4827 via an XDMC [87].

Content Information Watcher (CIW): The CIW is an entity that requests multimedia content information about a single content source or multiple content sources. The Watcher can be located in a user's terminal or within a network entity. The Watcher supports the following functions:

- Subscribes to a content source's multimedia content information according to RFC3265, RFC5839 and new event package;
- Subscribes to multiple content sources' multimedia content information according to RFC3265, RFC5839, RFC4662, RFC5367 [16, 88, 89];
- Compresses/decompresses the presence-related SIP messages when the Watcher resides in the terminal.

Watcher Information Subscriber (WIS) : The WIS is an entity that requests Watcher Information about entities that subscribe to a content source's multimedia content information. It can be located in a user's terminal or within a network entity. It supports the following functions:

- Subscribes to Watcher Information according to RFC3265, RFC5839, multimedia content event package, and other extensions;
- Subscribes to multiple subscribers' Watcher Information according to RFC3265, RFC5839 and RFC5367 [16];
- Subscribes to Watcher Information based on a trigger from the CIS;
- Compresses/decompresses the presence-related SIP messages when the Watcher Information Subscriber resides in the terminal.

Content List Server (CLS) : The CLS is a functional entity that accepts and manages subscriptions to resource lists containing a set of multimedia content sources, which enables a subscriber to subscribe to a list of multimedia content resources using a single subscription transaction. It may be re-used by services that make use of the SIP event notification mechanism defined in RFC3265 and the SIP event notification extension for resource lists defined in RFC4662. It supports the following functions:

- Authorizes Watchers' subscriptions and distributes Multimedia Content Information according to RFC3265, RFC4662, RFC5367, RFC5839 and the new multimedia event package;
- Accepts Watcher Information Subscribers' subscriptions and distributes Watcher Information according toRFC3265, RFC3857, RFC5367 and RFC5839;
- Performs back-end subscriptions on behalf of the Watcher according to RFC3265, RFC4662 and RFC5839;
- Performs back-end subscriptions on behalf of the Watcher Information Subscriber according to RFC3265,RFC3857, RFC4662 and RFC5839 [88];
- Regulates the distribution of Multimedia Content Information in the manner requested by Watchers;
- Regulates the distribution of Watcher Information in the manner as requested by Watcher Information Subscribers;
- Propagates the Watcher's request to regulate the distribution of Multimedia Content Information in the back-end subscriptions;

5.2. Content Delivery Core Components 125

- Propagates the Watcher Information Subscriber's request to regulate the distribution of Watcher Information in the back-end subscriptions;
- Subscribes to changes to documents stored in CLS XDMS; and
- Fetches documents from the CLS XDMS.

XML Document Management Client (XDMC): The XDMC interacts with the SDMS depending on its different instantiations either as a CIS XDMC or a CLS XDMC. It is in charge of the following functions:

- Manage related XML documents (e.g., multimedia content information authorization rules). Content provider may define different rules for each multimedia content information source.
- Subscribe to SIP event package for changes to XML documents stored in any XDMS

The XDMC includes an XCAP client and a SIP User Agent.

CIS XML Document Management Server (CIS XDMS): The Content Information Server XDMS is an XCAP server and SIP Notifier, as defined in RFC3265, that supports the following functions:

- Manages XML documents (e.g. multimedia content information authorization policies) specific to the provisioning service Enabler.
- Enables subscriptions to changes to documents stored in the CIS XDMS
- Notifies subscribers of changes to the CIS-specific documents stored in the network.

Content List Server XML Document Management Server (CLS XDMS): The CLS XDMS is an XCAP server and SIP Notifier, as defined in [RFC3265], that supports the following functions:

- Manages the multimedia content list presented in XML documents, which are specific to the use of a CLS.
- Enables subscriptions to changes to documents stored in the CLS XDMS; and
- Notifies subscribers of changes to such documents stored in the network.

5.2.1.2 Multimedia Content Information Data Model

The key to understanding how the provisioning service enabler works is to conceive the underlying resource model of event notification. In general, this model is similar to the resource model introduced in the RFC4479, with some key differences [90]. This section explains in detail the model as it applies to multimedia content information events. Figure 5.3 illustrates the model.

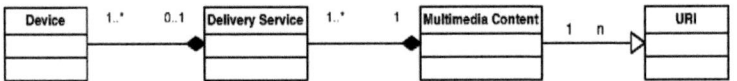

Figure 5.3: Content information data model

Multimedia content information conveys the availability of multimedia content to be consumed across a set of devices. The data model of the PSE follows the models defined in the RFC 4479 and RFC5839. The model is categorized in four classes:

1. The Content URI component indicates the content identifier (SIP URI, http URI, RTSP URI, RTP URI, etc.)

2. The Content component models the information about the content

3. The Service component models the delivery mechanism through which the content can be transmitted

4. The Device component models the physical pieces of equipment that captures, process or deliveries the content.

Therefore, multimedia content information combines devices, services and content information for a complete picture of a multimedia content's status on the network. We adapted the terms defined the RFC4479 with the scope of a multimedia content information data model. These new terms are as follows:

- **Data Component**: One of the device, service, or content parts of a multimedia content information document.

- **Status**: Availability information about a service, content, or device that typically changes over time, in contrast to characteristics, which are generally static.

- Characteristics: Information about a service, content, or device that is usually fixed over time, and descriptive in nature. Characteristics are useful for providing context that identifies the service or device as different from another service or device.

5.2. Content Delivery Core Components

- **Attribute**: A status or characteristic. It represents a single piece of content information.

- **Composition**: The act of combining a set of content and event data about multimedia content into a coherent picture of the state of that content.

The data model for multimedia content information is shown in Figure 5.3. The model seeks to describe the content, as identified by content URI. There are three components in the model: the content, the service, and the device. These three data components contain information (called attributes) that provides a description of some aspect of the service, content, or device. Detailed descriptions of these components can be found in Appendix C.1.

5.2.2 Content Management Enabler

Content Management Enabler (CME) controls the delivery of multimedia content from the content providers to the services providers and maintains related information. Referring to the analysis conducted in 4.5, the CME is in charge of managing the relationship between the service and content provider. It utilizes the CIPE functions to retrieve multimedia content information and the current status and interacts accordingly with the corresponding content provider.

The interaction communication styles between the CME and the content provider follow a session-based pull or push model using the SIP, the HTTP or the RTSP for session negotiation and the HTTP, the FTP and the RTP for content delivery as classified in Table 4.19 introduced in subsection 4.5. The CME makes use of the IMS core to interact with the content providers that can be a professional content provider or an ordinary IMS subscriber (to facilitate hosting and managing user generated content). The CME uses the media delivery functions to fetch or receive multimedia content from the content providers over IMS Mb reference point as introduced in 3.3.1 and thus triggers the MDF via the IMS ISC interface following either the back-to-back or third party call control SIP model. Figure 5.4 illustrates the logical architecture of the CME, functional entities are described in more detail in the next subsection, and the external functional entities and interfaces are discussed in Appendix C.2.

The CME may interact with other subsystems such as charging subsystem, user profile, BSS and OSS, but the related interfaces are not considered in the depicted logical architecture.

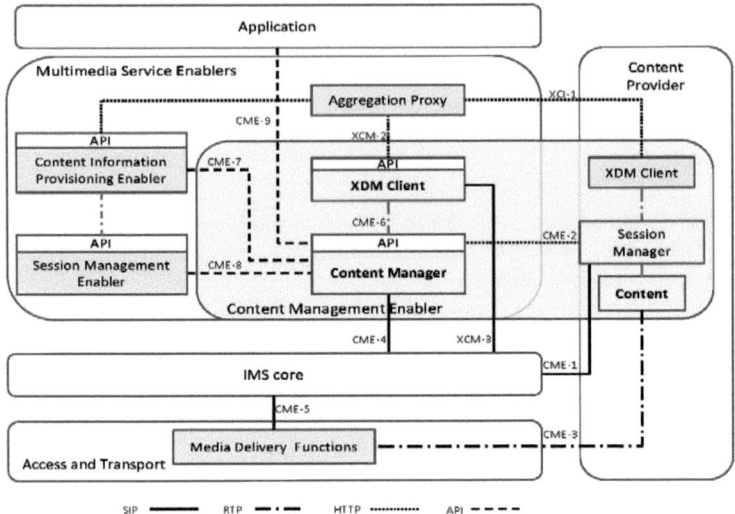

Figure 5.4: Content Management Enabler architecture

5.2.2.1 Content Manager

The Content Manager (CM) is the main functional component that interacts with different internal and external components and provides the following functions:

- Fetching multimedia content list from the XDM client via APIs

- Subscribing to the CIPE for any changes to the multimedia content information via APIs or SIP

- Receiving notification from the CIPE about any changes to the multimedia content information via APIs or SIP

- Interacting with the content provider to request or receive multimedia content either through pull or push communication style according to the classification defined in Table 4.19.

- Authorizing push multimedia content requests initiated by any content provider

5.2. Content Delivery Core Components

- Triggering media delivery functions to fetch or receive multimedia content from a dedicated resource following the back-to-back or third party call control SIP model. The related control method will follow the mechanism discussed in 4.2.7.3.

- Enabling the Session Management Enabler to retrieve information about available multimedia content

5.2.2.2 XDM Client

The XDM Client interacts with the XDM CIS to fetch content lists and the related multimedia content components via the XCAP. It also subscribes to the XDM CIS for any changes to the content list via SIP or APIs.

5.2.2.3 Content Provider

The Content Provider is the entity that provides the multimedia content. It is in charge of the following functions:

- Providing required content information to the CIPE via the XDM client and possibly publishing content status as specified above in Content Information Source.

- Pushing live or stored multimedia content to the CME after session setup via SIP or HTTP

- Enabling the CME to pull multimedia content after session setup via SIP, HTTP or RTSP

After session establishment, multimedia content is always transmitted to the media delivery nodes.

5.2.3 Session Management Enabler

The Session Management Enabler (SME) controls the delivery of multimedia content from the service provider to the consumers. In reference to the analysis discussed in 4.5, the SME is in charge of managing the relationship between the service provider and content consumers. The SME supports two content delivery services: live content streaming and stored content streaming. It interacts with the CME to retrieve multimedia content objects available in the network (i.e. MDF). Contents available in the MDF are either stored content or real-time stream that is received from certain content provider and can be relayed to any output bearers (e.g. to unicast or multicast bearers).

Based on the available content objects, the SME selects the suited delivery service for each content object, as it supports linear or on-demand delivery service. Therefore, it uses the CIPE to publish the related content information, as the CIPE is in charge of the composition of the available content information published by the content provider and the service-delivery-related information published by the SME.

According to user capabilities obtained during session establishment, the SME selects the appropriate delivery mode and then triggers the MDF for delivering the content to the consumer.

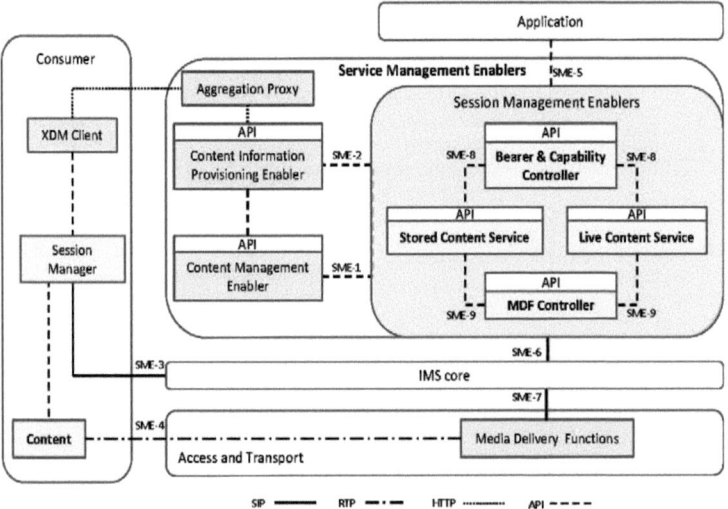

Figure 5.5: Session Management Enabler architecture

Figure 5.5 illustrates the logical architecture of the SME with functional entities described in more detail in the next subsection, while the external functional entities and interfaces are discussed in Appendix C.3. Note that the SME may interact with other subsystems such as charging subsystem, user profile, Business Support System (BSS) and OSS, but the related interfaces are not considered in the depicted logical architecture.

5.2.3.1 Live Content Service

The Live Content Service (LCS) is in charge of controlling the delivery of live content streams to the end users. The consumer can setup the session

5.2. Content Delivery Core Components

for content delivery by issuing a single SIP Invite request. In the case that the LCS maintains several content streams, to switch between several delivery channels, the user may perform one of the following scenario:

- Issuing a SIP re-Invite message in case of unicast content delivery mode or
- Leaving previous multicast group and then joining the target multicast group in case of multicast delivery mode, thereafter issuing a SIP Info or a SIP Publish message, as discussed in more detail in subsection 4.3.2.2.

The LCS may allow other service enablers or applications to push live multimedia content to a set of users through defined open interfaces. In such delivery use cases, two scenarios are possible:

- Inviting all users to this delivery session and triggering the MDF to start the delivery. However, such a use case is not recommended as we have found that the push method is neither efficient nor satisfies user-perceived multimedia experience (refer to detail discussion in subsection 4.5).
- Applying the event-induced session, in which the CIPE is in charge of distributing multimedia content information containing - among other parameters - content description, the status of multimedia content, content ID and the service URI of the LCS (i.e. the PSI in an IMS network). As a consequence, interested consumers can issue the SIP Invite request or directly join the multicast session (if the live session has been established before).

However, scenario one can be considered only if the application wants to address a determined set of users and wants to distinguish them from other users that might subscribe to the corresponding content list or the content provider list.

The LCS is in charge of the following functions:

- Receiving users' SIP Invite requests to start live delivery sessions following the procedure introduced in subsection 4.3.2.2.
- Receiving application requests to push multimedia content to a set of IMS end users
- Inviting end-users to a content delivery session with a dedicated multimedia content

- Interacting with the CME to retrieve multimedia content information about the available content in the MDF

- Publishing recent LCS delivery properties for each multimedia content to the CIPE

- Triggering media delivery and processing functions provided by the MDF

The primary distinction between the Live Content Service and the Stored Content Server (SCS) in general is that the LCS might serve a large number of users interested in particular live event. The SCS, on the other hand, mainly serves users that individually acquire multimedia content, which is delivered over a unicast transmission mode.

5.2.3.2 Stored Content Service

The Stored Content Service (SCS) is in charge of controlling the delivery of stored content streams to the end users. The consumer can setup the session for content delivery by issuing a single SIP Invite request. In the case that the LCS maintains several content streams that switch between several delivery channels, the user shall issue a dedicated SIP Invite message for each content delivery request.

The SCS may allow other service enablers or applications to push stored multimedia content to a set of users through defined open interfaces. The delivery may follow the Invite-based or event-induced session setup, as described in the previous subsection and in detail in 4.3.2.3 and in 4.3.2.4, respectively. The SCS is in charge of the following functions:

- Receiving users SIP Invite requests to start the delivery of a stored session following the procedure introduced in subsection 4.3.2.2.

- Receiving application requests to push multimedia content to a set of IMS end users

- Inviting end-users to a content delivery session with a dedicated multimedia content

- Interacting with the CME to retrieve multimedia content information about the available content in the MDF

- Publishing SCS as a delivery service for each multimedia content to the CIPE

- Triggering media delivery and processing functions provided by the MDF

5.2. Content Delivery Core Components

Although the SCS is mainly uses unicast transmission mode, the multicast mode might be used for delivering multimedia content to a set of users in linear mode (i.e. no support for trick functions mode).

5.2.3.3 Bearer Selection and Capability Controller

The Bearer Selection and Capability Controller (BSC) is in charge of the following functions:

- Validating user capabilities included in the SDP body against the content properties and the MDF capabilities
- Determining delivery properties of multimedia content according to users capabilities
- Selecting a transmission mode (unicast or multicast) according to user context (device capabilities and the available network condition)

5.2.3.4 MDF Controller

The MDFC is in charge of the following function:

- Discovering the delivering and processing capabilities of the MDF by issuing a SIP Option message
- Triggering the MDF to relay or stream multimedia content to one or a set of end users according to the RFC4240 [20].

5.2.4 Media Delivery Function

Media Delivery Function (MDF) provides capabilities for conveying multimedia content from the content provider to the end consumers while applying media processing functions if required. Referring to 4.2.7, the MDF supports two classes of content delivery:

- File-based content delivery using the HTTP, FTP or FLUTE protocols
- Streaming functions using the RTP over UDP

Figure 5.6 illustrates the logical architecture of the MDF, which consists of a Media Server Controller (MSC) and a Media Server Processor (MSP). However, in order to support scalable and distributed network, the MSC may control a set of MSPs. Each MSP has an input and output port for receiving

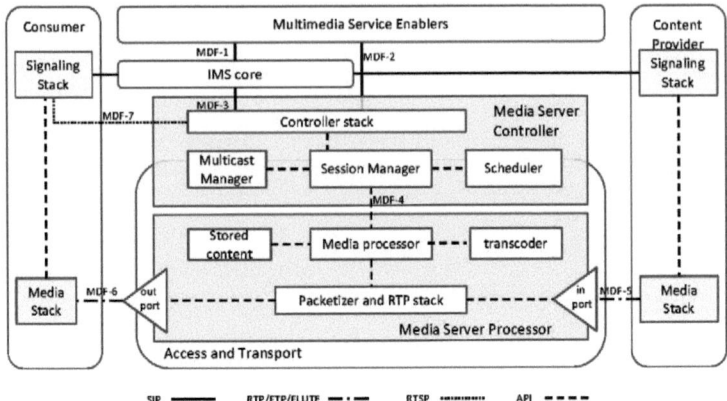

Figure 5.6: Media Delivery Function architecture

and transmitting multimedia content, respectively. The MSC enables application servers (e.g. SME, CME or any multimedia service enabler) to make use of the media delivery and processing functions provided by the MSP.

The application server may interact with the media server controller via the IMS core following the IMS architecture or via a direct interface. The advantage of the IMS-based interface is that the MDF networks can serve multiple application servers transparently, while the direct interface implies that the MDF is restricted to serve only a set of defined interfaces and shall implement all security aspects that can be provided by the IMS core.

The interface between the MSC and the MSP is not defined in this work. Therefore, a basic form of APIs is used to trigger the required media delivery and processing functions. However, this form of control does not constrain how an application server triggers the required functions or decrease the efficiency of content delivery. The following subsection describes the related functional entities, while the external functional entities and reference points will be discussed in Appendix C.4.

5.2.4.1 Media Server Controller

The MSC is in charge of the following functions:

- Enabling the application server to trigger multimedia delivery and processing functions following the RFC4240 as described in 4.2.7.3.

5.2. Content Delivery Core Components 135

- Controlling media delivery and processing functions on the Media Server Processor (MSP) via defined APIs

- Controlling the contemporary multimedia content stream and the available stored multimedia content

- Managing multicast delivery bearers for each multimedia content delivery

- Scheduling multimedia content for content delivery based on application server request

- Managing media control messages for controlling on-demand content stream according to the RFC2326 [18].

5.2.4.2 Media Server Processor

The MSC supports the following functions:

- Enabling the MSC to trigger media delivery and processing functions

- Fetching multimedia content from the Content Provider via FTP or HTTP

- Storing multimedia content fetched or streamed from the content provider

- Receiving content stream from a dedicated content provider or a multicast transmission mode

- Relaying stored or contemporary content streams to a set of end users over unicast or multicast bearer

- Streaming multimedia content in a linear or on-demand mode according to MSC request

- Transcoding multimedia content according to required output properties defined by the MSC

- Adapting content rate according to processor capabilities and MSC requests

- Downloading multimedia content over a multicast bearer via FLUTE protocol according to the RFC3926 [79].

5.3 Summary

In this chapter, the design principles and consequent framework for efficient delivery of multimedia content in an NGN environment are introduced. Furthermore, the design of all core functional components and related interfaces are comprehensively explained. The framework is in line with NGN principles and defines four layers and two planes as follows:

- The layers include access and transport, IMS-based service control functions, multimedia service enablers and third party multimedia applications.

- The planes encompass the content provider and the content consumer.

On the access layer, the platform takes into account the integration of bidirectional and unidirectional transport technologies such as DSL/PON, 3GPP networks and DVB. On the transport layer, IP multicast is considered to be used when applicable. The IMS core is used as is, without any modification in order to allow simple integration of the proposed functional components in an NGN environment.

According to the design guideline proposed in the previous chapter, the event-induced session is the most efficient model for multimedia content delivery. Based on this, a dedicated enabler called the Content/Service Information Enabler is defined. With this context in mind, the proposed framework is composed of four functional components, as depicted in Figure 5.1:

1. **Content Information Provisioning Enabler**(CIPE), which aggregates and distributes multimedia content information between content provider, service provider and consumers. The event-pull interaction model via the SIP and the HTTP is used, which relies on the SIP subscription and notification and the HTTP GET methods. The design of the CIPE follows the OMA presence and XDMS enablers, but using a different event-package and data model, as specified in subsection 5.2.1.

2. **Content Management Enabler**(CME), which controls the delivery of multimedia content from the content providers to the services providers and maintains the related information. It manages the multiple source multimedia content received from a DVB receiver or from user streaming or an upload content stream. It utilizes the CIPE functions to retrieve multimedia content information and the current status and accordingly interacts with the corresponding content provider and MDF for content delivery, as specified in subsection 5.2.2.

5.3. Summary

3. **Session Management Enabler** (SME) which controls the delivery of multimedia content from the service provider to the consumers in an IMS-based network. Referring to the analysis conducted in 4.5, the SME is in charge of managing the relationship between the service provider and content consumers. The SME supports two content delivery services: live content streaming and stored content streaming. It interacts with the CME to retrieve multimedia content objects available in the network (i.e. MDF). Contents available in the MDF are either stored content or real-time streamed content that is received from certain content providers and can be relayed to any output bearers (e.g. to unicast or multicast bearers) based on user context. Therefore, the SME realizes the vision of multimedia content delivery from multiple sources to several users over various channels. The detailed description can be found in subsection 5.2.3.

4. Media Delivery Function(MDF), which provides delivery capabilities for conveying multimedia content from the content providers to the end consumers while applying media processing functions if required. Referring to 5.2.4, the MDF supports two classes of content delivery: First, file-based content delivery using the HTTP, FTP or FLUTE protocols and content streaming using the RTP over UDP. The detailed specification can be found in subsection 5.2.4.

For efficient content delivery, these four enablers are used during the entire life-cycle of multimedia content delivery defined in 4.2.1. The architectural design of these enablers satisfies the most desirable properties and recommendations defined in chapter 4. The enablers, by design, are highly aligned with most standardization bodies like OMA, IETF, 3GPP and ETSI TISPAN.

There are additional functions, such as authorization, charging, accounting and digital rights management, that are also essential in any commercial deployment of a multimedia content delivery solution, however, the design in this work limits the scope only to those four enablers that are considered the core content delivery enablers.

The next chapter describes how the defined reference architecture was followed in the development of a prototype implementation for delivering multimedia content in an NGN environment.

CHAPTER 6
Implementation of Multimedia Content Delivery Core Enablers

6.1 Introduction

Following the specification of the IMS-based multimedia delivery framework as described in chapter 5, this chapter presents, in detail, how the specification was implemented in a prototype solution. The reference implementation consists of distributed components, which are the Content Information Provisioning Enabler (CIPE), Session Management Enabler (SME), Content Management Enabler (CME) and Media Delivery Function (MDF). The first three enablers are considered to be part of the multimedia service enabler layer and their entire implementation was based on JAVA. The implementation follows the paradigm of Object Oriented Programming. The MDF was part of the access and transport layer and was developed in C. In order to focus on the implementation aspect, the use cases and all message flows of these enablers have been moved to Appendix C.

6.2 Multimedia Service Enablers

The CIPE, the SME and the CME are implemented based on the SIP servlet APIs described in 2.3.4.1. Therefore, the implementation can be deployed in any application server that supports SIP servlet APIs. The interactions between these enablers in the current implementation are limited to those between the SME and the CME as the CIPE is still under development. Therefore, the XDM client and the interfaces towards the CIPE are not included.

In order to enable 3rd party applications to make use of these enablers, the supported capabilities are exposed through open programmable APIs specified with Web Service Description Language (WSDL). The realization of the related web services are based on the Axis libraries, which is an open source implementation for the web service communication protocol Simple Object Access Protocol (SOAP). SOAP is a lightweight protocol for exchanging structured information in a decentralized, distributed environment. Axis (Apache

EXtensible Interaction System) [91] is a SOAP framework for constructing SOAP communication entities.

In addition, the platform Java EE (Java Platform, Enterprise Edition version) is used for the realization of Web services and SIP Servlets. The related components are merely deployed in particular containers that implement the Java EE specification.

6.2.1 Content Information Provisioning Enabler

The logic of the CIPE is based on a general event-based handler that manages the SIP Publish, the Subscription and the Notification messages distributed among the data source, data consumers and the application. The event-based handler makes use of SIP Servlet APIs to interact with the content information provider and consumer, as depicted in Figure 6.1.

The event-based handler is implemented as a general container, handling the event messages, namely the SIP Publish, the SIP Subscription and the SIP Notification messages, independently of the event package, which is processed by additional application logic provided by plug-ins. Therefore, multiple applications can be run on the top of the event-based handler. Plug-ins can be added, removed and (de-)activated at runtime.

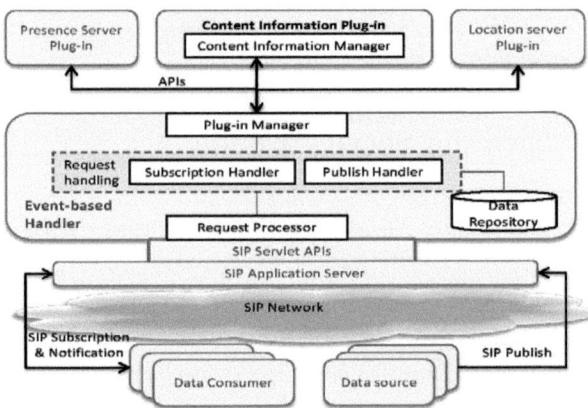

Figure 6.1: Content Information Provisioning Enabler reference implementation

The CIPE includes the following components:

6.2. Multimedia Service Enablers 141

Request Processor : in charge of receiving incoming SUBSCRIBE and PUBLISH requests and sending the related notifications to the subscriber. It consists of a SIP servlet that decides if an incoming request is an initial request or an update of an existing subscriber session.

Plug-in Manager : responsible for deleting, storing, activating and deactivating plug-ins and acquiring active plug-ins. It is designed to make changes to the plug-in configuration at runtime, which means that the server does't need to be restarted after adding, removing or (de-)activating a plug-in. After deployment, the plug-in is instantly operational.

Plug-ins : The actual application logic of the server is performed by the Plug-in, which is in charge of processing a particular event-package. Each plug-in decides for itself the Notification messages if it is responsible for a request or not by checking all necessary preconditions (e.g. header values, content type, SIP Method of the request). Furthermore, each plug-in provides information about its supported content types, SIP header, SIP Methods and general functionality. The Content Information Provisioning Plug-in processes the content information event-package according the specification defined in subsection 6.2.1.

Content Information Manager : provides management functions for multimedia content information as specified in subsection 6.2.1. It is in charge of merging several published information related to certain content sources into a single content information document.

Request Handlers : responsible for assigning the plug-ins when a SUBSCRIBE or PUBLISH request is received. They manage the timer handling, authorization of subscriber, storing and removing the requests from the data repository, and also delegate published user data to the plug-ins of a subscription.

Data Repository : stores published data, subscriptions to resources and the relationships between subscriptions and publisher.

The event-based handler can use the RLS (Resource List Server) in order to allow data consumers to subscribe to a set of data sources (Publishers) using a single subscription message. However, the RLS and the integration with the XDMS are not depicted in Figure 6.1. The RLS is further considered as a plug-in integrated into the event-based handler.

6.2.2 Content Management Enabler

The Content Management Enabler (CME) is responsible for managing the delivery of multimedia content from the content provider to the MDF, as described in subsection 6.2.2. The CME implementation makes use of SIP Servlet APIs to interact with content provider and the MDF.

Therefore, it can be deployed in any SIP application server hosting the SIP Servlet container that is confirmed with SIP Servlet specifications. With regards to this, the CME accepts content provider SIP requests for content the delivery (push-mode) or initiates SIP requests towards the content provider according to an application or SME request (pull-mode).

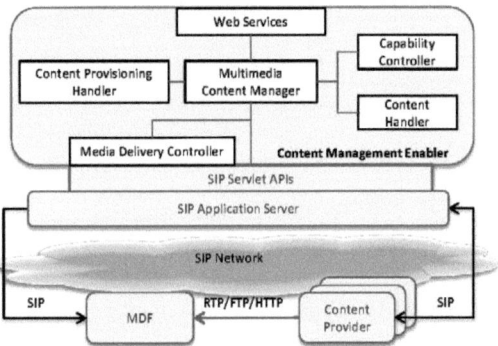

Figure 6.2: Content management Enabler reference implementation

Figure 6.2 shows the reference implementation of the CME components, which is based on the SIP Servlet APIs that abstract the SIP stack from the CME logic and expose its supported capabilities through web services APIs. The CME includes the following components:

Multimedia Content Manager : This component is the main component of the CME and thus performs most CME tasks with the aid of the other CME components. The primary task of this component is accepting or initiating SIP requests from and to the content provider, respectively. Therefore, it implements the corresponding SIP servlet APIs. For content delivery, it triggers the MDF on behalf of the Media Delivery Controller to receive or fetches the associated content. Furthermore, it enables the SME or other application to check the availability of any multimedia content, as depicted in the activity diagram Figure 6.3.

6.2. Multimedia Service Enablers

Content Provisioning Handler : This component interfaces with the CIPE in order to obtain the content information for all multimedia content already published by the associated content providers. In the current implementation, this handler read the provisioning information from local configurable file as the interface for the CIPE was not available yet.

Multimedia Delivery Controller : This component is used to trigger the MDF with requested delivery or processing functions such as store or prepare-for-relay functions. Therefore, it implements the corresponding SIP servlet APIs.

Content Handler : This component maintains all multimedia objects already available in the MDF either as stored or live content.

Capability Controller : This component checks the content provider capabilities against the MDF capabilities and selects the appropriate delivery parameters between the content provider and the MDF node.

Web Services : This component exposes all CME supported functions as web services in order to allow the seamless integration of the CME in an open environment.

Figure 6.3 illustrates the activity diagram for obtaining content availability information by the SME or other service enabler. First, the CME makes use of the CRID (Content Resource Identifier) passed by the SME to check if a content object is already maintained by the Content Handler or not. If it is not available, the CME invokes the Content Provisioning Handler to obtain the related content information. If content information does not exist, a null object is returned. Otherwise, a new content object is constructed and passed to the Content Handler to be stored.

Thereafter, the CME checks if the content is already available in the MDF or not. If it is available, the CME returns the content object to the caller. If it is not, it evaluates content status. If it is not ready, it returns a null object. Otherwise, it further checks the content delivery mode in order to trigger the MDF to either fetch the content from the content provider server or receive content stream from the associated content source (IP address, port, media type, codec, rate, etc.). Finally, the CME returns the content object, with the associated content information, to the caller.

6.2.3 Session Management Enabler

The Session Management Enabler (SME) is responsible for managing the delivery of multimedia content from the MDF to a set of end users, as described

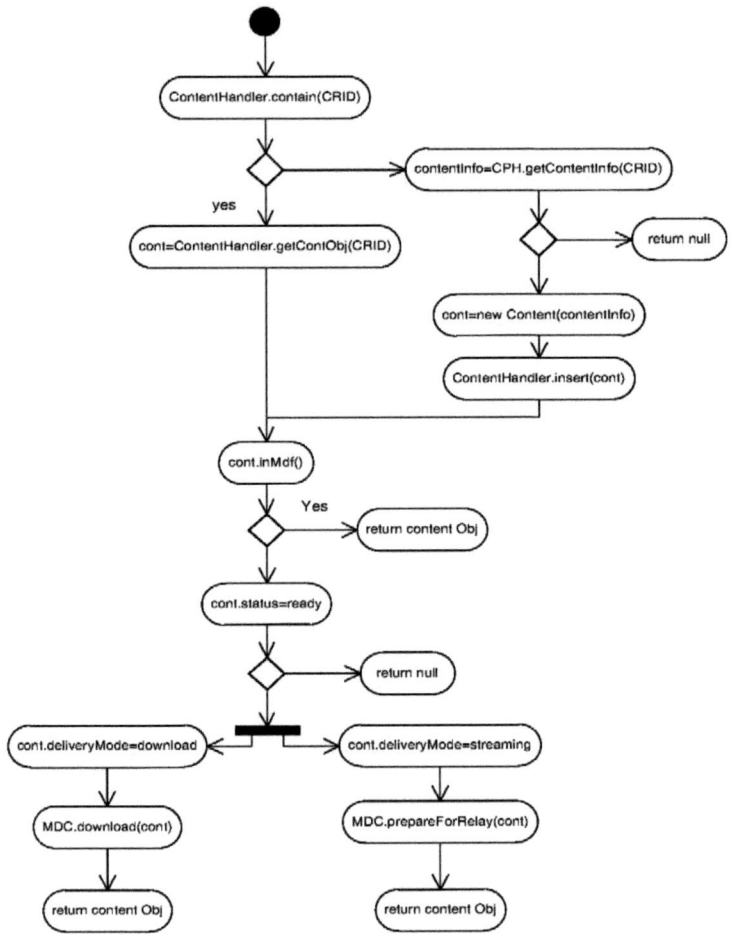

Figure 6.3: Content Management Enabler activity diagram

in subsection 5.2.3. The SME implementation makes use of SIP Servlet APIs to interact with IMS users and the MDF. Therefore, it can be deployed in any SIP application server, hosting a SIP Servlet container confirmed with SIP Servlet specifications.

With regards to this, the SME accepts application requests through web

6.2. Multimedia Service Enablers

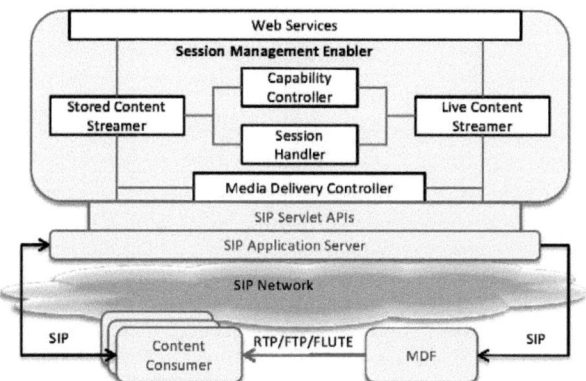

Figure 6.4: Session management Enabler reference implementation

services APIs for triggering content delivery to a set of IMS users and, accordingly, the SME initiates the session by issuing SIP invite messages to these users (push-model) and the MDF, as described in more detail in Appendix C.3. On the other hand, the SME accepts user-initiated SIP requests for certain multimedia content based on previous provisioning (pull-model).

Figure 6.4 shows the reference implementation of the SME components, which is based on the SIP Servlet APIs that abstract the SIP stack from the SME logic and expose its supported delivery services through web services APIs. The SME includes the following components:

Live Content Streamer : This component manages the delivery of live multimedia content available in the MDF to content consumers. Therefore, it implements the related SIP Servlet APIs in order to accept user SIP requests and trigger the MDF to relay the content to the consumers with specific delivery characteristics (transmission mode, codec, rate, etc.). With this context it uses the capability controller and the media delivery controller components. The activity diagram depicted in Figure 6.5 illustrates the processing routine of the LCS component in more detail.

Stored Content Streamer : This component manages the delivery of stored multimedia content available in the MDF for end consumers. Therefore, it implements the related SIP Servlet APIs in order to accept user SIP requests and to trigger the MDF to stream the content to the corresponding user according to its device's capabilities. In this context, it uses

Chapter 6. Implementation of Multimedia Content Delivery Core Enablers

the capability controller and the media delivery controller components. The activity diagram depicted in Figure 6.6 illustrates the processing routine of the SCS component in more detail.

Session Handler : This component is a utility component used by both LCS and SCS components. It controls, stores and organizes multimedia delivery sessions. It performs several functions: first, checking whether a particular session exists or not; second, updating or terminating existing sessions and finally, adding a new leg (e.g. new user) to an existing streaming session.

Capability Controller : This component is a utility component invoked by both LCS and SCS components, as well as the CME in order to match the delivery parameters of the incoming content stream, user equipment capabilities and MDF capabilities. In addition, it is in charge of selecting bearer mode in the case that the MDF supports different transmission modes (unicast, multicast and broadcast).

Media Delivery Controller : This component is a utility component invoked by both LCS and SCS components in order to trigger the media delivery and processing functions provided by the MDF (e.g. relay content stream with a dedicated transmission mode, transcoding, rate-scaling, recording, etc.).

Web Services : The LCS and the SCS expose their supported delivery services through web services APIs, which enable third party applications or other service enablers to push multimedia content to a set of end users.

Figure 6.5 illustrates the LCS activity diagram which shows one of the main LCS delivery services through which the user triggers content delivery via a SIP Invite request. Upon receiving user-initiated SIP Invite requests the LCS SIP Servlet checks user authorization. If the user is not authorized, it sends the SIP error code 402 message (*Payment Required*) or error code 488 (*Not Acceptable Here*).

Then LCS makes use of the Content Resource Identifier (CRID) obtained from user request to check if a delivery session already exists in the Session Handler or not. If it is not available, the LCS invokes the CME for acquiring the related content information. If the return value is a null, the SIP error code 404 (*Not Found*) is sent to the user. Otherwise, a new multimedia content object is constructed and passed to the Session Handler to be stored. Thereafter, the LCS matches content

6.2. Multimedia Service Enablers

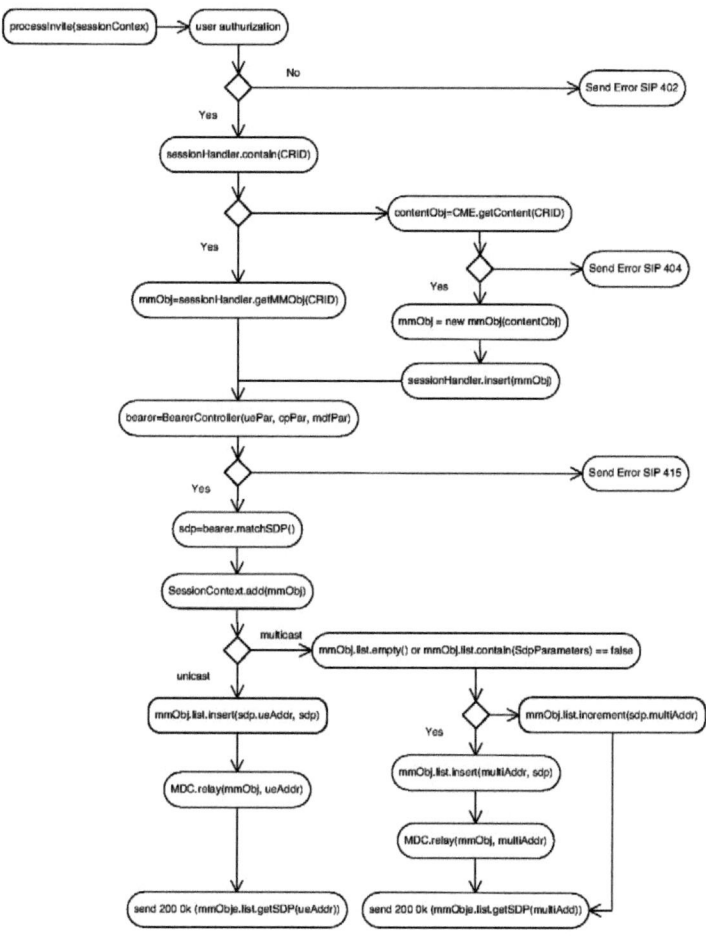

Figure 6.5: Live Content Streamer activity diagram

parameters against user equipment capabilities and the MDF capabilities. If UE capabilities could not be supported, the LCS sends the user the SIP error code 415 (*Unsupported Media Type*). At this point, session information is stored in the session context object, in order for the LCS to be able to access session information when the MDF or the end user sends back the response messages (as different methods are invoked by the SIP Servlet container). According to the interaction with the capability controller, the LCS distinguishes between only two transmission modes, either unicast or multicast. However, the integration of broadcast transmission mode (e.g. over DVB-T/H) is based on a tunneling content stream from the MDF to the broadcast station (e.g. the DVB-T/H playout center) over an IP multicast.

As most live content delivery sessions include multiple consumers, the LCS maintains the information of all output channels (using either uincast or multicast bearer) for each content delivery in one object which is managed by the session handler. In the case that the capability controller has decided for unicast bearer, the LCS adds the related session parameters (IP, port, codec, content type, etc.) to the Multimedia Object list maintained by the session controller, and then triggers the MDF to relay the associated content to the associated output channel. In the case of a multicast bearer, the LCS checks if a multicast channel with the same properties already exists in the session controller or not. Therefore the LCS verifies first if the Multimedia Object list is empty, or if a multicast bearer with the same delivery parameters (i.e. codec, rate and media types) is unavailable. If one of both conditions is valid, the LCS adds this channel to the Multimedia Object list and triggers the MDF to relay the associated content with the required parameters to a defined multicast address. But if a multicast bearer is already active, the LCS increments the number of receivers associated with this multicast session. Finally, the LCS responds to user request with the related SDP parameters in the 200 OK message. Furthermore, the LCS completes the session setup towards the user and the MDF following the Back-to-Back SIP user agent model.

In the case of the SCS, the related activity diagram depicted in Figure 6.6 is almost similar to the LCS activity diagram, but with a few distinctions. First, the SCS uses, in this case, only a unicast delivery mode. Second, it supports on-demand content streaming by providing the consumer with an RTSP resource for controlling media sessions through trick functions. Therefore, the SCS distinguishes between *linear* or *on-demand* content delivery and that based on user subscription or the configuration of the service delivery properties. In the case of linear streaming, the SCS triggers the MDF to relay the associated content after evaluating user equipment capabilities. But, in the case of on-demand streaming, the SCS requests that the MDF controller provides an RTSP resource for the associated content. Finally, the SCS responds

6.2. Multimedia Service Enablers

to the end user with the identified session parameters in the 200 OK message.

Note that not all the LCS and the SCS activities are exactly illustrated in these diagrams, but both diagrams but both diagrams understanding how the LCS and the SCS work.

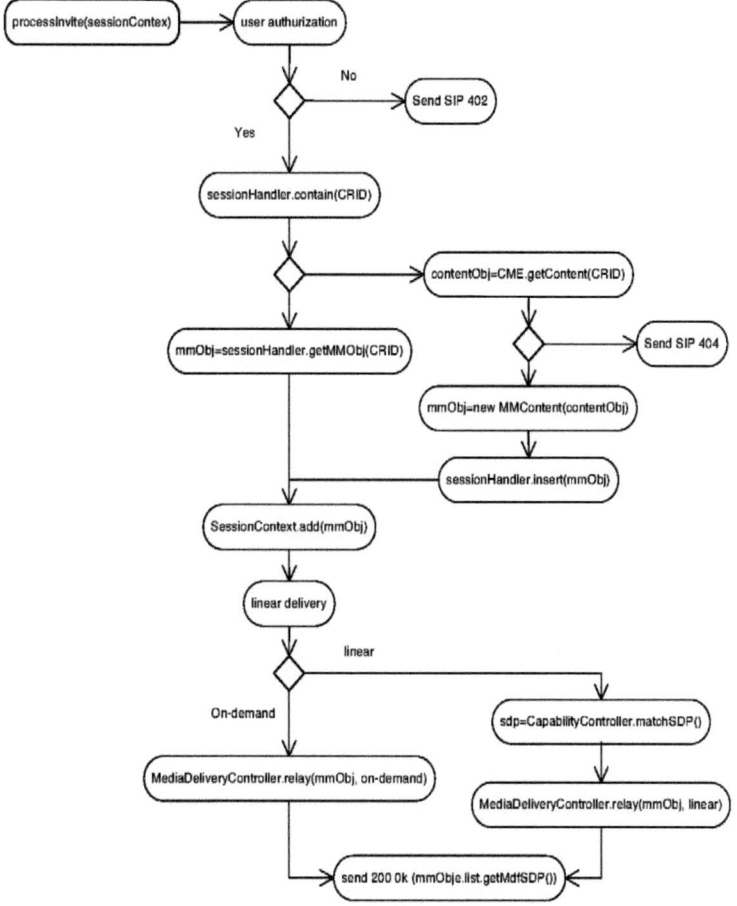

Figure 6.6: Stored Content Streamer activity diagram

6.2.4 Media Delivery Function

The Media Delivery Function (MDF) provides a set of delivery and processing functions that can be utilized in a SIP-based network, as specified in subsection 5.2.4. The delivery and processing functions can be triggered via SIP protocol and multimedia media content is received. It supports several delivery protocols. It uses the RTP for receiving and sending content stream and FTP/HTTP and FLUTE for fetching and downloading content. Furthermore, it supports the RTSP for controlling media streaming.

The MDF is developed mainly in C programming language using the library Glib and can be deployed in a Linux operating system. It is based mainly on the GStreamer libraries [92], which offer most of the needed media processing and delivery capabilities, and the Sofia-SIP library [93] for the realization of the control interface. However, other libraries are used such as libcurl and FLUTE to provide special functionalities. The GStreamer main advantages are that the pluggable components can be mixed and matched into arbitrary pipelines so that it's possible to write a full-fledged video or audio editing application. It supports various codecs and a wide variety of formats, including MP3, Ogg/Vorbis, MPEG-1/2, AVI, Quicktime, mod, and more.

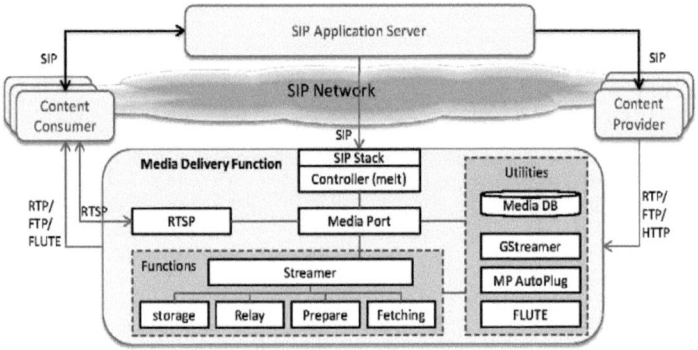

Figure 6.7: Media Delivery Function reference implementation

Figure 6.7 shows the reference implementation of the MDF and the essential components which are:

Controller (melt) : This component is in charge of processing SIP messages and triggers the requested media and delivery functionalities. Therefore, it is based on the top of the Sofia-SIP stack. Media processing and delivery functions are triggered via SIP following the specification defined in

6.2. Multimedia Service Enablers

the subsection 2.3.3.2, where the required media delivery and processing functionality is indicated in the SIP URL and each multimedia content is identified by a unique identifier included in the SDP message.

Media Port : This component is the main function which parses the configuration file, initializes the external libraries (e.g. the GStreamer and Sofia-SIP) and starts the SIP stack.

Streamer : This component initializes the media pipelines for each media delivery and processing functionalities.

Media Delivery and Processing Functions : These functions are developed as standalone components that can be integrated or excluded from the MDF. The current implementation supports the following functions:

- Remote content fetching: This is a delivery function capable of downloading content from FTP or HTTP servers.

- Prepare for Relay: This is a delivery function that prepares the required resources for receiving content streams within a media session to a determinate port at the MDF.

- Relay: This is a delivery and processing function that streams an incoming content stream or stored content. The former content stream has to be available in the MDF as live content and processed by the Prepare for Relay function. In the latter case, the content has to be downloaded or recorded in the MDF. Note that the delivery is linear (without support of trick functions).

- Storage: This is a processing function which stores live content within a live session at the MDF. The multimedia information is stored in an AVI container. The video is transcoded to MPEG4 and the audio to MP3 format.

- RTSP relay functionality: This function enables the content consumer to control the delivery of content stream using the RTSP protocol. This function is similar to the Relay function, but with support of trick functions using RTSP.

Utility Functions : A set of functions used by different MDF components in order to complement its work. These functions - among others - are:

- Media DB: This function implements the database utility for managing multimedia content

- Media Port Auto-Plug-in: This function performs the procedures to create the send and receive functionalities for each available codec for the Gstreamer pipelines. They are extensible and are based in the codec name or the payload type.

- FLUTE: This component provides the implementation for the server side of the FLUTE protocol.

In fact, delivering interactive and personalized multimedia services (e.g. live TV) to huge numbers of IMS subscribers with different terminal capabilities in an efficient way requires advanced media processing capabilities. The implementation of the MDF fulfills these requirements and offers the necessary processing functions for multimedia content as well as supporting seamless and creative collaboration between content providers, network operators and service providers. Furthermore, it is flexible enough to be deployed on IMS networks or other multimedia platforms, provided that the required processing functions can be dynamically triggered and/or modified within a multimedia session. Therefore, it can be customized quickly in order to be used, for example, as a home server, media proxy or even as a media player.

6.3 Discussion

Following the specification of the session-based multimedia content delivery framework and the involved functional elements described in the Chapter 5, this chapter presented a detailed implementation of a prototype solution. This prototype consists of distributed enablers: the Content Information Provisioning Enabler (CIPE), the Session Management Enabler (SME), the Content Management Enabler (CME) and the Media Delivery Function (MDF). The first three enablers are considered to be part of the multimedia service enabler layer and their entire implementation was based on JAVA EE. They were implemented based on the SIP servlet APIs described in 2.3.4.1. Therefore, the implementation can be deployed in any application server supporting SIP servlet APIs. The implementation followed the SOA paradigm with the objective of allowing other application enablers or third party applications to use the offered services through exposed open programmable APIs specified with WSDL. The MDF supported several delivery protocols. It used RTP for receiving and sending the content stream, FTP/HTTP and FLUTE for fetching and downloading content, and RTSP for controlling media streaming. A SIP stack was also integrated in order to trigger and control the content delivery and adaptation functions. The entire implementation was developed in C language in a Linux operating system.

6.3. Discussion

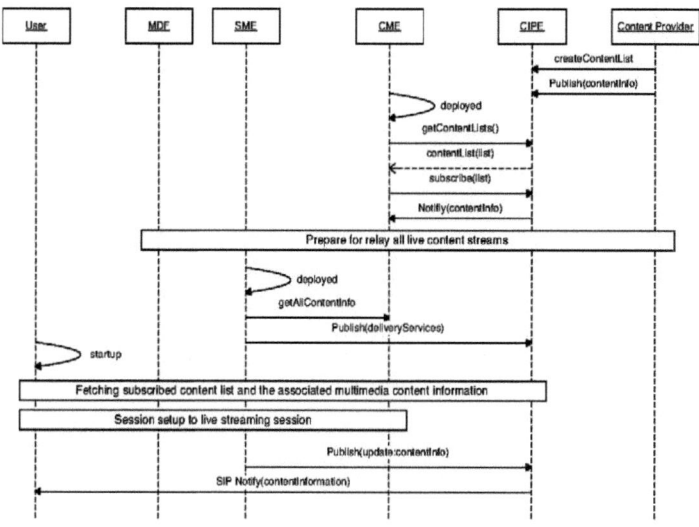

Figure 6.8: Message flows of integrating all multimedia service enablers

The interactions between these enablers in the current implementation were limited to those between the SME and the CME, as the CIPE is still under development. Figure 6.8 illustrates one possible scenario of how all multimedia service enablers, the MDF, the content provider and the consumer interact, however, other scenarios are also possible. The objective of this diagram is to understand how these enablers work in concert for the delivery of personalized multimedia content. The related detailed message flows are presented in Appendix C.

Ultimately, the content provider and multimedia content information are the key elements that are essential for this scenario, where the content provider (or administrator) creates a content list including a set of content sources and defines (publishes) the related content information to the CIPE.

Once the CME is deployed in an application server, it interacts with the CIPE through its exposed APIs in order to obtain all (authorized) content lists and the associated content information. Then the CME triggers the prepare-for-relay function on the MDF in order to receive all live content streams from the coupled content providers (for details see Appendix C.4). When the SME is deployed in an application server, it requests the CME for all available content information and consequently publishes the delivery services

Chapter 6. Implementation of Multimedia Content Delivery Core Enablers

as content information for each associated content stream to the CIPE. When a user starts up the IMS client, it registers with the IMS core (not depicted in this diagram), fetches the content information from the CIPE (for details see Appendix C.1) and subscribes to the changes in the content information. If the user wishes to watch a live content stream, the client establishes a SIP-based session to the SME (LCS) which triggers the MDF to relay the required content steam, as discussed in subsection 6.2.3. Accordingly, the SME may update the service delivery information associated with this session by invoking the publish method on the CIPE.

In the next chapter, this prototype implementation is validated in different deployment scenarios and used for performance evaluation with the objective of understanding the performance impact on the IMS core and the service enablers under different load and test scenarios.

CHAPTER 7
Validation and Evaluation

7.1 Introduction

Based on the system implementation discussed in chapter 5, we will now describe the validation environment where the functionalities of all components are integrated in an IMS-based delivery playground. As portability is one of the design requirements of these components, several validation environments are addressed; namely at Fraunhofer Institute testbeds and on C-Mobile (and later on C-CAST) project[1] [61]. Furthermore, several performance evaluations have been conducted under different system conditions and traffic loads. We conclude the chapter with a suggestion for a possible optimization method for the cases where test results show low performance. Unless noted otherwise, all performance measurements show the mean values of multiple test runs.

7.2 COSMIC Deployments

The prototype implementation is deployed in different environments with different testbed setups and with various targeted scenarios. The following subsections introduce a few of these setups that validate the functionalities of the reference implementation for delivering advance multimedia services. The objective is to verify the support of personalization, interactivity and merging multimedia experience with telecommunication services.

7.2.1 Testbeds

During the last few years, Fraunhofer Institute FOKUS has established several testbeds with the objective of develop technologies and related know-how in different research aspects of fixed and wireless next generation networks and IMS-based multimedia service delivery platforms. In addition, FOKUS has coined the notion of technology-focused "playgrounds", which can be considered as open environments to be used by academic and industrial partners for

---
[1]C-Mobile and C-CAST projects are a European Information Society Technology (IST) research project that aims to provide enhancements to the MBMS for systems beyond 3G at Radio, RAN and Core Network levels.

early prototyping of new multimedia services, related components, protocols, and applications.

Two of these playgrounds are the "Open IMS Playground @ FOKUS" and "FOKUS Media Interoperability Lab (MIL)" [94, 95]. Both playgrounds consist of the IMS core over different access technologies, SIP application servers and various IMS services. Furthermore, these playgrounds have been extended to support the delivery of multimedia services over heterogeneous access networks. The Open IMS Playground focuses mainly on the IMS core and IMS services, while the MIL addresses primarily the IMS-based IPTV frameworks and thus can be considered as proof of concept for the IMS-based IPTV architecture. MIL is regarded as a show room for the future converged multimedia services covering TV services, and NGN services and represents the state-of-the-art research activities.

The IMS-based multimedia service enablers are deployed in both playgrounds in different scenarios addressing certain requirements or demonstration applications. The most important of these applications are described in the next subsection.

7.2.1.1 FOKUS OpenIMS Playground

The first application that was based on the prototype implementation and was deployed in the Open IMS Playground is the integration of DVB-H and UMTS access networks with delivery multimedia streaming, with the objective of supporting seamless mobility. Figure 7.1shows an overview of the IMS-based integration of the DVB-H and UMTS by illustrating the signaling and session data flows between the IMS components, the DVB-H Playout Center, content provider, and the user equipment. The Session Management Enabler (SME) maintains the session and switching logic and is the entity keeping track of service utilization, making the decision for the optimal transmission medium (e.g. broadcast via DVB-H or unicast via UMTS bearer). It further controls the MDF for media processing and must be aware of the user context, in order to set up the suitable bearer mode (i.e. unicast or broadcast).

The DVB-Playout Center (DVB-POC) systems are responsible for the broadcast of multimedia content using DVB-H. Due to the nature of the DVB as a broadcast technology mobility, is not supported. However, the implementation facilitates vertical mobility between several access bearer technologies in such a system.

In this validation scenario, the mobile device is equipped with a UMTS radio interface and a DVB-H receiver both controlled by the IMS-based streaming client. COSMIC SME is deployed in a SIP application server, which was developed at Fraunhofer FOKUS and known by the name SIP Servlet Execu-

7.2. COSMIC Deployments

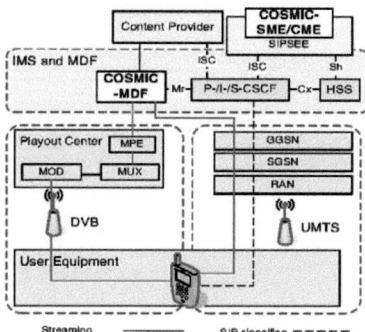

Figure 7.1: IMS-based DVB-H and UMTS integrated streaming scenario

tion Environment (SIPSee) [96]. The key triggering point for vertical mobility is the number of mobile devices interested in receiving a content stream within a service area (in this scenario, the radio signal coverage area in the testbed). Therefore, the demonstration starts with one mobile device connected over UMTS to establish the IMS-based multimedia streaming session. After session setup with certain numbers of mobile devices (configurable value in the SME), the SME decides to use a DVB-H bearer to serve all users available at the same serving area instead of multiple UMTS bearers. Figure 7.2 shows the related SIP message flows, as follows:

- Upon receiving the SIP Invite request from user (n+1) the SME updates the relay session on the MDF by adding the DVB-H bearer as an additional multicast leg.

- Based on this multicast stream the DVB-H POC receives the incoming traffic and broadcasts it over an associated DVB-H frequency, which is also known by the SME.

- Then the SME responds to the Invite request with the DVB-H frequency and informs the already connected user(s) via the UMTS channels about the DVB-H channel and related parameters (DVB-H frequency, multicast address, etc.).

The IMS core is based on the FOKUS open source implementation of the P-/I-S-CSCF and the HSS [53]. This work has been published in several papers like [97, 98].

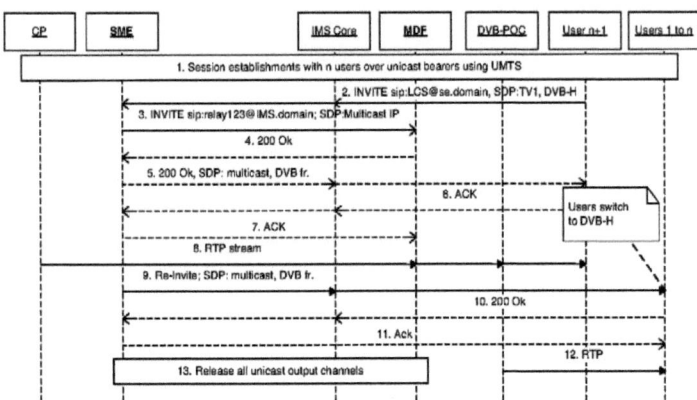

Figure 7.2: Message flow of the IMS-based DVB-H and UMTS integration

Based on the prototype implementation, we conducted several measurements with the target of evaluating the switching delay of content stream from LAN and UMTS to DVB-T and vice versa. All results are based on the statistical average of 10 record sets. Table 7.1 represents the total delay including signaling delay (user → SME → MDF and content streams (audio and video track) (MDF → user-LAN, MDF → UMTS → user or MDF → DVB-POC → user) as illustrated in Figure 7.1.

| Content | Switching delay between different technologies in ms | | | |
Stream	LAN→DVB-T	DVB-T→LAN	UMTS→DVB-T	DVB-T→UMTS
Audio track	4415	386	4116	3385
Video track	4435	654	4328	3884

Table 7.1: Switching delay from LAN and UMTS to DVB-T

It is clear that the switching delay to the DVB-T is much higher than to the other access networks. This is because the DVB-T receiver on the UE takes a long time to tune the receiver to the right DVB-T channel and then encapsulate RTP streams from the DVB-T signal.

7.2.1.2 Media Interoperability Lab

Furthermore, scenarios are developed and deployed in the Media Interoperability lab (MIL) with the target of merging multimedia streaming services with telecommunication services with support of personalization and interac-

7.2. COSMIC Deployments

tivity. MIL setup is very similar to the FOKUS IMS playground, as depicted in Figure 7.3, where the SME/CME and the MDF are integrated.

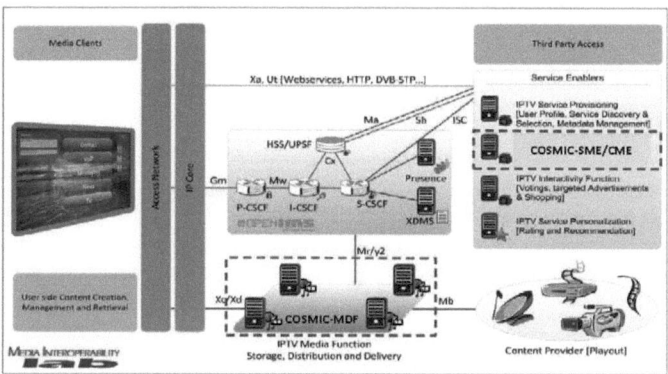

Figure 7.3: Media Interoperability Lab testbed setup

On the user side, an advanced IMS-based multimedia client has been developed for the Windows operating system running on a PC, notebook or set-top-box and based on .NET libraries. The client makes use of all framework functionalities through the Gm, Mb and Ut reference points. The client supports multimedia streaming services (live TV and VoD), telecommunication services (telephony, chat, messaging and presence), as well as advanced features such as displaying incoming calls, pausing the stream of a VoD movie, muting the audio of live TV during a call, watching what your friends are currently watching and enabling session mobility of the TV session.

Figure 7.5 shows two multimedia applications:

- The first application (on the left) shows an IMS subscriber with both mobile and fixed terminals, each of which are equipped with two different or cloned IMS SIM (ISIM) cards that contain one or two IMS Private Identities (IMPIs), respectively, and two IMS Public Identities (IMPUs). The user is subscribed to the IMS-based Video-on-Demand (VoD) service with session continuity feature supported by the SME and the IMS service profile stored in the HSS. The scenario is divided in two phases: In the first phase, the subscriber uses his fixed terminal to initiate a request for watching a movie within a VoD session and then pauses the stream (step 1) when he decides to leave the house (step 2). In the second phase, he uses his mobile terminal to continue watching the same movie at the same position he paused the stream (step 3 and

160   **Chapter 7. Validation and Evaluation**

4), which was maintained by the SME. Once the subscriber successfully registers with the IMS core, the SME is notified about the registration process following the third party registration procedure. Accordingly, the SME sends the subscriber his personalized VoD service profile that includes the last movies that he watched and the specific position at which he paused the stream. This work is published in [60].

- The second scenario (on the right) illustrates a converged scenario. The objective is to explain how a combination of TV services and IMS services through the activity sharing service can be realized based on our prototype implementation. The scenario is demonstrated through the activity sharing service, which enables the end-user to share his multimedia activity (like the TV channel or VoD movie he is watching) with his friends stored in the buddy list. The screen shot in the figure above shows Bob sharing his activity with one of his buddy members. The client makes use of the IMS presence enabler deployed in the lab for distributing such kinds of information, but without any change in our enabler implementations. This demo illustrates how multiple service enablers interact with each other during service delivery and the correlation between TV services and NGN services. The cross-fertilization of multimedia services and telecommunication services is published in several papers and journals like [62, 99, 100].

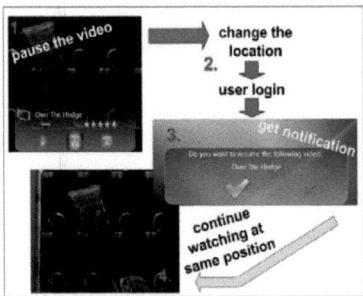 

Figure 7.4: Session Mobility Application   Figure 7.5: Sharing Multimedia Activities

7.2.2 Projects

This research has contributed to several research projects with an industry partner and the European Commission, Information Society Technologies

7.2. COSMIC Deployments

(IST). The industry partner is a global telecommunications vendor that does not want its name mentioned. The goal of the project is to specify an end-to-end IMS-based IPTV framework with the end target of personalization and interactivity. The project lasted for two years and part of the project results were contributed to several Standard Development Organizations (SDOs) like ETSI TISPAN, ITU-T Focus Group IPTV [10], Also, furthermore, contributions were published by our partner itself.

C-Mobile and C-CAST (Context Casting) [101] are both IST projects each of which lasted for two years.

- C-Mobile aimed at enhancing the MBMS for systems beyond 3G at Radio, RAN and Core Network levels. Furthermore, it worked on the core network evolution and integration of interactive mobile services in an IMS-based delivery framework ensuring a smooth migration path for the subsequent releases. Our main contribution was the integration of IMS with the MBMS framework.

- C-CAST was the successor of the C-Mobile project and its main objective was to evolve multimedia multicasting to exploit the increasing integration of mobile devices in our everyday physical world and environment. Our contribution was the further improvement of the Session Management Enabler that was initially within the C-Mobile project and extended with further features and open interfaces in C-CAST.

7.2.2.1 Deployment Scenarios

The main target of the contribution to these projects was to enhance the IMS network with advanced multicast and broadcast content distribution in mobile cellular networks. Therefore, the concept of Session Management Enabler (SME), Content Management Enabler (CME), Content Information Provisioning Enabler (CIPE) and Media Delivery Function (MDF) was applied in these projects. As the CIPE was not completely developed during C-Mobile project, the announcement functionality was realized via a simple HTTP server.

Unfortunately, IMS and MBMS are separated subsystems sharing no common interfaces. Therefore, the main requirement is to enable the delivery of multimedia content to a group of IMS users using a multicast/broadcast bearer where appropriate. Since IMS delivery is restricted to unicast transmissions, it would obviously benefit from using several multicast and broadcast technologies like DVB-H, as defined in subsection 7.2.1, and MBMS.

There are two different approaches to integrate IMS with MBMS. The first is to maintain the BM-SC and extend functionalities by adding SIP signaling, whereas the second approach tries to distribute the BM-SC functionalities among enhanced IMS entities. In C-Mobile the latter option was considered and a service provisioning architecture was developed. The identified MBMS BM-SC functionalities are mapped onto the IMS layered architecture. Hence, the BM-SC is removed from the architecture and a long term solution for the next generation multimedia content distribution is envisaged instead.

A simplified version of IMS-MBMS integrated framework is depicted in Figure 7.6 in which COSMIC components are depicted in a continuous black line, namely the SME and the MDF. A detailed description of this architecture is provided in Appendix D, where MBMS functions are distributed on different layers of the IMS networks. Furthermore, C-MOBILE architecture and project results are published in different papers like [62, 102, 103, 104].

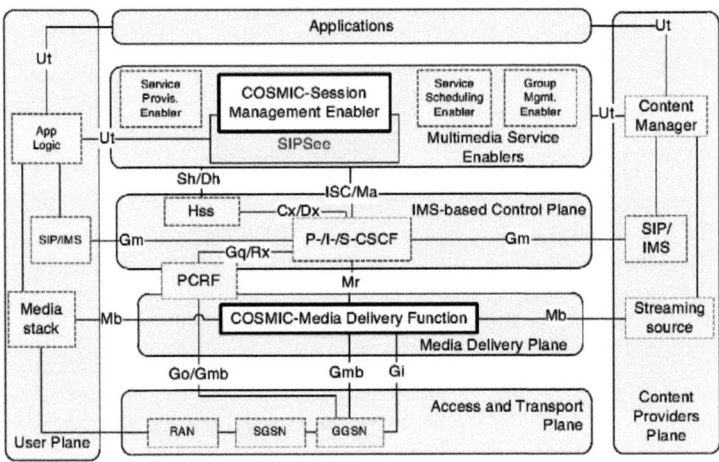

Figure 7.6: IMS-MBMS integrated architecture

In C-Mobile, the procedure for accessing multimedia content distinguishes between session establishment and start transmission. The session establishment phase covers the SIP session setup (between the UE and the SME) and the MBMS PDP context activation. While in the start transmission phase the SME (or the CP) triggers the delivery in accordance with content availability (or defined schedule). The related procedures are discussed in details in Appendix D.

As the CIPE was not yet developed according to the scope of the analysis discussed in 4.3 during the C-Mobile project, the event-induced multicast

7.2. COSMIC Deployments

session reduced the two phases into one phase, in which the SME (Application Server) does not maintain the SIP Invite session for long time. In this case, the UE does not need to establish a SIP session and then proceed with the MBMS PDP context activation procedure. This leads to a reduction in the total signaling messages and thus improves network performance.

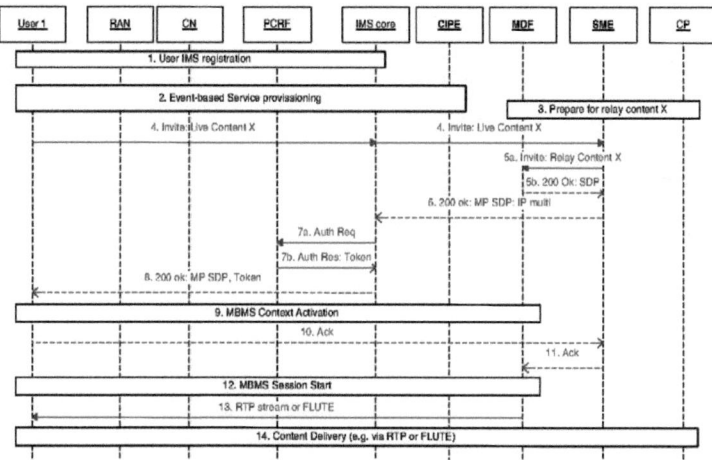

Figure 7.7: Message flows of the IMS-MBMS session

Figure 7.7 illustrates the adapted session establishment phase and the start transmission phase, as follows:

- After the IMS subscriber registers with the IMS core, the CIPE provides him with provisioning information of all multicast sessions that the user subscribed to.

- If there is multimedia content available (i.e. ready for delivery), the SME first performs the prepare-for-relay procedure and then updates the pertaining service delivery parameters (i.e. IP multicast address) for the CIPE (step 3).

- As a result, interested users can initiate SIP Invite request to the SME (or perform the MBMS Join procedure directly). The SIP INVITE message is routed by the CSCF to the corresponding SME, which provides the desired MBMS service (step 4).

- At this time, the SME triggers the MDF to relay the associated content to a defined MBMS bearer (i.e. IP multicast) (step 5).

- Thereafter, the MDF sends the 200 OK message to the SME including the SDP parameters, which is forwarded to the user. The P-CSCF then performs resource authorization with the PCRF (step 7).

- Based on SDP parameters, the UE performs the MBMS context activation procedure, as defined in the MBMS specification then sends the SIP Ack message (step 9).

- At this time, the SME sends the SIP Ack message confirming the relay session. As a consequence (step 11), the MDF starts the MBMS session start procedure followed with the content delivery (either as content stream or download via RTP or FLUTE, respectively).

Furthermore, deployment scenarios were developed within the C-Mobile project, and in particular the implementation of the push delivery mode. In this mode, other enablers, such as the group management, enabler trigger the SME to initiate the MBMS delivery session according, for example, to context updates of the targeted group, content provider availability or service scheduling. For this reason, the SME APIs are used to allowing the enabler to invoke session setup.

7.3 Performance Evaluation

One of the main reasons to focus on styles for IMS-based applications is because component interactions can be the dominant factor in determining user-perceived performance and network efficiency, as defined in 3.2.2. Since the communication style (push-mode, pull-mode or event-induced mode) influences the nature of those interactions, selection of an appropriate architectural style can make the difference between success and failure in the deployment of an IMS-based application. The performance of an IMS-based application is bound first by the application requirements, then by the chosen interaction style, followed by the realized architecture, and finally by the implementation of each component, as discussed in detail in section 4.3. For this reason, we will initially evaluate a set of SIP transaction models, focusing on the performance of the IMS network in general.

The limiting factor for performance in our prototype implementation is the SME, as this is the entity where massive load in terms of SIP signaling and processing power (due to serving a large number of users) is expected. We therefore concentrate on testing the limits of the SME node. However,

7.3. Performance Evaluation 165

the system to be tested includes all the multimedia service enablers, the MDF and the IMS core.

The next subsection provides a detailed description of the test cases conducted in the Fokus IMS Playground mentioned above. First, the test environment and related configuration is presented. The parameters that should be modified on the system under the test are then discussed. The expected results and metrics that should be gathered during the test and used to identify the performance of the system under the test are also given. The test cases are then defined, followed by the discussion of test results.

7.3.1 Test Environment

The test environment focuses on six components that can be distributed in different physical nodes, as depicted in Figure 7.8. These are:

1. User Equipment (UE), which acts as an IMS client to initiate or receive any IMS-based request for obtaining multimedia content from the IMS-based network. A set of UEs are emulated in one host to receive or initiate a session invitation. The UEs are emulated by SIPNuke testing tools that were developed at FOKUS [105].

2. Content Provider (CP), which is the source of multimedia content. The content is transmitted to the IMS network for further media processing or content delivery. The source of multimedia content can be from separated nodes (e.g. an IMS client, Video LAN Client or a web camera) or from a file stored in the MDF.

3. The IMS core, which is the SIP control network between the system components. It manages UE registration, triggering applications, and forwarding requests among the system components. Therefore, the IMS core should be configured to forward the following requests: (1) UEs' requests to application servers (e.g. SME), (2) AS requests to the UEs and (3) AS media processing requests to the MDF. FOKUS Open IMS core is deployed in this environment [53].

4. The Multimedia Service Enablers (MSE), which are composed of the SME, the CME and the CIPE. One or all of these enablers were deployed according to the requirements of the targeted test scenarios. These enablers were hosted in a particular SIP application server, which ran a SIP container and a Web-Service container. Several application servers have been deployed in the testbed such as the SIPSee [96], Sailfin [106] and BEA WebLogic Sip Server [107].

5. The Web-based application, which makes use of the MSE functions (like the SME) to trigger the delivery of any multimedia content to a set of UEs. The related web-service APIs are invoked according to a SOA paradigm.

6. The Media Delivery Function (MDF), which provides media delivery and processing functions to any IMS-based application server. Two deployment scenarios were considered between the SME and the MDF:

    - The SME sends media processing requests via the IMS core, in which the related filter criteria were defined on the HSS.
    - The SME sends the media processing requests directly to the MDF without the IMS core in between.

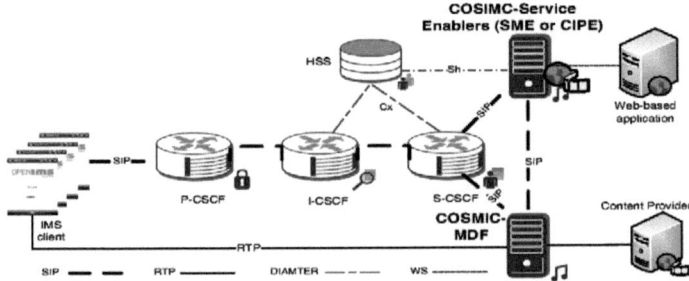

Figure 7.8: Test environment

Note that not all of these components may occur in all the test scenarios, but each is deployed in the test environment according to the need or availability.

7.3.1.1 Parameters

There are several parameters considered during the execution of the test. These parameters are described in the next subsections.

Number of Users : To guarantee a sustained rate of requests initiated by the SME or the UEs, a set of IMS UEs has to be emulated. Therefore, the number of required users can be obtained by applying the following formula: $ue = r \times t + offset$; where Ue: number of required users; r : call/request rate; t: time taken for content streaming and $offset$: additional users

7.3. Performance Evaluation

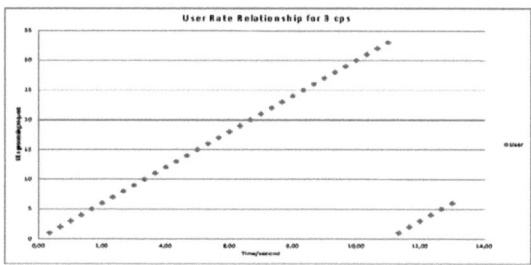

Figure 7.9: Relationship between the number of UEs and generated request over the time

For instance, $r = 3 request/second$, $t = 10 second$, and $Offset = 3$, then $ue = 3 \times 10 + 3 = 33 users$

Figure 7.9 illustrates the relationship between the total required users against time according to the previous example. Once the first user processes request 1, he receives the content stream for 10 seconds. In order to keep the rate at 3 cps, the remaining users (user 2 to user 33) process the next requests (time=2/3=0.67 sec to 11 sec). After 11 seconds, user 1 processes request 34 at 11.33 and so on.

Session duration : After each request initiated by the UE or sent by the enabler to a particular UE, content streaming lasts for a certain time (e.g. 10 seconds), this time is referred to as content stream time. Session duration is the sum of session establishment time and content stream time.

In general, the longer the test duration is the more precise the measurement results are. Therefore, a series of tests have to be conducted where each UE processes only one request in each sequence. Figure 7.9 illustrates one complete series of tests and the second series in part (only six requests). The following formula is applied to calculate the test duration:

$$t_{total} = ue \times n = r \times t \times n, \text{ where}$$

t_{total}: test duration; ue: number of required users; n: test iteration; r: call/request rate and t: time it takes for content streaming. The n denotes the number of iterated test sequences generated during the whole test period where each UE processes only one request during each set of test sequences, as depicted in Figure 7.9. Therefore, it represents the number of requests processed by each UE during the whole test period. For instance: call_rate=3 request/second, media_session_duration=10 seconds and test_series = 10, then the Test_duration becomes 300 seconds

Call rate specifies how often requests are generated either from the SME or from the UEs. The call rate can range from 3, 5, 7, 10, 15, 20, etc. Call per Seconds (cps).

7.3.1.2 Performance Metrics

The main objective of this test is to evaluate the performance of the SME, as well as the evolved components ranging from the IMS core, the MDF and the WS. Therefore, the following key metrics are of interest:

1. **session setup delay** (D_{sig}), which includes the delay of each SIP request initiated by the SME or by the UE. The measurement can be done by the SME or by the UE.

2. **Total setup delay** (D_{total}), which includes the session establishment delay and the time required until the first RTP packet is received by the UE (in case of addressing the QoE, then the time measured should be up to displaying the whole picture on the UE screen).

3. **SME Maximum Processing Sessions**, which represents the number of existing sessions on the SME by taking into account the number of served UEs and the average session/media establishment delay.

Figure 7.11 illustrates the session and the total establishment delay by requests initiated by the UEs (e.g. Bob and Alice). The SME maximum processing sessions will be calculated by the SME itself.

7.3.1.3 Testing Tools

The test is performed in the FOKUS playground, which represents a real IMS-based infrastructure. However, in order for the performance test to emulate multiple IMS clients, two testing tools were used, SIPp [108] and SIPNuke [105]. In addition, the Wireshark tool was used for tracing and analyzing the IMS traffic. It is the world's foremost network protocol analyzer [109] and allows for the capturing of network data and packet browsing.

7.3. Performance Evaluation 169

SIPp : SIPp is a free Open Source test tool and trace generator for the SIP protocol. It establishes and releases multiple calls with the INVITE and BYE methods. It emulated the IMS clients and the MDF. This test tool was initially used to evaluate the implementation in the early stage of this work, 7.3.3. However, for the latter part of the testing, the SIPNuke was used due to its higher level of performance and flexibility than SIPp.

SIPNuke : SIPNuke is a flexible IMS load generator developed at the Fraunhofer FOKUS institute. Its key features are performance, flexibility and ease of use. It was mainly used to emulate IMS clients to generate multiple SIP sessions with different call rates.

7.3.2 SIP Transactions Evaluation

In session-based content delivery in an IMS network, several SIP transactions may occur, as discussed in several scenarios in chapter 4. However, the evaluation of these transactions was mainly based on a mathematical formulation that does not reflect the behavior of both the IMS core and the application over time in respect of various SIP transactions. Following the pull-based scenarios defined in subsection 4.3.2.3, the users interact with the AS using different SIP transactions, especially in a multicast delivery session. In this regard, various SIP transactions are generated at different rates within a SIP-based session. Three types of SIP transactions are considered: SIP Re-INVITE message, INFO message and SUBSCRIBE/NOTIFY message, as depicted in Figure 4.8, Figure 4.9 and Figure 4.10, respectively. As the SIP PUBLISH method comprises only one SIP transaction similar to the SIP INFO transaction, it is not considered in this measurement. Since we are interested in understanding the impact of the SIP transactions, the session does not include a content stream. A set of SIP User Agents (SUA) were emulated with SIPnuke and simple SIP Servlet logic was deployed in a Sailfin application server.

After session setup via a SIP INVITE message, one of these SIP transactions is generated at a specific configurable rate (5, 10, 15, 25 or 35 request per second). Initially, we set the number of SUAs and the request rate as variable, however, then we found that the system being tested gave stable results with 1000 SUAs at different request rates. As we are interested in the performance of the SIP transactions as opposed to the performance of the system being tested, we conducted the measurements with a fixed number of the SUAs (i.e. 100) while varying the request rate. For each SIP transaction, the corresponding delay measured at the SUA is the total time beginning with the initial SIP request (e.g. INVITE, Re-INVITE, INFO or SUBSCRIBE/NOTIFY) and going up to the SIP OK response from the application server. For each

SIP	5 rps		10 rps		15 rps		25 rps		35 rps	
Transaction	μ/ms	σ/ms	μ/ms	σ/ms	μ/ms	σ/ms	μ/ms	σ/ms	μ/ms	σ/ms
Re-Invite	26.8	5.7	26.7	5.9	26.7	5.7	**27.4**	**6.1**	1741	1313
Info	20.0	3.7	19.9	3.6	19.9	3.5	**19.9**	**3.6**	21.9	14.4
Sub/Notify	20.0	3.6	20.0	3.5	20.0	3.6	**19.8**	**3.6**	22.2	14.5

Table 7.2: SIP transactions evaluation

transaction type, the measurements at each rate were performed 10 times with 100 emulated SUAs and the mean value of the measured delay was calculated.

Table 7.10 represents the average signaling delay (μ) of each transaction between the SUA and the application server at different request rates. There is no significant difference between the INFO and SUBSCRIBE/NOTIFY transactions at all request rates. At loads up to 25 requests per second, the delay of the SIP Re-INVITE transaction is approximately 25% higher than the delay of the other two transactions. However, at a load of 35 requests per second, the delay of the Re-INVITE transaction was observed to increase exponentially, while the delay of the other two transactions remains small. However, the standard deviation (σ) remains small.

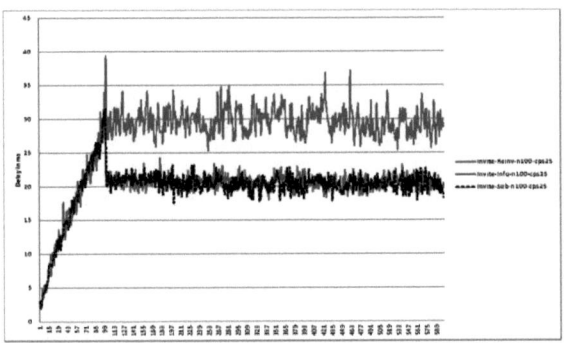

Figure 7.10: Delay of several SIP transactions at rate 25 cps

Figure 7.10 depicts the delay of these three transactions measured with 25 requests per second (rps). The delays of the Re-INVITE, INFO and SUBSCRIBE/NOTIFY are depicted by the continuous grey line, continuous red line and dashed line, respectively. The total number of sessions is represented in the horizontal axis. In all test scenarios, the delays of the initial 100 re-

7.3. Performance Evaluation

quests increases linearly as they represent the delay in session setup via the SIP Invite message. The delay of the following 500 requests represents the delay of the corresponding SIP transaction, and remains approximately constant for all transactions, as shown in Table 7.2. However, the delay of the Re-INVITE transaction is higher than the other two transactions.

As the Re-Invite transaction consists of three messages in contrast to the other two transactions that consist of two messages only, its associated delay is expected to be higher than the delay of the other two transactions. According to the analysis performed in subsection 4.5, the SIP INFO is considered, in theory, to be better in terms of performance than the SUBSCRIBE/NOTIFY transaction, while the measurement results show that both transactions have similar behavior even at higher request rates.

7.3.3 End-to-End Signaling Evaluation

To understand the impact of the IMS signaling overhead on a linear streaming session using a unicast or a multicast transmission mode, a unicast linear streaming session will be considered according to user initiated requests. Figure 7.11 shows the related call flow diagram. Note the impacts of the associated SIP transactions were discussed in 4.3.2.2. The objective of the end-to-end evaluation was to determine the signaling delay in the following three aspects:

1. Total signaling delay (D_{sig}): $UE \leftrightarrow SME \leftrightarrow MDF$ (steps 1 - 10 or 11 - 18 in Figure 7.11)

2. Signaling delay in the ISC interface (D_{sig_ISC})(steps 2 - 5 or 12 - 14 in Figure 7.11)

3. MDF triggering delay (D_{sig_MDF})(steps 3, 4 or 13). Although the SIP messages pass the IMS core, it is not depicted in Figure 7.11.

The test case was performed according to the message diagram depicted in Figure 7.11 by taking into account the environmental characteristics and the parameters defined in Table 7.3. The processing time inside the MDF is set to zero, so the signaling delay measurements cover only the signaling portion and ignore the content and resource allocation times within the MDF. This would decrease the performance of the SME. The tables below contain all or a selection of the following information:

- statistical average value (μ)
- standard deviation σ)

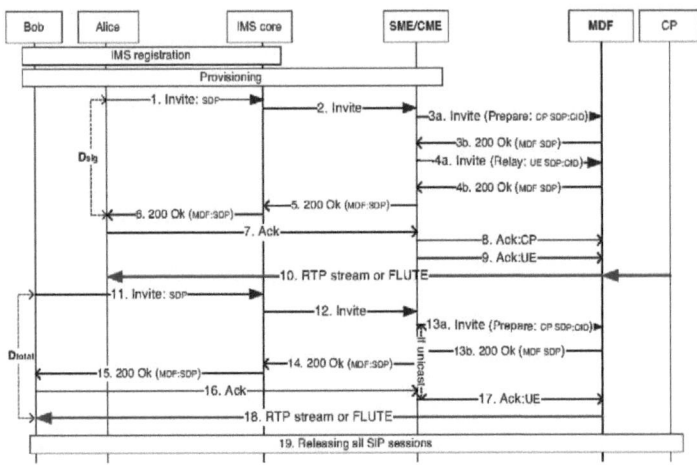

Figure 7.11: End-to-end message flows of a live content session

- coefficient of variation (c_v) to evaluate the ratio of $\frac{\mu}{\sigma}$
- median ($\widetilde{x}$) to exclude statistical outliners

The measurement does not focus on the performance of the implementation as this subject will be considered in the next sections. However, the environment considered two different access networks (WLAN and LAN) and two SIP application servers (SIPSee and BEA), in which the SME/CME is deployed and executed.

Test case	Environment	Parameters	Metrics
Unicast linear	SME and CME deployed in SIPSee LAN and WLAN access network	Ue = 1, r=const., n=20, t=0	D_{sig}, D_{sig_ISC}, D_{sig_MDF}

Table 7.3: End-to-End evaluation test cases

Table 7.3 summarizes the test case and the related test environment, test parameters and evaluation metrics. The results of this work have been published in [60, 110, 99].

7.3.3.1 Test Diagram

This test case can be described based on Figure 7.11 that illustrates the detailed sequence flows between the IMS UEs, the SME/CME and the IMS-

7.3. Performance Evaluation

based network. Only two IMS subscribers (Alice and Bob) are shown, however the test may include sets of subscribers. All these UEs are subscribed to the SME streaming service and the related service profiles and the associated Initial Filter Criteria (iFC) are stored in the HSS. The scenario is divided into six phases:

1. All UEs must register themselves with the IMS core before session establishment. Therefore, all test UEs have to be defined in the HSS and have to be subscribed for all SME services (not depicted in this figure).

2. The first UE (e.g. Alice) sends a SIP Invite request carrying the SME PSI, the CRID and terminal capabilities (step 1). Based on the PSI, the S-CSCF routes the request to the SME deployed on the SME AS. The SME checks first if a delivery session associated with this CRID already exists (which is not the case at this time). Therefore, it requests that the Content Management Enabler (CME) or the database obtain the related content information and possibly request the content from the content provider and prepare it for delivery.

3. The CME behaves as a SIP back-to-back user agent between the CP and the MDF. It requests the MDF initiate a *"prepare for relay"* session via a SIP Invite message that includes (step 2-3):

    - The SIP URL of the relay service (e.g. *relay@CDCF-ims-domain.com*)
    - A new CRID that identifies the relay session for further requests
    - CP session parameters (e.g. content type, codecs, IP address and ports)

4. After the SME receives the content information with the CRID from the CME, it makes use of the CRID to trigger the MDF to relay this content to Alice's unicast IP address or IP multicast address (if multicast is supported on the network and on Alice's device)(step 4-5). The relay session parameters offered by the MDF are forwarded to Alice's terminal. Once Alice's terminal receives the 200 OK message, it allocates the required local ports (or joins a multicast group if required) to receive the content stream (step 6-7).

5. Successive users' requests (here Bob) follow the same path of the first SIP invite message. In this case, both Alice and Bob are using the same multicast bearer to receive the content. The SME provides Bob with the identical session parameters as Alice. Otherwise (step 9-11), the SME triggers the MDF to relay the content to Bob's terminal by

inserting Bob's session parameters and the same CRID. Later, based on the MDF response, the SME forwards the session parameters of the allocated bearer to Bob (step 12-13).

6. In the case of multicast content delivery, the UE shall join the multicast group ID, including the SDP part of the 200 Ok message (before step 13, but not depicted in this figure).

7. At the end of each delivery session (e.g. in our test cases after few seconds, say 10 sec) each UE issues a SIP Bye message to release the session, which causes the SME to release the delivery session (either unicast or multicast).

In this scenario, the SME may use unicast, multicast or both modes for content delivery. Furthermore, the content can be stored or live content.

7.3.3.2 Total Signaling Delay

Results: The total signaling delay refers to the total time beginning with the user SIP INVITE request up to the SIP OK response from the infrastructure (both detected at the client side). This time contains the processing time within the SME and the content stream signaling to the MDF. As already mentioned within this performance test, the allocation time within the MDF is set to zero. Actually, the pure signaling time is the point of interest here. The processing time may differ between different MDF implementations.

Interface	μ in ms		σ in ms		c_v in %		$\widetilde{x}$ in ms	
	BEA	SIPSee	BEA	SIPSee	BEA	SIPSee	BEA	SIPSee
WLAN	54	84	28	30	51	35	42	84
LAN	49	76	2	7	4	10	48	77
IMS ISC	40	69	4	4	10	6	39	71
SME - MDF	49	66	3	4	9	6	35	67

Table 7.4: Total end-to-end signaling delay of user-initiated multimedia session

Evaluation: The signaling delay can be considered from the following two perspectives.

- The first perspective addresses the access network. There is so far no appreciable difference between LAN and WLAN regarding the signaling delay. This stems from the low volume of traffic generated by the signaling and has therefore insignificant influence on the RAN. However, with the respect to the standard deviation, the values concerning the

7.3. Performance Evaluation

WLAN access network are quite variable. But as the median is quite close to the average value, it becomes evident the variance results from statistical outliers.

- The second perspective addresses the performance of BEA AS versus SIPSee. The signaling delay using BEA AS is approximately 66% of the delay of using SIPSee AS. Concerning absolute values, the higher delay of using SIPSee AS is negligible as the absolute values are in an imperceptible range.

Table 7.4 represents the total signaling delay between the UE, the SME and the MDF for a unicast content delivery in which the MDF has to be invoked explicitly for each single request. Therefore, there is no difference between unicast and multicast content stream invocation (when multicast delivery is not signaled yet). However, when the SME already knows the proper multicast address and the MDF already delivers the requested content via multicast, the signaling delay is significantly smaller than the unicast session, where the content stream had to be activated toward the MDF. For this reason, it is not explicitly mentioned here.

7.3.3.3 ISC interface signaling delay

Results: These performance tests target the signaling delay at the IMS service control (ISC) interface between S-CSCF and AS in IMS. The delay quantifies the time between sending the SIP Invite message from the S-CSCF to AS and the SIP OK response from the AS (both detected at the S-CSCF). This value covers the processing time within the AS and the time for triggering the MDF. The processing time of the MDF is set to zero.

Evaluation: Similar to the previous result, BEA AS based content delivery approach results in 57% of the processing time of SIPSee AS based approach. Within the range of 20 record sets, the standard deviation is relatively small. Thus, it can be assumed the values are significant and steady, as presented in Table 7.4.

7.3.3.4 SME and MDF Signaling Delay

The MDF initiation signaling delay indicates the time from the first received SIP Invite (detected at the SME), triggering the MDF, receiving the SIP OK response from the MDF and creating and sending the final SIP ACK to the MDF (detected at the SME).

Evaluation: Table 7.4 shows measurement results in which the BEA AS again has clearly a smaller signaling delay compared to the SIPSee. But the absolute difference is marginal (see previous comment). Both Application Servers behave very similarly in the context of signaling delay performance measurements. However, the delay is almost the same as the ISC signaling delay. According to further MDF specific performance measurements, which will be presented in more detail in subsection 7.3.5, the IMS core consumes more than 80% of the processing time of the SIP Invite message due to the MDF iFC evaluation by the IMS core.

Performance measurements with respect to different user load and the associated signaling delay are essential to understand the impact on the components to be tested. The next measurements concentrate on this case.

7.3.4 Multimedia Service Enablers

In order to understand the limit of the SME we conducted two test cases; user-initiated and application-initiated content stream session, as specified in Table 7.5. The message diagram of the user initiated content stream session follows the diagram depicted in Figure 7.11.

Test case	Environment	Parameters	Metrics
User-initiated unicast session	SME and CME deployed in SIPSee, LAN access network, VLC as CP, MDF and SIPNuke emulating UEs	Ue=variable, r=variable, n=variable, t=10 sec	D_{sig} and D_{total}
application-initiated unicast session	WS, SME and CME deployed in SIPSee, LAN access network, VLC as CP, MDF and SIPNuke emulating UEs	Ue=variable, r=variable, n=variable, t=10 sec	D_{sig} and D_{total}

Table 7.5: Performance measurement use cases

According to the analysis provided in 4.4, event-induced multimedia content delivery improves user-perceived multimedia experience. Therefore, we focus only on one push delivery mode, namely the unicast mode, as specified in Table 7.5. The related message diagram is illustrated in Figure 7.12. The results of this work have been published in [100, 111].

7.3.4.1 Test Diagram

To estimate the performance of the end-to-end delay for session set-up of an application initiated content delivery using a WS application, the SME, the CME, the IMS core, the MDF and the IMS subscriber are involved in the process. Figure 7.12 shows the sequence diagram of message flows for a single session. For sake of simplicity, only one user is depicted; however the test

7.3. Performance Evaluation

case includes multiple IMS subscribers according to the generated call rate as explained in 7.3.1.2. Furthermore, the IMS core and the registration phase of the IMS subscribers are not shown.

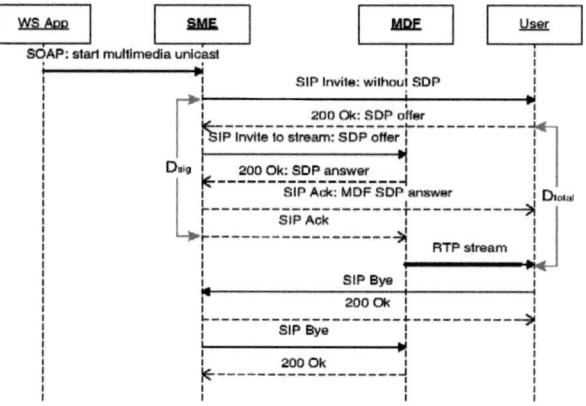

Figure 7.12: Application-initiated content delivery

The test case was performed as follows:

1. The WS application initiates the test session by invoking the start multimedia unicast API exposed by the SME, in order to stream multimedia content to a set of IMS subscribers.

2. Consequently, the Multimedia Service Enablers (MSE) acts as third party call controller following RFC 3725 [112] and hence initiates a SIP invite message for each IMS subscriber without SDP parameters. The IMS core forwards the Invite request to the IMS subscriber based on a previous successful registration (not depicted in the diagram). The SME sets a time to measure the signaling delay (D_{sig}).

3. The IMS subscriber, emulated by the SIPNuke tool, responds with a 200 Ok message with an SDP offer and sets a timer to measure the total delay (D_{total}).

4. Upon receiving the 200 Ok message, the SME triggers the MDF to stream the requested multimedia content indicated in the SDP offer over a unicast bearer.

5. The MDF responds with a 200 Ok message that includes the corresponding delivery parameters stored in the SDP answer.

6. In turn, the SME confirms both sessions by sending two SIP Ack messages to the IMS subscriber with the MDF SDP parameters and to the MDF. Then it logs the measured signaling delay (D_{sig}).

7. At this time, the MDF starts streaming the content.

8. Once the IMS subscriber receives the first RTP packet, it stops the timer and logs the measured total delay (D_{total}).

9. Then the IMS client suspends the session for a certain time (e.g. 10 seconds) and then issues a SIP Bye message to release the delivery session.

10. Upon receiving the SIP Bye message, the SME terminates the associated MDF session.

7.3.4.2 User-initiated unicast session

The performance measurement aim is to determine the total signaling delay (D_{total}), including the round trip time of the first RTP packet. The time for setting up the stream towards the MDF and relaying to the user is denoted as D_{sig}. We consider a test scenario setting up one single session for content delivery towards MDF (*prepare-for-relay*) and a unicast transmission session for each user request (*relay*). The test case is performed according to the message diagram depicted in Figure 7.11 by taking into account the environmental characteristics and the parameters defined in Table 7.5 and denoted with a user-initiated unicast session. These nodes are connected via a fast-Ethernet LAN (100Base-T) network, where there are 6 hops between the user terminals and the SME/CME, 2 hops between the SME/CME and the MDF, 1 hop between the CP and the MDF, and 6 hops between the MDF and user terminals.

Results: Figure 7.13 to Figure 7.14 depict different measurements calculated on the client with increasing calls per second rates. The total session delay D_{total} is depicted in red and the signaling delay D_{sig} is depicted in blue. The total number of simultaneous sessions for each realization is represented in the horizontal axis. The duration of each media session is 10 seconds, in which the client receives RTP traffic then issues the SIP Bye message to terminate the session. Each delay value in the graphs corresponds to the median of a series of repeated 10 executions of the test case. Regarding the $Dsig$ value, the measurement is done when the first 200 OK arrives at the user terminal. This duration is the sum of the network delays over the tested communication media and the processing delay introduced by the IMS core network, the SME and the MDF. The D_{total} depicts the time when the first RTP packet arrives

7.3. Performance Evaluation

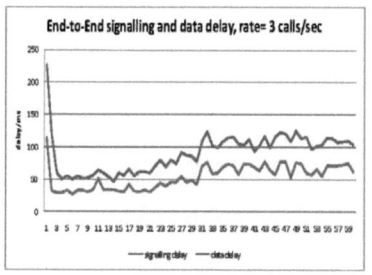

Figure 7.13: Delay of user-initiated session at 3 cps

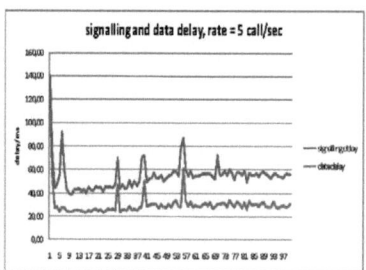

Figure 7.14: Delay of user-initiated session at 5 cps

at the user terminal. However, this is not taking into account when the first complete video frame is to be displayed at the terminal.

Figure 7.15: Delay of user-initiated session at 7 cps

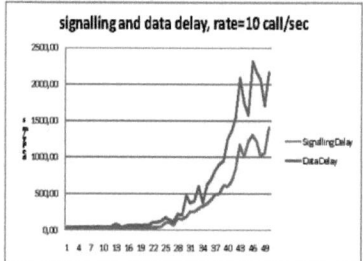

Figure 7.16: Delay of user-initiated session at 10 cps

Evaluation: As we see in the measurements, from a certain total simultaneous number of sessions (here from 60 up to 100), both signaling and total media delay grow constantly when the call rate is 3 and 5 calls per second. At a rate of 7 and 10 calls per second, the media delay increases gradually at the beginning and then exponentially from the middle. However, the end-to-end delay does not increase much and is still acceptable enough to keep all users very satisfied or satisfied. Based on these results we can make four important observations:

- The signaling delay has a significant impact on the total delay when several nodes are involved in the signaling path, including the UE, IMS core, the SME/CME and MDF.

- The delay of the first request (clearly in Figure 7.13 and Figure 7.14) is always higher than the subsequent messages due to two additional processing delays: the first is introduced by the IMS core, where the S-CSCF needs time to download the user profile from the HSS, as this request is the first SIP Invite message issued by the user to the SME after the IMS registration. The second delay is due to the preparation for the relay session between the content provider (VLC) and the MDF and the setting up of the related pipeline on the MDF (step 3 in Figure 7.11).

- Processing time on the SME/CME has a big penalty at high call rates especially when several sessions already exist on the SME (more than 60 and 30 sessions on the rate of 7 and 10 cps, respectively). This means that retransmission of previous requests (either Invite or Bye messages) occurs only after a certain time, which is less than the total end-to-end signaling delay. As a result of that, the actual rate of received requests on the SME is much higher than the 7 or 10 cps and consequently the measured delay increases exponentially (clearly in Figure 7.15 and Figure 7.16).

- On the SME with a high processing time, retransmissions are triggered by the IMS core, as well as by the clients even if the packet was successfully delivered, because the retransmission timers are smaller than the total latency.

Furthermore, the results indicate that, while the SME performs well under a low rate, the latency would be at an acceptable limit (less than 200ms) with a high request rate, only if a load balancing process is applied for incoming requests. However this is not the case in the current implementation and this issue has to be considered for future work.

7.3.4.3 Application-initiated unicast session

The performance measurement aim is to determine the total signaling delay (D_{total}), which includes the signaling delay (D_{sig}) plus the round trip time of the first RTP packet. For each initiated session multimedia content (audio and video tracks) streams for a certain time (e.g. 10 seconds). This time is considered media stream time. Session duration covers session establishment and media stream. In general, the longer the test duration, the more precise the measurement results are. Therefore, a series of tests were conducted, where each UE processes only one request in each sequence.

Results: Figure 7.17 and Figure 7.18 depict different measurements calculated with 5 and 7 calls/requests per second, respectively. The tests were

7.3. Performance Evaluation

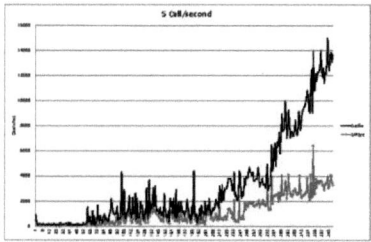 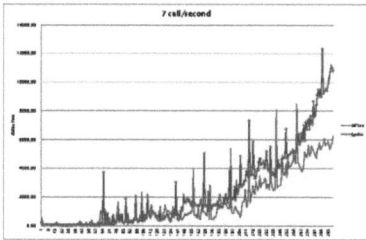

Figure 7.17: Delay of application-initiated session at 5 cps

Figure 7.18: Delay of application-initiated session at 7 cps

conducted using two different application servers: the SIPSee and the Sailfin [106]. The related measurement results are depicted in red and green, respectively. The total number of sessions is represented in the horizontal axis. The duration of each session is 10 seconds. Each delay value in the graphs corresponds to the median of a series of repeated measurements. Regarding the D_{total} value, the measurement is finished when the first RTP packet arrives at the user terminal. However, this delay does not include the depacketization, decoding and the display processing time.

Evaluation: As we see in the measurements, from a certain total simultaneous number of sessions (here from 60 up to 200), at the beginning the delay grows slowly and constantly for both 5 and 7 call per second rates and exponentially from the middle. Based on these results, we should make three important observations:

- The signaling delay has a significant impact on the total delay, where several nodes are involved in the signaling path including the UE, IMS core, the SME and MDF.

- The delay of the first request (not very clear in Figure 7.17 and Figure 7.18) is always higher than the subsequent messages due to the processing delay on the IMS core and the preparation for the relay session on the MDF, as described above in the previous test case.

- Processing time on the SME was a big penalty at high rates and especially when multiple sessions already exist on the SME (more than 60 sessions on the 5 and 7 cps rates). This means that retransmission of previous requests (either Invite or Bye messages) occurs only after a certain time, which is less than the total end-to-end signaling delay. As a result, the actual rate of received requests on the SME or on the UEs is much higher than the actual rate (i.e., 5 or 7 cps) and consequently the measured delay increases exponentially.

Moreover, the results indicate that while the SME performs well under low load, the latency would be at an acceptable limit (less than 400ms) with a high request rate, only if a load balancing process would be applied for incoming requests. However, this is not the case in the current implementation and this issue has to be considered for future work.

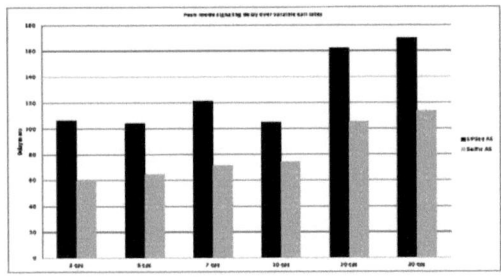

Figure 7.19: Push-mode signaling delay over various call rates

Figure 7.19 shows the performance measurement for the push-mode session by deploying the SME in a SIPSee and a Sailfin SIP servlet container. The measurement considers only up to 100 sessions with variable call rates (3, 5, 7, 10, 20 and 30 cps). It is obvious that the platform performance of the Sailfin SIP AS with the same load is more than 55% better than the SIPSee AS. This shows that the performance of the SIP AS can have a direct impact (positively or negatively) on the total signaling delay of a multimedia session. Therefore, it is important to consider which SIP AS should be used in the real deployment.

7.3.5 Media Delivery Control

To estimate the performance of both the MDF and the signaling interface, we measured the triggering latency of the relay function on the MDF, as well as its complete processing time against variable call rate throughput. To do so, we prepared several media streams in MPEG-TS format to simulate different

7.3. Performance Evaluation

content providers that stream media content directly to the MDF. Increasing relay requests are simulated by the SME. In order to evaluate the MDF control interface, two interfaces are considered in the test environment:

1. Routing through the IMS core where, due to the hiding of the IMS network topology, the I-CSCF receives all SIP messages and contacts the HSS for each new SIP dialog in order to resolve the appropriate S-CSCF from the database. The S-CSCF then forwards the SIP message to the MDF based on the iFC downloaded only once from the HSS.

2. Messages are forwarded to the MDF directly and without the IMS core.

Test case	Environment	Parameters	Metrics
Prepare for Relay	SME emulated with SIPp, IMS core, VLC as CP, MDF	r=variable, n=variable, t=const.	D_{sig} and D_{MDF_PT}
Prepare for Relay	SME emulated with SIPp, direct control, VLC as CP, MDF	r=variable, n=variable, t=const.	D_{sig} and D_{MDF_PT}
Relay	SME emulated with SIPp, IMS core, VLC as CP, MDF	r=variable, n=variable, t=const.	D_{sig} and D_{MDF_PT}
Relay	SME emulated with SIPp, direct control, VLC as CP, MDF	r=variable, n=variable, t=const.	D_{sig} and D_{MDF_PT}

Table 7.6: MDF performance test cases

Based on the available MDF implementation, two performance test cases have been conducted that cover the service activation of the input leg "*prepare for relay*" as well as the output legs "*relay to UEs*" of a relay function. Table 7.6 summarizes both test cases with the related test environment, test parameters and evaluation metrics. The metrics used to evaluate the performance of the MDF and the signaling interface between the AS and the MDF - directly or through the IMS Core - are as follows:

1. Average/median triggering delay of the incoming and outgoing leg (AS↔MDF input-RTT and AS↔MDF output-RTT "*Round Tripe Time*"): the average RTT delay time measured by the AS for initiating the incoming and outgoing leg(s) of a relay function.

2. Average/median processing delay of the setup incoming and outgoing leg on the MDF (MDF-input-PT and MDF-output-PT): the average delay time for initiating the incoming and outgoing leg of a relay function on the MDF and the time needed for allocating the required processing resources.

The measured triggering delay (AS↔MDF-in-RTT and AS↔MDF-out-RTT) includes the local processing on the AS, the round trip time between the AS and MDFP, and the latency introduced by the MDFP for session management and resource allocation. We encountered the problem that we could not directly measure the delay introduced by the MDFP's SIP stack (Sofia-SIP [93]), which necessarily will grow at increasing call per second rates.

The measurements consist of 100 records of each scenario. A record set of 100 values contains statistical outliers (as we have seen by analyzing the standard deviation), so our evaluation is based on the median value which disregards statistical outliers.

In case of the IMS deployment, SIP messages arrive at the MDF after 6 hops in a fast-Ethernet LAN (100Base-T) environment. The MDF host is an Intel Core Duo T2400 at 1.83 GHz with 1 GB RAM (2 MB L2 cache). The Open IMS Core host is a Dual Pentium III at 933 MHz with 512 MB RAM. The SME has been emulated with the SIPp test tool. The results of this work have been published in [113].

7.3.5.1 Test Diagram

Figure 7.20 illustrates the message flows between the AS and the MDF in three phases as follows:

1. The SME on the AS side triggers the MDF to receive content from a content provider as incoming leg of the relay function (step 1 to 4)

2. Then the AS determines the outgoing leg of the relay function, which could be assigned to a multicast or a unicast bearer (step 5 to 8)

3. At this time, the MDF relays the content from the incoming leg to the outgoing leg.

After one test iteration, the SME releases all the outgoing legs and the associated incoming leg by issuing two SIP Bye messages (not depicted in the message flow).

7.3.5.2 Prepare For Relay Function

The SME triggers the MDF for the preparation of the relay function once for each input channel and is used to setup the internal pipelining of the MDF. Figure 7.21 illustrates the measurement result of our test for setting up the internal pipeline.

Evaluation: As the preparation of relay function is used to setup the internal pipelining of the MDF, it takes more time for the MDF to invoke

7.3. Performance Evaluation

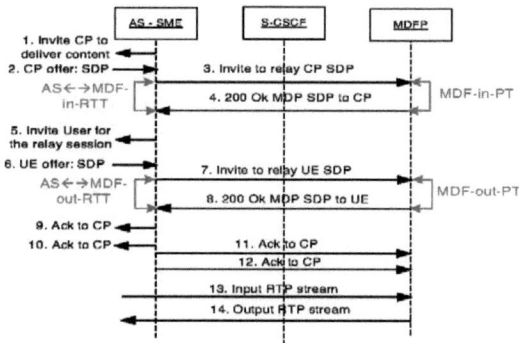

Figure 7.20: Message flows of the MDF relay function

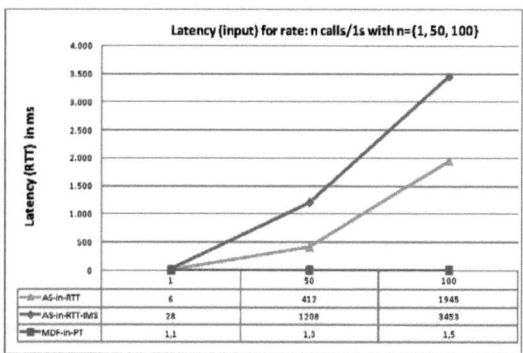

Figure 7.21: MDF prepare for relay performance measurement results based on calls/1s

the related processing entity that it takes to to setup the output channels, as presented in the next subsection. The measurement of 50 channels per second represents a worst case scenario. It is not necessary to evaluate more than 50 input channels per second (in parallel) in a real condition use case. Concerning the processing time inside the MDF, it is not the component that is creating the most latency, but the SIP Stack at the MDF, together with the delay introduced by the IMS components. Furthermore, it is obvious that the signaling via IMS Core produces a big latency (blue line), which is about 1.2 seconds, at rate of 50 calls per second. In the case when the IMS is bypassed, the latency is 0.4 seconds. The former latency is attributed to the I-CSCF connecting for each SIP request to the HSS which generates 7 SQL queries towards the database. In this regard, *the connection to the HSS (database) has to be minimized. This can be achieved through caching the last used S-CSCF for a specified amount of time (e.g. 5s)*.

7.3.5.3 Relay Function

Results: The SME triggers the MDF for relaying a dedicated multimedia content that has been provided during the preparation phase. Figure 7.22 and Figure 7.23 illustrate the measurement result of the test for setting up a set of output channels (5, 50, 100, 200, 400 and 500) at 1 and 10 calls per seconds.

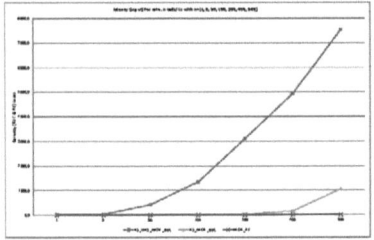 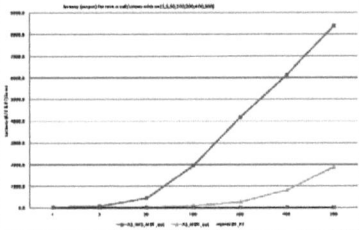

Figure 7.22: Triggering relay function at 1 cps   Figure 7.23: Triggering relay function at 10 cps

Evaluation: Figure 7.22 and Figure 7.23 show the output delay for parallel setup of the output channels. Considering the MDF architecture, it is obvious, that the output streaming is far less time consuming as there is no pipeline setup required in this step. It consists only of a mapping of the already prepared processing chain with a target sink (unicast/multicast) based on the channel id.

However, one can see that the signaling via IMS Core produces a big latency, which is about 0.4 seconds at rate of 50 calls per second, as depicted with the blue line. In the case of bypassing the IMS, it is 0.006 second. This is due to the I-CSCF connecting each SIP request to the HSS, which generates 7 SQL queries towards the database. In this regard, the connection to the HSS (database) has to be minimized. This can be achieved by caching the last used S-CSCF for a dedicated amount of time (e.g. 5s).

7.4 Discussion and Comparison with other Solutions

The IMS is a new and emerging technology enabling the realization of FMC. It is passing through an evolutionary and development phase. TISPAN, Open IPTV Forum and the ITU-T have defined an IMS-based IPTV solution that enables the convergence of classical IMS services and TV services. However, part of this research work has contributed to the standardization in particular subjects and has considered additional interfaces not within the scope of the standardization bodies (e.g. the interface towards the Content Provider). On the other hand, the research community has studied several content delivery approaches with the objective of enriching IMS applications with multimedia experience.

In this section we survey different multimedia delivery solutions and approaches developed or proposed by the standardization bodies or other researchers that have been published in scientific literature and compare them to our solution as specified in chapter 5.

7.4.1 Standardization Bodies

ETSI TISPAN, Open IPTV Forum and the ITU-T have been working on standardizing the IMS-based IPTV delivery framework for the past few years, and the specification process is still ongoing. On other hand, there are interfaces that are either under development (e.g. the MDF control interface) or beyond the scope of the standard (e.g. the interface between the service provider and the content provider). Furthermore, these three organizations focus on the delivery of TV services via fixed access networks, but do not consider mobile access technologies and related aspects.

The OMA BCAST (Mobile Broadcast) [114] defines an enabler for the delivery of content stream and file distribution functionality over mobile networks, but it does not consider the integration of the BCAST within the IMS network.

Also, there are several multimedia solutions that make use of the public Internet to deliver applications with rich and interactive video content, but the delivery lacks QoS and overall control of the service offer and flexible charging models. However, the IMS-based delivery framework can overcome these deficiencies. Table 7.7 shows a comparison between the current two multimedia delivery platforms, namely the public Internet and the classical fixed and mobile IPTV platforms, and the IMS-based Solution. Currently, there are just a few commercial IMS-based IPTV platforms offered only by two vendors, namely Ericsson and Huawei, as stated in their website, but there has been neither commercial deployment, nor public evaluation results.

Feature	Web-based streaming	Classical IPTV	COSMIC Approach
Platform Geographical Reach	Public Internet Globally	Closed platform Within operator domain	Integrated framework Within operator domain and possibly globally
Ownership of the platform	Any content or service provider	Network operator	Network operator, service provider or shared
Content provisioning mechanism	Based on user's search or web advertisement (e.g. email)	Electronic Program Guide (EPG) following pull model	Combination of event-based and pull interaction model
Content management	Administrative	Administrative	Administrative or dynamic
Content sources	Professional content provider or user generated content	collaboration between operator and content providers	Professional content provider or user generated content
Interworking with content provider	Hosting and providing multimedia content directly to the consumer	No specified interface available between operators and CP	Defined interworking interface towards the content provider
Delivery mechanism	Unicast streaming or file download	Unicast and multicast streaming	Unicast, multicast and broadcast
Awareness of access technology	Not	Yes	Yes (in managed content delivery)
Mobility support	Not	Not	Yes
Personalization and Interactivity	Not supported	limited support	Full support
Service openness	Within public Internet	Operator policy and platform capabilities	Defined open interface to access delivery capabilities
QoS	Best-effort	Manageable	Supported (in managed content delivery)
Convergence of Multimedia Services	Client-oriented	Limited support	Full support
Utilization of deployed nodes	Shared resources	Single platform with dedicated resources	Shared resources

Table 7.7: Comparison between current multimedia delivery frameworks and COSMIC

In this work, several interfaces that are beyond the scope of the standard-

7.4. Discussion and Comparison with other Solutions

ization bodies or not even considered, are studied and evaluated in depth. Furthermore, a prototype implementation was presented and several performance measurements have been conducted and discussed. The integration with several access networks is explained and demonstrated in a distributed and scalable testbed.

It is obvious that multimedia content delivery based on the IMS control differs from Web-based delivery in that the former is a highly-managed system, offering guaranteed QoS and involving user subscriptions. Compared with classical fixed IPTV and mobile TV, it provides a great avenue for converged rich multimedia services due to its personalized and interactive nature. Furthermore, this work enhances the IMS with multiple delivery capabilities that smoothly facilitate the integration of different players such as the content provider and the service providers in the value chain of multimedia content delivery applications.

7.4.2 Research Community

Here we present several solutions that have been proposed by various researchers. The countermeasures are presented in order of publication. Each proposal is summarized according to the alignment with this work. We base this summary on available facts in the publication and do not judge any of the proposed ideas here.

7.4.2.1 Cagenius

T. Cagenus et al. proposes Ericsson IMS-based architecture for the delivery of interactive IPTV services [42]. They introduce an overall architecture with distributed functionalities among the IMS core, the IMS enablers, the IPTV application servers and the Service Delivery Platform. The paper discusses the interfaces between the user equipment (IPTV Terminal Function) and the network side comprehensively. However, it does not explain the IPTV application server and how it interacts with the other nodes (e.g. the content provider, the media servers for content delivery and media processing).

7.4.2.2 Ambient Networks Project

Within the Ambient Networks project [45], a service-specific overlay network for content delivery and content adaptation has been designed, which is based on a peer-to-peer communication model for service discovery, and service path management for media delivery. Project results have been published in several papers as follows:

- Niebert N. et al. [45] introduce service specific overlay networking for adapting multimedia content within the ambient networks project. Such as overlay is based on the peer-to-peer communication model for service discovery and service path management for media delivery. Although this solution has been evaluated in simulation, there has not been any realization yet.

- Mathieu et al. and Hartung et al. [46, 78] proposes an approach to the integration of media processing based on the overlay-networking paradigm, in which how such a concept could be applied within a SIP-based session in an IMS environment is described. This content delivery approach implies that session participants or the IMS core are registered with the overlay network, which is in charge of media processing as well as the required QoS. Conversely QoS and media processing are key features supported by the IMS network. This concept will introduce additional delay to the session setup between session participants. Unfortunately the work does not provide any evaluation result for this concept.

- Tariq et al. [77] propose a proxy-based dynamic configurable multimedia processing entity, but the integration of such a proxy within an IMS-based network has not been considered.

Although the Ambient Networks Project provides a solution for media processing in a peer-to-peer content delivery approach, the proposed integration with the IMS core is not efficient and no reference implementation or evaluation is provided.

7.4.2.3 ScaleNet Project

E. Mikoczy et al. [115] presents an architecture to provide IMS based IPTV, according to ETSI-TISPAN deployed in the ScaleNet project [44] consisting of functional elements and the description of basic call flows to provide IMS based IPTV according to ETSI TISPAN. Their work describes an IPTV service called "*Click to Multimedia Service*". The proposed solution does not consider the session management or the content management functions, which are both important in an IMS-based content delivery network. Furthermore, the service discovery and provisioning functions are based only on the pull method (using http request), which cannot satisfy user perceived multimedia experience under continuous changes in the availability of new multimedia content, compared to event-based content provisioning. Furthermore, the implementation considers only the session mobility and related delay, but does not provide detailed evaluation, as included in this work.

7.4. Discussion and Comparison with other Solutions 191

7.4.2.4 Interactivity and Personalization in IMS-based Network

Chatras et al [43] outlines the motivations behind, benefits of and feasible technical challenges in the IMS-based IPTV framework, but neither implementation nor evaluation is presented.

E. Marilly et al. [116] proposes a solution for content adaptation and service personalization of Interactive Mobile TV Services. They present use cases of different technologies and a functional architecture supporting the adaptation and personalization of service applications. The proposed architecture follows the OMA BCAST architecture and provides an integration option with the IMS network by considering the interactive mobile TV solution as part of the media server functionality. However, from a scalability point of view, the entire architecture should therefore be analyzed by breaking-down its set of supported functionalities and distributing them into different IMS functional elements, namely the IMS application servers and the IMS media server.

7.4.2.5 University of Cape Town IMS-based IPTV

The University of Cape Town (UCT) has recently developed an IMS-based IPTV system that is based mainly on four components [117]:

1. UCT IMS client [118] which offers the necessary client side IMS features, such as registration, service selection, call setup, media preference settings and IPTV viewing

2. IMS core, which is based on the FOKUS Open IMS Core that provides the call session control and HSS.

3. Media Server, which is a third party RTSP-based media server to deliver the media stream

4. IPTV application server, which is a basic SIP-based indirection server implemented as a user agent. It maintains a hash-table with a list of content resources (SIP resources) RTSP resources each of which is associated wiht an RTSP address.

It is obvious that this system provides only a basic IMS-based VoD delivery service instead of a comprehensive IPTV solution, because it lacks essential IPTV functionalities like session management, content management, content provisioning functions and further media delivery and processing functions (e.g. multicast support, relying feature, transcoding, etc.). Furthermore, the media server is loosely-coupled with the AS, where the MDF control interface is not considered in the current solution.

Recently, UCT IMS-based solution has been extended to deliver personalized advertisements to the user upon service, request and schedules subsequent advertisements during the lifetime of an active session [119]. Therefore, the IPTV AS is extended for the implementation of the advertisement application server functionalities.

7.4.2.6 Rating of Multimedia Delivery Approaches

One of this thesis objectives is to develop an open interactive multimedia delivery framework for delivering multimedia content in an IMS-based network. The related work we present in this chapter targets different delivery approaches. For a rating in comparison to our work we limit the related work to those that also address multimedia content delivery. Therefore, we leave out the work Chatras [43].

We will assign marks in four categories. For the *novelty* of the idea we consider a work that describes a completely new approach to multimedia content delivery (++), a new delivery approach but defined already by the standard (+), an enhancement of an already existing delivery approach (o) or a variation of a known delivery approach (-).

For supporting various *delivery services*, we distinguish between *linear* delivery and *on-demand delivery*. The difficulty in linear delivery service lie in the support of multiple transmission modes over different access networks with the objective of serving a large number of users. We give a mark (+) for supporting each transmission mode (unicast, multicast and broadcast), (++) in the case of supporting fixed and wireless access network (e.g. DSL/FTTH, 3GPP MBMS and DVB-H) and (o) in the case that the approach does not support linear delivery. For on-demand service delivery we give a (+) if the approach supports this feature, (++) fixed and mobile network is considered and (o) if the approach does not support the on-demand delivery service.

Furthermore, the approach of *managing multimedia content* (i.e. content provider integration) into the system content is one aspect of this dissertation . Therefore, if the delivery approach/framework defines dynamic mechanisms for content feeding, discovery and provisioning, we give for each supported feature, in the case of supporting the certain feature efficiently (+), simple support (o) (e.g. pull-based delivery for content provisioning) and if none of these features are supported (-).

For the openness, we distinguish between open framework and closed framework, where we give a (+) if the framework supports open interfaces, to enable a third party service provider to make use of framework capabilities. This will enable an easy integration with other domain-oriented applications in the IP cloud. On the other hand, we give (o) if it does not provide any

7.4. Discussion and Comparison with other Solutions

Approach	Novelty	Delivery services		Content Management			Openness	Validation
		linear	On-Demand	Cont. Feeding	Provisioning	Discovery		
Cagenus	+	++	+	-	o	o	-	++
Ambient Networks	++	+	o	o	-	o	-	o
ScaleNet	+	+	+	-	o	o	-	++
Marilly	+	++	o	-	-	-	-	+
UCT IPTV	o	-	+	-	o	o	-	++
COSMIC-MSE	++	++	+	+	+	+	+	++
COSMIC-MDF	+	++	+	+	o	o	o	++

Table 7.8: Rating of multimedia delivery approaches

open interfaces.

Finally, we rate how the approach/framework is validated, ranging from no validation at all (- -), some theoretical projections (-), simulations (o), implementation with test bed (+) to real-life tests (++).

A summary of rating these delivery approaches is given in Table 7.8. The main conclusions are:

- Content delivery approach proposed by the ambient network project and the collaboration of SME/CME and CPE approach is based on completely new ideas (denoted in the table with the term SME/CME/CPE).

- Event-based multimedia content delivery relying on event-based content provisioning and session management shows better performance than the other approaches. All other works are variations of previous works or represent a reference implementation of a defined standard (e.g. IMS-based IPTV or OMA BCAST).

- For delivery services, most of the available approaches consider either fixed or mobile networks or the support of linear or on-demand content delivery. However, this work considers both approaches and defines new enhancements for extending the IMS network in order to support unicast, multicast and broadcast transmission modes.

- From a content management point of view, most of the research work or standardization specifications define simple provisioning and discovery mechanisms based on pull requests using mainly the HTTP protocol.

However, this work provides a novel concept based on even-based content provisioning that facilitate the management of multimedia content information (e.g. content status) for the entire multimedia content delivery life-cycle. Furthermore, most of these approaches are often presumed to have multimedia content stored and available in the delivery platform in advance. In contrast the MDF developed in this work provides an open interface to feed multimedia content to the delivery channels at any time.

- Regarding service openness, all delivery solutions are primarily closed system and do not offer open interfaces to make use of its delivery capabilities. However, this work provides open programmable interfaces that enable third party applications to easily integrate the delivery capabilities into its service logic.

- Most of the mechanisms defined in this work have been validated and evaluated in testbeds, which we evaluate as the bare minimum to show the validity of an approach. Only half of the related works are validated or evaluated with test results.

CHAPTER 8

Conclusions

This dissertation has extensively studied multimedia content delivery in the NGN environment, discussed large-scale multimedia content delivery in the NGN, evaluated different delivery approaches, and proposed a novel session-based content delivery approach with the objective of enhancing network efficiency and improving the user perceived quality of experience. In the course of the research for this dissertation, several related papers and other writings have been published that deal with the same problems:

1. Two published journal papers

2. Twenty-one conference papers as first author (two of which are still in review process) and fourteen papers as co-author

3. Co-author of one chapter of a book

This research work contributed to several research projects, such as C-Mobile and C-CAST as discussed in 7.2.2. This chapter summarizes the achievements of this work and describes the on-going future extensions of this work in several research projects.

8.1 Summary and Impacts

This dissertation developed an efficient session-based multimedia content delivery framework in an NGN environment. The objective of this framework was to enrich the multimedia experience of NGN/IMS subscribers and enable personalization and interactivity, while also considering network resource efficiency and optimization. It offers a prototype implementation of the framework reference architecture. This work can therefore be considered as a foundation for any NGN-based delivery architecture and provides guidance for the development of IMS-based multimedia applications.

The framework is a coordinated set of enablers that provides general delivery capabilities either for transmitting multimedia content or the associated multimedia content information (metadata). The objective was to minimize latency and signaling messages, while at the same time maximizing the efficiency and scalability of component implementations. This was achieved by defining different communication models between the involved nodes.

Based on these facts, this work provides enhancements for IMS-based networks with the objective of supporting rich multimedia content delivery capabilities, in order to serve as as a foundation for all social interactions. What makes the IMS-based content delivery so promising for personalized applications like IMS-based IPTV, is that it has the potential to be directed at consumers with certain desirable characteristics. For example, from the advertisement point of view, the advertising messages will be delivered directly to the targeted user only, thus saving money on mass advertising when compared to the traditional advertisement model. This characteristic would result in a higher turnover and is therefore much more attractive to marketers than the mass marketing model [116]. The following contributions to the field of Telecommunications and Information Technology have been made as part of this dissertation:

- A formalized description for understanding several communication models in IMS/NGN-based applications.

- A classification and analysis of several SIP methods and communication models that can be used in any IMS-based multimedia applications

- A generic framework for delivering IMS-based interactive and personalized multimedia applications and enabling cross-breeding of multimedia content and telecommunication services

- A reference implementation of basic core delivery functionalities that have been validated in several testbed deployments and evaluated under several test conditions

The challenging aspect of this work has been the study of and development of solution for delivering multimedia content to high number of IMS subscribers in an efficient and optimized manner. In fact, IMS was initially developed to manage one-to-one communication sessions rather than one-to-n or n-to-n communication sessions. IMS is supposed to be an overlay technology on top of different access networking and emerging All-IP Networks, and the IMS session is based on the unicast transmission mode and does not make use of multicast or broadcast capabilities of the transport and access networks.

IMS enables the merging of fixed and mobile networks as well as telecommunications and multimedia applications on a single platform. However, the complexity of multimedia applications, different IMS session management

8.1. Summary and Impacts

models, various access and transport delivery capabilities, provide clear evidence for the need for improvement to IMS in order to support the delivery of real-time multimedia applications more efficiently.

Multimedia applications are time sensitive applications that have a set of constraints that should be considered during application development as well as execution. Therefore, we distinguish between distinct types of properties: real-time delivery properties and architectural properties. The first type defines a set of key performance indicators that have to be monitored and maintained during the delivery of multimedia applications. These properties are delay, jitter, packet loss, etc. The latter type defines a set of architectural properties such as - among others - network performance, user-perceived performance and scalability. These properties shall be considered a measure for guiding the design of IMS-based multimedia applications. The properties of both types are discussed in detail in chapter 3.2 and have been taken into account during the development of this work.

With the complexity of multimedia frameworks along with the increasing demand for multimedia content, the old and existing closed and standalone delivery frameworks solutions are not enough to offer multimedia delivery capabilities for different players in distributed domains. In chapter three, the requirements for a set of management and delivery capabilities are identified that are essential for any multimedia delivery framework and are specifically considered in this work. These capabilities are classified into three categories: *content management, session management* and *content delivery*.

Chapter 4 discussed these requirements and provided a detailed analysis from the architecture and signaling perspectives. First, the functional requirements for multimedia content delivery were identified on the basis of a defined life-cycle of multimedia content delivery. The functional requirements were grouped into five categories: *IMS core, service provisioning, content management, multimedia session management* and *media delivery functions*. Second, different traffic profiles of IMS-based multimedia services were introduced and aligned with a mathematical formulation of each of these profiles. Based on the defined analysis guidelines and the comprehensive study of message flows of several delivery use cases, several recommendations were deduced, in particular which protocols or protocol combinations for several multimedia content delivery approaches can be applied.

A reference implementation of a set of basic media delivery functional components, so-called service enablers, were developed as an integrated framework for delivering multimedia content in a distributed infrastructure administered and operated by multiple service domains. As service openness is one of the main design requirements in SOA-based infrastructure, these enablers (e.g. the media delivery function or the Content Information Provisioning function) can be deployed for a standalone service and provide their delivery and processing functions for other applications or enablers through defined interfaces (e.g. SIP protocol or SOAP API). Furthermore, the developed enablers can jointly work to deliver personalized and interactive multimedia content among IMS subscribers with minimal administration and operational effort, as content provider, services provider and media delivery providers can interwork dynamically and easily compared to the current solutions, in which the content provider is still not well-integrated with the services provider platform.

For IMS-based multimedia applications, system performance was dominated by signaling messages. For a distributed multimedia application, component interactions consist of a high amount of signaling messages among system entities rather than computation-intensive tasks. The event-induced content delivery was developed in response to those needs. It focuses on providing users with personalized multimedia content information updated according to the delivery state of the multimedia content. User subscriptions to any particular multimedia service or content can be used at different levels in the network, in order to prepare the expected required resources (either delivery or processing resources). The measurement results discussed in 7.3.4 show that the pull model is more efficient and the system can serve more subscribers than the push model.

This research work can be justified by the successful track of publications that were published during the development of the IMS-based multimedia delivery framework, which has been deployed in different testbeds and international projects, as discussed in chapter 7. At every step in carrying out this research, the state of the art solution was presented and defended in a particular article or paper in a reputed and referenced journal and/or in well-known IEEE/IFIP/ACM international IT security and communication conferences. The list of publications appears throughout the references used in this work, as listed in the Bibliography.

8.2 Outlook

This section explores those issues that were not been addressed in detail within this work. These issues are beyond the scope of this dissertation, and outline the basis for future work. The significant contribution of this work was the integration of a set of multimedia content delivery enablers that facilitate the delivery of personalized multimedia content from content provider to consumers in an IMS-based network with the objective of efficiency and resource optimizations. For that purpose, three service enablers and one media delivery enabler have been developed; the Session Management Enabler, Content

8.2. Outlook

Management Enabler, Content Information Provisioning Enabler and Media Delivery Function, respectively. However, the initial implementation of the service/content provisioning enabler only supported pull mechanisms and the event-based model is still under development. The future recommendation should consider two directions, first on the service and content provisioning functions and second on the media delivery and processing functions.

In the first case, the content provisioning enabler can play an important role in the service provider domain, as it stores content information, service delivery information and user subscriptions. Based on this information, the service provider will have the ability to develop personalized services or allow third party applications to make use of such information. On the other hand, as service subscription along with the related network demand can guide resource reservation functionality to estimate the anticipated media flows, the service provider may interact with the connectivity provider to prepare the required resources or to request additional connectivity resources for particular users at a particular time and place. To support a new feature, it is presumed that the Content Information Provisioning Enabler shall interact with the resource reservation functionality (e.g. 3GPP PCRF) to establish the pre-reservation procedure.

The design of the content provisioning enabler is based on the event-based communication model which is a generic communication style that can be applied to other applications managing presence, location, context or sensor information among several network entities. In this regard, the implementation shall separate the communication part from the processing part of the event information, so that the reference implementation can be used as a base framework for integrating or developing any network-based application that uses an event-based communication style between its network entities. As Hypertext Markup Language 5 (HTML5) will support the event-based communication model, the framework may abstract the protocol semantics from the application logic and thus support several protocols such as SIP or HTTP.

In this, work the media processing and delivery functions are developed to enable the delivery of the multimedia content stream efficiently through the use of multicast and broadcast transport capabilities. However, the distribution of processing and delivery functions among a set of media servers and the related control functionality are not defined. Therefore, both issues are still valid research aspects to be considered in future work. The research effort conducted in Michael K. dissertation [120] introduces a cooperative provisioning of media delivery functions using peer-to-peer principles. This approach is used for distributing multimedia processing functions across the network. The integration of this approach with the COSMIC framework could also be considered for future work.

The Peer-to-Peer (P2P) content sharing and streaming approach could utilize the advantages of the session-based content delivery concept proposed in this work. As P2P networks have shown a clear lack of mechanisms that ensure QoS and support authorization and accounting mechanisms, the integration of the session-based content delivery model for controlling content delivery between the peers following the P2P model will combine the benefits of the advantages of both models.

The COSMIC framework offers core multimedia content delivery functionalities that can be integrated in an IMS-based infrastructure or any IP-based environment. In this regard, the multimedia service enablers and the MDF can be considered as basic building blocks for delivering personalized multimedia content. As advertising and interactivity are expected to be part of the most influential business and revenue models in the future, the COSMIC framework provides a suitable basic architecture for converged multimedia content delivery built on a generic multi-access framework. Therefore, the targeted architecture can rely on the COSMIC framework and the associated delivery mechanisms.

IMS-based content delivery differs from Web-based delivery in that it is a fully managed system, offering guaranteed QoS and involving user subscriptions. Furthermore, it provides an excellent avenue for advancing multimedia services due to its personalized and interactive nature. However, the ongoing increase in bandwidth offered through various access technologies aligned with the improvements on the IP layer will enable the Over-the-Top providers to delivery multimedia content with acceptable QoS and usually with no or minimal charges to the end user. Therefore, the OTT delivery model of multimedia content, combined with its mainly advertisement based revenue, may diminish the need for an IMS-based delivery system in the near future.

While the hype phase of the IMS is over and small-scale IMS-based NGN rollouts have begun all over the world, IMS operators still need quantifiable incentives to adopt the IMS on a much larger scale. One of the reasons why IMS has not yet received wide scale adoption is the lack of revenue generating opportunities to complement current telecommunications services. Moreover, it is essential for IMS operators to recoup the costs of IMS investments within viable time frames. Also, video content is forecasted to represent 66% of all mobile data traffic by 2014, increasing 66-fold from 2009 to 2014-the highest growth rate of any mobile data application tracked in the Cisco Visual Networking Index: Forecast [121]. Therefore, we hope that this work will provide guidance to the research community towards the definition of more open, personalized and context-aware content delivery networks.

CHAPTER 9
Acronyms

3GPP	3rd Generation Partnership Project
3GPP2	3rd Generation Partnership Project 2
AAA	Authentication, Authorization, and Accounting
AF	Application Function
ALM	Application Layer Multicast
API	Application Programming Interfaces
ATIS	Alliance for Telecommunications Industry Solutions
AVPs	Attribute-Value Pairs
BBERF	Bearer Binding and Event Reporting Function
BGCF	Breakout Gateway Control Function
BM-SC	Broadcast/Multicast Service Centre
BSS	Business Support System
BSC	Bearer Selection and Capability Controller
CAPEX	Capital Expenditures
CGI	Common Gateway Interface
CID	Content Identifier
CIP	Content Information Publisher
CIS	Content Information Server
CIW	Content Information Watcher
CIPF	Content Information Provisioning Functions
CIPE	Content Information Provisioning Enabler
CLS	Content List Server
CMF	Content Management Functions
CME	Content Management Enabler
COSMIC	effiCient sessiOn-baSed MultImedia Content Delivery in Next Generation Network
CP	Content Provider
CPL	Call Processing Language
CRID	Content Resource Identifier
CSCF	Call Session Control Function
DRM	Digital Rights Management
DVB	Digital Video Broadcasting
DVB-C	DVB-Cable
DVB-H	DVB-Handheld

DVB-POC	DVB-Playout Center
DVB-T	DVB-Terrestrial
DVB-S	DVB-Satellite
DVB-IPTV	DVB-IPTV
DVB-MHP	DVB-Multimedia Home Platform
DHCP	Dynamic Host Configuration Protocol
E-CSCF	Emergency CSCF
EPC	Evolved Packet Core
EPG	Electronic Program Guide
ETSI	European Telecommunications Standards Institute
FMC	Fixed Mobile Convergence
FLUTE	File Delivery over Unidirectional Transport
FTP	File Transfer Protocol
GEM	Globally Executable DVB-MHP
GSM	Global System for Mobile Communications
GPRS	General Packet Radio Service
GGSN	GPRS Support Node
GEPON	Gigabit Ethernet-PON
HLR	Home Location Register
HSS	Home Subscriber Server
HTML5	Hypertext Markup Language 5
HTTP	Hypertext Transfer Protocol
IBCF	Interconnection Border Control Function
ICID	IMS Charging Identifier
I-CSCF	Interrogating CSCF
IETF	Internet Engineering Task Force
iFC	Initial Filter Criteria
IGMP	Internet Group Management Protocol
IGMPv3	IGMP Version 3
IGP	Interior Gateway Protocol
IMD	IP Multimedia Domain
IMS	IP Multimedia Subsystem
IMPI	IMS Private User Identity
IMPU	IMS Public User Identity
IP	Internet Protocol
IPTV	IP Television
ISIM	IMS Subscriber Identity Module
ITU-T	International Telecommunication Union, Telecommunication Standardization Sector
IVR	Interactive Voice Response
JAIN	Java API for Integrated Networks

LCS	Live Content Service
LTE	Long Term Evolution
MBMS	Multimedia Broadcast Multicast Services
MRB	Media Resource Broker
MSC	Media Server Controller
MSCML	Media Server Control Markup Language
MSE	Multimedia Service Enablers
MCF	Media Control Functions
MDF	Media Delivery Function
MDFC	MDF Controller
MGCF	Media Gateway Control Function
NGMN	Next Generation Mobile Network
MGW	Media Gateway
MLDv2	Multicast Listener Discovery Version 2
MOS	Mean Opinion Scores
MPF	Media Processing Function
MRFC	Media Processing Function Controller
MRFP	Media Processing Function Processor
MSP	Media Server Processor
MSEr	Mean Square Error
MTU	Maximum Transmission Unit
NGN	Next Generation Network
NGMN	Next Generation Mobile Network
OIF	Open IPTV Forum
OMA	Open Mobile Alliance
OPEX	Operating Expenses
OSA	Open Service Access
OSS	Operating Support System
OTT	Over-The-Top
P2P	Peer-to-Peer
PCC	Policy and Charging Control
PCEF	Policy and Charging Enforcement Function
PCP	Professional Content Producer
PCRF	Policy and Charging Rules Function
P-CSCF	Proxy CSCF
PDN-GW	packet data network gateway
PDP	Packet Data Protocol
PIM	Protocol Independent Multicast
PIDF	Presence Information Data Format
PLMN	Public Land Mobile Network
PoC	Push-to-talk over Cellular

PON	Passive Optical Network
PSI	Public Service Identifier
PSTN	Public Switched Telephone Network
PNA	Presence Network Agent
PSNR	Peak Signal to Noise Ratio
PUA	Presence User Agent
PVR	Personal Video Recorder
QoE	Quality of Experience
QoS	Quality of Service
RACS	Resource and Admission Control Subsystem
RLS	Resource List Server
RSVP	Resource Reservation Protocol
RTCP	Real-Time Control Protocol
RTP	Real-Time Transport Protocol
RTSP	Real-Time Steaming Protocol
S-CSCF	Serving CSCF
SCS	Stored Content Service
SCTP	Stream Control Transmission Protocol
SDF	Service Discovery Function
SDOs	Standards Development Organizations
SDP	Session Description Protocol
SeIP	Service Information Publisher
SIP	Session Initiation Protocol
SCF	Service Control Functions
SIW	Service Information Watcher
SLEE	Service Logic Execution Environment
SLA	Service Level Agreement
SME	Session Management Enabler
SMF	Session Management Functions
SOA	Service Oriented Architecture
SOAP	Simple Object Access Protocol
SP	Service Provider
SSF	Service Selection Functions
TCP	Transmission Control Protocol
TDM	Time-division multiplexing
TISPAN	Telecoms & Internet converged Services & Protocols for Advanced Networks
UDP	User Datagram Protocol
UGC	User Generated Content
UMTS	Universal Mobile Telecommunications System
UPSF	User Profile Server Function

URI	Uniform Resource Identifier
VDSL	Very-High-Data-Rate Digital Subscriber Line
WIS	Watcher Information Subscriber
WSDL	Web Service Description Language
XDMC	XML Document Management Client
XDMS	XML Document Management Server
XML	Extensible Markup Language

Bibliography

[1] TISPAN ES 282 001: NGN Functional Architecture; Release 1, August 2005. (Cited on pages 2, 30 and 119.)

[2] ITU-T Recommendation: NGN Framework Reference Architecture, 2006. (Cited on pages 2 and 30.)

[3] Multimedia Delivery in the Future Internet A Converged Network Perspective; Version: 1.0, 2008. White Paper produced by the Media Delivery Platforms Cluster; Available at: HTTP://www.ist-sea.eu/Dissemination/MDP_WhitePaper.pdf visited on 27.12.2010. (Cited on pages 2, 3, 17 and 25.)

[4] ATIS-0800007: IPTV HIGH LEVEL ARCHITECTURE, 2007. (Cited on pages 2 and 41.)

[5] Open IPTV Forum: Functional Architecture; v1.2, December 2008. (Cited on pages 2 and 66.)

[6] R.T. Fielding. *Architectural styles and the design of network-based software architectures*. PhD thesis, Citeseer, 2000. (Cited on pages 4, 10, 50, 53, 54, 61, 66 and 68.)

[7] BitTorent P2P client, 2008. Available at http://www.bittorrent.com/ visited on 27.12.2010. (Cited on pages 16 and 17.)

[8] K. Savetz, N. Randall, and Y. Lepage. *MBONE: Multicasting Tomorrow's Internet*. IDG Books Worldwide, Inc. Foster City, CA, USA, 1995. (Cited on page 16.)

[9] AB Roach. RFC3265: Session Initiation Protocol (SIP)-Specific Event Notification. *RFC Editor United States*, 2002. (Cited on pages 18, 20 and 122.)

[10] High level architecture overview for IMS-based solution for IPTV standardization. Contribution during the meeting held in Sophia Antipolis 16-20 October 2006; 11Ter; 11tTD245, October 2006. (Cited on pages 18 and 161.)

[11] R. Fielding, J. Gettys, J. Mogul, H. Frystyk, L. Masinter, P. Leach, and T. Berners-Lee. RFC 2616: Hypertext Transfer Protocol–HTTP/1.1. *RFC Editor United States*, 2(1):2–2, 1999. (Cited on pages 19 and 230.)

[12] J. Klensin. RFC2821: Simple mail transfer protocol. *RFC Editor United States*, 2001. (Cited on page 19.)

[13] S.J. Rosenberg. RFC5411: A Hitchhikers Guide to the Session Initiation Protocol (SIP). 2006. (Cited on pages 19 and 21.)

[14] J. Rosenberg. RFC 3856: A presence event package for the session initiation protocol (SIP). *IETF. Ago. de*, 2004. (Cited on pages 20 and 122.)

[15] A. Niemi. RFC3903: Session initiation protocol (SIP) extension for event state publication. In *Publication, RFC 3903, IETF*. Citeseer, 2004. (Cited on page 20.)

[16] A. Niemi and D. Willis. RFC5839: An Extension to Session Initiation Protocol (SIP) Events for Conditional Event Notification. *IETF RFC5839, May*, 2010. (Cited on pages 20, 123, 124 and 228.)

[17] M. Handley, V. Jacobson, and C. Perkins. RFC4566: SDP: Session Description Protocol, July 2006. (Cited on pages 21 and 76.)

[18] H. Schulzrinne, A. Rao, and R. Lanphier. RFC2326: Real time streaming protocol (RTSP). *IETF (April 1998)*. (Cited on pages 22, 135 and 247.)

[19] N. Greene, M. Ramalho, and B. Rosen. Media gateway control protocol architecture and requirements. *Request for Comments*, 2805. (Cited on page 23.)

[20] RFC4240: Basic network media services with SIP, December 2005. (Cited on pages 23, 117, 133, 239 and 247.)

[21] J. Van Dyke, E. Burger, and A. Spitzer. RFC5022: Media Server Control Markup Language (MSCML) and Protocol. Technical report, RFC 5022, Nov. 2007. (Cited on page 23.)

[22] H. Schulzrinne, S. Casner, R. Frederick, and V. Jacobson. RFC3550 RTP: A Transport Protocol for Real-Time Applications, July 2003. (Cited on pages 23, 24 and 245.)

[23] R. Braden, L. Zhang, S. Berson, S. Herzog, and S. Jamin. RFC2205: Resource ReSerVation Protocol (RSVP)-Version 1 Functional Specification. *IETF, September*, 1997. (Cited on page 24.)

[24] P. Calhoun, J. Loughney, E. Guttman, G. Zorn, and J. Arkko. RFC3588: Diameter Base Protocol. *Internet RFCs*, 2003. (Cited on page 24.)

Bibliography

[25] C. Rigney, S. Willens, A. Rubens, and W. Simpson. Remote authentication dial in user service (RADIUS), 2000. (Cited on page 24.)

[26] 3GPP TS 23.246: Multimedia Broadcast/Multicast Service (MBMS), Architecture and functional description, 2005. (Cited on page 26.)

[27] ETSI TR 102 377: Digital Video Broadcasting (DVB); DVB-H Implementation Guidelines, November 2005. (Cited on page 26.)

[28] PacketCable Architecture Framework Technical Report, 2006. (Cited on pages 27 and 30.)

[29] MHP and GEM. Available at: http://www.mhp.org/ visited on 11.01.2011. (Cited on page 27.)

[30] 3GPP TS 23.401: General Packet Radio Service (GPRS) enhancements for Evolved Universal Terrestrial Radio Access Network (E-UTRAN) access, 2009. (Cited on page 28.)

[31] 3GPP TS 23.402: Architecture enhancements for non-3GPP accesses, 2009. (Cited on page 28.)

[32] TS 23.228:IP Multimedia Subsystem; stage 2; (Release 8). (Cited on pages 29, 31, 78 and 87.)

[33] Bharat Book Bureau. IP Multimedia Subsystem (IMS): The Market for Components and User Equipment. Technical report, Bharat Book Bureau, January 2008. (Cited on pages 29 and 47.)

[34] 3GPP TS23.002: Technical Specification Group Services and Systems Aspects; Network architecture; (Release 8), 2006. (Cited on page 33.)

[35] IP Multimedia (IM) session handling; IM call model; Stage 2; (Release 8). (Cited on page 35.)

[36] JAVA Specification Requests, JAIN SLEE (JSLEE) v1.1. http://jcp.org/en/jsr/detail?id=240. [Online: accessed 28.12.2010]. (Cited on page 36.)

[37] SIP Servlet API. Available at: http://jcp.org/en/jsr/detail?id=116 visited on 28.12.2010. (Cited on page 36.)

[38] OMA-AD-Presence: OMA Presence SIMPLE; Architecture Document, 2006. (Cited on page 38.)

[39] ETSI and Parlay. Open Servcie Access and Parlay specification, 2010. Available at: http://www.etsi.org/WebSite/Technologies/OSA.aspx visited on Dec 2010. (Cited on page 40.)

[40] ETSI RTS 182 027: IPTV Architecture; IPTV functions supported by the IMS subsystem. Draft ETSI RTS 182 027 V3.3.0, August 2009. (Cited on pages 42, 63, 88, 116 and 228.)

[41] A. Al-Hezmi, O. Friedrich, S. Arbanowski, and T. Magedanz. Requirements for an IMS-based quadruple play service architecture. *Network, IEEE*, 21(2):28–33, 2007. (Cited on pages 43 and 64.)

[42] T. Cagenius, A. Fasbender, J. Hjelm, U. Horn, I.M. Ivars, and N. Selberg. Evolving the TV experience: Anytime, anywhere, any device. *Ericsson review*, 3:107–111, 2006. (Cited on pages 43 and 189.)

[43] B. Chatras and M. Sa
"id. Delivering quadruple play with IPTV over IMS. *The Journal of The Institute of Telecommunications Professionals Volume*, 1(Part 2):10. (Cited on pages 44, 191 and 192.)

[44] ScaleNet. The ScaleNet project, 2005-2009. Available at: http://www.pt-it.pt-dlr.de/de/1038.php visted on Dec 2010. (Cited on pages 44 and 190.)

[45] N. Niebert, A. Schieder, H. Abramowicz, C. Prehofer, and H. Karl. Ambient Networks-an architecture for communication networks beyond 3G. In *IEEE Wireless Communications*. Citeseer, 2004. (Cited on pages 44, 82, 189 and 190.)

[46] B. Mathieu, M. Song, J. Rey, and S. Schmid. A service specific overlay network for adapting SIP multimedia calls. In *Proceedings of the International Conference on Intelligence in Service Delivery Networks (ICIN06)*. (Cited on pages 44, 82 and 190.)

[47] A. Munir. Analysis of SIP-based IMS session establishment signaling for WiMax-3G networks. In *Networking and Services, 2008. ICNS 2008. Fourth International Conference on*, pages 282–287. IEEE, 2008. (Cited on page 44.)

[48] H. Fathi, S.S. Chakraborty, and R. Prasad. Optimization of SIP session setup delay for VoIP in 3G wireless networks. *Mobile Computing, IEEE Transactions on*, 5(9):1121–1132, 2006. (Cited on page 44.)

Bibliography 211

[49] 3GPP TS 24.228: Signaling flows for the IP multimedia call control based on Session Initiation Protocol (SIP) and Session Description Protocol (SDP), stage 3 - Release 5, September 2006. (Cited on page 44.)

[50] M. Ulvan and R. Bestak. Delay Performance of Session Establishment Signaling in IP Multimedia Subsystem. In *Systems, Signals and Image Processing, 2009. IWSSIP 2009. 16th International Conference on*, pages 1–5. IEEE, 2009. (Cited on page 44.)

[51] G. Camarillo, R. Kantola, and H. Schulzrinne. Evaluation of transport protocols for the session initiation protocol. *Network, IEEE*, 17(5):40–46, 2003. (Cited on page 45.)

[52] D. Vingarzan and P. Weik. End-to-end performance of the IP multimedia subsystem over various wireless networks. In *Wireless Communications and Networking Conference, 2006. WCNC 2006. IEEE*, volume 1, pages 183–188. IEEE, 2006. (Cited on page 45.)

[53] D. Vingarzan, P. Weik, and T. Magedanz. Development of an open source IMS core for emerging IMS testbeds. *Special Issue on IMS, Journal on Mobile Multimedia (JMM)*, 2(3). (Cited on pages 45, 157 and 165.)

[54] L. Xing-feng, Y. Bao-ping, and L. Wan-ming. Overlay multicast network optimization and simulation Based on Narada Protocol. In *Advanced Communication Technology, 2008. ICACT 2008. 10th International Conference on*, volume 3, pages 2215–2220. IEEE, 2008. (Cited on page 45.)

[55] JF Buford and M. Kolberg. Hybrid overlay multicast simulation and evaluation. In *Consumer Communications and Networking Conference, 2009. CCNC 2009. 6th IEEE*, pages 1–2. IEEE, 2009. (Cited on page 45.)

[56] R. Pantos. IETF Draft: HTTP Live Streaming. November 2010. Availble at: http://tools.ietf.org/html/draft-pantos-http-live-streaming-05 visited on 31.01.2011. (Cited on page 46.)

[57] A. Zambelli. IIS smooth streaming technical overview. *Microsoft Corporation*, 2009. Availble at: http://www.iis.net/community/files/media/smoothspecs/[5BMS-SMTH].pdf visited on 31.01.2011. (Cited on page 46.)

[58] Adobe Flash. HTTP Dynamic Streaming on the Adobe Flash Platform. *Adobe Flash Platform Technical White Paper*, 2010. Availble at: http://www.adobe.com/products/httpdynamicstreaming/pdfs/httpdynamicstreaming_wp_ue.pdf visited on 31.01.2011. (Cited on page 46.)

[59] Inc. MRG. IPTV Global Forecast 2010 to 2014 Semiannual IPTV Global Forecast Report. Technical report, Multimedia Research Group Inc., June 2010. (Cited on page 47.)

[60] A. Al-Hezmi, C. Riede, O. Friedrich, S. Arbanowski, and T. Magedanz. Cross-fertilization of IMS and IPTV services over NGN. In *Innovations in NGN: Future Network and Services, 2008. K-INGN 2008. First ITU-T Kaleidoscope Academic Conference*, pages 153–160. IEEE, 2008. (Cited on pages 48, 160 and 172.)

[61] A. Al-Hezmi, M. Knappmeyer, B. Ricks, FC Pinto, and R. Tonjes. Enabling IMS with multicast and broadcast capabilities. In *Personal, Indoor and Mobile Radio Communications, 2007. PIMRC 2007. IEEE 18th International Symposium on*, pages 1–5. IEEE, 2007. (Cited on pages 48 and 155.)

[62] A. Al-Hezmi, F. Carvalho de Gouveia, and T. Magedanz. Enabling triple play services over NGN. In *Information and Communications Technology, 2007. ICICT 2007. ITI 5th International Conference on*, pages 91–97. IEEE, 2008. (Cited on pages 48, 116, 160 and 162.)

[63] ITU-T G.1080: Quality of experience requirements for IPTV services, December 2008. (Cited on page 52.)

[64] Consideration on Channel Zapping Time in IPTV Performance Monitoring, May 2007. Availble at: http://www.itu.int/md/dologin_md.asp?lang=en&id=T05-FG.IPTV-C-0545!!MSW-E visited on 28.01.2011. (Cited on page 52.)

[65] V. CE, A. KA, D. CA, and P. GV. Live Broadcasting of High Definition Audiovisual Content Using HDTV over Broadband IP Networks. *International Journal of Digital Multimedia Broadcasting*, 2008, 2009. (Cited on page 52.)

[66] 3GPP TS 23.207: End-to-end Quality of Service (QoS) concept and architecture, 2008. (Cited on page 52.)

[67] R. Sparks et al. RFC3515: The session initiation protocol (SIP) refer method, 2003. (Cited on page 59.)

Bibliography

[68] TS 183 063: Telecommunications and Internet converged Services and Protocols for Advanced Networking (TISPAN) IMS-based IPTV stage 3 specification. (Cited on pages 66, 91, 93 and 223.)

[69] J. Rosenberg, H. Schulzrinne, and P. Kyzivat. RFC3840: Indicating user agent capabilities in the session initiation protocol (SIP). Technical report, RFC 3840, August 2004. (Cited on page 68.)

[70] J. Rosenberg, H. Schulzrinne, and P. Kyzivat. RFC3841: Caller preferences for the session initiation protocol (SIP). *RFC3841, http://www. ietf. org/rfc/rfc3841. txt.* (Cited on page 69.)

[71] Miikka P., Hisham K. Georg M., and Aki N. *The IMS IP Multimedia Concepts and Services in the Mobile Domain.* John Wiley & Sons Ltd, 2004. (Cited on page 69.)

[72] H. Kosch, L. Boszormenyi, M. Doller, M. Libsie, P. Schojer, and A. Kofler. The life cycle of multimedia metadata. *Multimedia, IEEE*, 12(1):80–86, 2005. (Cited on page 70.)

[73] D. Garlan and M. Shaw. An introduction to software architecture. *Advances in software engineering and knowledge engineering*, 1:1–40, 1993. (Cited on page 73.)

[74] E. Nebel and L. Masinter. RFC1867: Form-based File Upload in HTML. *RFC Editor United States*, 1995. (Cited on pages 74 and 77.)

[75] J. Rosenberg, H. Schulzrinne, G. Camarillo, A. Johnston, J. Peterson, R. Sparks, M. Handley, and E. Schooler. RFC3261: Session Initiation Protocol, 2002. (Cited on pages 75 and 76.)

[76] B. Quinn and K. Almeroth. RFC3170: IP Multicast Applications: Challenges and Solutions. *RFC Editor United States*, 2001. (Cited on page 81.)

[77] M.A. Tariq and M. Kampmann. A Dynamic Configurable Multimedia Processing Proxy for IPTV Services in Ambient Networks. In *Mobile and Wireless Communications Summit, 2007. 16th IST*, pages 1–5. IEEE, 2007. (Cited on pages 82 and 190.)

[78] F. Hartung, N. Niebert, A. Schieder, R. Rembarz, S. Schmid, and L. Eggert. Advances in network-supported media delivery in next-generation mobile systems. *Communications Magazine, IEEE*, 44(8):82–89, 2006. (Cited on pages 82 and 190.)

[79] T. Paila, M. Luby, R. Lehtonen, V. Roca, and R. Walsh. RFC 3926: FLUTE File delivery over unidirectional transport. *Network Working Group*, 2004. (Cited on pages 84, 86 and 135.)

[80] 3GPP TS 26.090: AMR speech Codec; Transcoding Functions, January 2005. (Cited on page 85.)

[81] 3GPP TS 26.190:Speech codec speech processing functions; Adaptive Multi-Rate - Wideband (AMR-WB) speech codec; Transcoding functions, June 2005. (Cited on page 85.)

[82] G. Yu, T. Westholm, M. Kihl, I. Sedano, A. Aurelius, C. Lagerstedt, and P. Odling. Analysis and characterization of IPTV user behavior. In *Broadband Multimedia Systems and Broadcasting, 2009. BMSB'09. IEEE International Symposium on*, pages 1–6. IEEE, 2009. (Cited on pages 89, 90 and 223.)

[83] G. Camarillo. The Stream Control Transmission Protocol (SCTP) as a Transport for the Session Initiation Protocol (SIP). 2005. (Cited on page 111.)

[84] B. Wang, J. Kurose, P. Shenoy, and D. Towsley. Multimedia streaming via TCP: An analytic performance study. *ACM Transactions on Multimedia Computing, Communications, and Applications (TOMCCAP)*, 4(2):1–22, 2008. (Cited on page 112.)

[85] E. Burger. RFC 4483: A Mechanism for Content Indirection in Session Initiation Protocol (SIP) Messages. Technical report, RFC 4483, May 2006. (Cited on pages 115 and 117.)

[86] H. Mehta, R. Walsh, IDD Curcio, J. Peltotalo, and S. Peltotalo. Internet-Draft: SDP Descriptors for FLUTE. *Work in Progress*, 2010. (Cited on page 117.)

[87] M. Isomaki and E. Leppanen. RFC4827: An Extensible Markup Language (XML) Configuration Access Protocol (XCAP) Usage for Manipulating Presence Document Contents. *IETF RFC4827, May*, 2007. (Cited on page 123.)

[88] Roach A. B., Campbell B., and Rosenberg J. RFC4662: A Session Initiation Protocol (SIP) Event Notification Extension for Resource Lists, 2006. (Cited on pages 123 and 124.)

Bibliography 215

[89] G. Camarillo and AB Roach. RFC5367: Subscriptions to Request-Contained Resource Lists in the Session Initiation Protocol (SIP). Technical report, IETF RFC5367, October 2008. (Cited on page 123.)

[90] J. Rosenberg. A data model for presence. Technical report, RFC 4479, July 2006. (Cited on page 126.)

[91] A. Server. The Apache Software Foundation, 2003. Available at: http://ws.apache.org/axis/ visited on 27.12.2010. (Cited on page 140.)

[92] GStreamer library. Available at: http://gstreamer.freedesktop.org visited on 27.12.2010. (Cited on page 150.)

[93] SIP Sofia library. Available at: http://sofia-sip.sourceforge.net/ visited on 27.12.2010. (Cited on pages 150 and 184.)

[94] FOKUS Open IMS Playground. Available at: http://www.fokus.fraunhofer.de/de/fokus_testbeds/open_ims_playground/index.html visited on 27.12.2010. (Cited on page 156.)

[95] FOKUS Media Interoperability Lab. Available at: http://www.fokus.fraunhofer.de/de/fokus_testbeds/mi_lab/index.html visited on 27.12.2010. (Cited on page 156.)

[96] K. Knuettel, T. Magedanz, L. Xie, and A. Al-Hezmi. SIP Servlet Execution Environment (SIPSEE)-An IMS/NGN SIP AS for Converged Applications. *Fraunhofer Institute FOKUS*. (Cited on pages 157 and 165.)

[97] A. Al-Hezmi, F. Carvalho de Gouveia, M. Sher, O. Friedrich, and T. Magedanz. Provisioning IMS-based seamless triple play services over different access networks. In *Network Operations and Management Symposium, 2008. NOMS 2008. IEEE*, pages 927–930. IEEE, 2008. (Cited on page 157.)

[98] A. Al-Hezmi, N. Blum, and T. Magedanz. IMS basiertes Triple Pay Toolkit-der FOKUS Open IMS Playground. pages 18–21, 2007. (Cited on page 157.)

[99] A. Al-Hezmi, O. Friedrich, S. Arbanowski, and T. Magedanz. Interactive multimedia services over open NGN testbed. In *Proceedings of the 4th International Conference on Testbeds and research infrastructures for the development of networks & communities*, pages 1–6. ICST (Institute for Computer Sciences, Social-Informatics and Telecommunications Engineering), 2008. (Cited on pages 160 and 172.)

[100] A.H. Adel, M. Thomas, J.P. Jordi, and R. Christian. Evolving the Convergence of Telecommunication and TV Services over NGN. *International Journal of Digital Multimedia Broadcasting*, 2008, 2008. (Cited on pages 160 and 176.)

[101] C-CAST IST project. Available online at: http://www.ict-ccast.eu visited on 27.12.2010. (Cited on page 161.)

[102] N. Baker, M. Zafer, A. Al-Hezmi, and Fucks M. Enabling Multimedia Broadcast/Multicast Services over Converged Networks. In *World Wireless Research Forum (WWRF) 17 Meeting*, 2006. (Cited on page 162.)

[103] M. Knappmeyer, B. Ricks, R. Tonjes, and A. Al-Hezmi. Advanced multicast and broadcast content distribution in mobile cellular networks. In *Global Telecommunications Conference, 2007. GLOBECOM'07. IEEE*, pages 2097–2101. IEEE, 2007. (Cited on page 162.)

[104] M. ZAFAR, N. BAKER, A. IKRAM, M. FUCHS, F. PINTO, A. AL-HEZMI, M. KNAPPMEYER, and T. MOTA. Design of NGN Mobile Multicast Group Service Enablers, 2008. (Cited on page 162.)

[105] SIPNuke, Fraunhofer Institut, FOKUS. Available at: http://www.sipnuke.org/ visited on 27.12.2010. (Cited on pages 165 and 168.)

[106] SailFin SIP Application Server. Available at: https://sailfin.dev.java.net/ visited on 27.12.2010. (Cited on pages 165 and 181.)

[107] BEA WebLogic Sip Server 3.0. Available at: http://www.oracle.com/us/corporate/Acquisitions/bea/index.html visited on 27.12.2010. (Cited on page 165.)

[108] SIPp, SIP testing tools. Available at: http://sipp.sourceforge.net/ visited on 27.12.2010. (Cited on page 168.)

[109] Wireshark. Available at: http://www.wireshark.org/ visited on 27.12.2010. (Cited on page 168.)

[110] C. Riede, A. Al-Hezmi, and T. Magedanz. Session and media signaling for IPTV via IMS. In *Proceedings of the 1st international conference on MOBILe Wireless MiddleWARE, Operating Systems, and Applications*, pages 1–6. ICST (Institute for Computer Sciences, Social-Informatics and Telecommunications Engineering), 2008. (Cited on page 172.)

Bibliography

[111] A. Al-Hezmi, G. Daher, J. Simoes, and T. Magedanz. SOA-based multimedia streaming enabler over IMS networks. In *Proceedings of the 7th International Conference on Advances in Mobile Computing and Multimedia*, pages 391–395. ACM, 2009. (Cited on page 176.)

[112] J. Rosenberg, J. Peterson, and H. Schulzrinne. RFC3725: Best Current Practices for Third Party Call Control (3pcc) in the Session Initiation Protocol (SIP). Technical report, BCP 85, RFC 3725, April 2004. (Cited on page 177.)

[113] C. Riede, JJ Pallares, A. Al-Hezmi, and T. Magedanz. Advanced media delivery in IMS-based networks. 2008. (Cited on page 184.)

[114] OMA-TS-BCAST: File and Stream Distribution for Mobile Broadcast Services, v1.0, 2007. (Cited on page 187.)

[115] E. Mikoczy, D. Sivchenko, B. Xu, and V. Rakocevic. IMS based IPTV services: architecture and implementation. In *Proceedings of the 3rd international conference on Mobile multimedia communications*, pages 1–7. ICST (Institute for Computer Sciences, Social-Informatics and Telecommunications Engineering), 2007. (Cited on page 190.)

[116] E. Marilly, G. Delègue, O. Martinot, S. Betgé-Brezetz, and S. Betgé. Adaptation and personalisation of interactive mobile TV services. *JOURNAL-COMMUNICATIONS NETWORK*, 6(1):33, 2007. (Cited on pages 191 and 196.)

[117] D. Waiting, R. Good, R. Spiers, and N. Ventura. Open source development tools for IMS research. In *Proceedings of the 4th International Conference on Testbeds and research infrastructures for the development of networks & communities*, pages 1–10. ICST (Institute for Computer Sciences, Social-Informatics and Telecommunications Engineering), 2008. (Cited on page 191.)

[118] D. Waiting, R. Good, R. Spiers, and N. Ventura. The UCT IMS client. In *Testbeds and Research Infrastructures for the Development of Networks & Communities and Workshops, 2009. TridentCom 2009. 5th International Conference on*, pages 1–6. IEEE, 2009. (Cited on page 191.)

[119] P.R. Wilson and N. Ventura. A Direct Marketing Platform for IMS-Based IPTV. In *Southern Africa Telecommunication Networks and Applications Conferences (SATNAC)*. SATNAC, August 2009. Available online at: http://satnac.org.za/proceedings/2009/papers/services/Paper%2038.pdf visited on 31.01.2011. (Cited on page 192.)

[120] Michael Kleis. *CSP, Cooperative Service Provisioning using Peer-to-Peer Principles*. PhD thesis, Technische Universität München, 2009. (Cited on page 199.)

[121] Cisco Visual Networking Index Forecast Predicts. Available online at http://newsroom.cisco.com/dlls/2010/prod_020910b.html visited on 27.12.2010. (Cited on page 200.)

[122] H. Sugano, S. Fujimoto, G. Klyne, A. Bateman, W. Carr, and J. Peterson. RFC 3863: Presence Information Data Format (PIDF). *Internet Engineering Task Force*, 2004. (Cited on page 235.)

[123] S.E. Deering. RFC1112: Host Extensions for IP multicasting. *RFC Editor United States*, 1989. (Cited on page 247.)

[124] B. Cain, S. Deering, I. Kouvelas, B. Fenner, and A. Thyagarajan. RFC3376: Internet Group Management Protocol, Version 3. *RFC Editor United States*, 2002. (Cited on page 247.)

Appendix A
IMS Interfaces

A.1 IMS Logical Architecture

A summary of the whole interfaces depicted in Figure A.1 is described in 2.3.3.1

A.2 IMS Interfaces

The following table provides the description of all 3GPP IMS interfaces and the related protocols.

Interface	Protocol	Description
Sh	Diameter	HSS↔AS: Transport user related information (Activate/deactivate initial filter criteria.
Cx	Diameter	HSS↔S-CSCF, HSS↔I-CSCF: S-CSCF assignment, Routing information, Authorization, authentication, iFC transfer
Dx	Diameter	SLF↔S-CSCF, SLF↔I-CSCF: To retrieve HSS address which holds subscriber profile.
Ma	SIP	I-CSCF↔AS: To forward SIP request destined to Public Service Id hosted by AS, and vice versa.
ISC	SIP	S-CSCF↔AS, S-CSCF↔MRB: Use to provide services for IMS
Cr	SIP	AS↔MRFC: Enable MRFC to fetch resource from AS, Media control request from AS to MRFC
Mw	SIP	P/I/S-CSCF↔P/I/S-CSCF: Forwarding of SIP signaling messaging between CSCF
Mi	SIP	S-CSCF↔BGCF: For forwarding of SIP message to BGCF
Mk	SIP	BGCF↔BGCF: For forwarding of SIP messages from BGCF to another BGCF/IBCF.
Mr	SIP	S-CSCF↔MRFC: Interaction between S-CSCF and MRFC
Mj	SIP	BGCF↔MGCF: Exchange of SIP message between BGCF and MGCF for interworking with CS or transit scenario.
Mg	SIP	MGCF↔I-CSCF, MGCF↔S-CSCF: To forward incoming SIP signaling from MGCF for CS interworking.
Gm	SIP	UE↔P-CSCF: SIP signaling between UE and IMS Core network.
Ut	HTTP/XCAP	UE↔AS: Enable user to manage service related information, for example: contact list in presence/messaging application.
Rx	Diameter	P-CSCF↔PCRF: Allow QoS and charging related information for controlling service data flow and IP bearer resources.
Gx	Diameter	PCRF↔PCEF: Transfer policy and charging rules from PCRF to PCEF.
Gxx	Diameter	PCRF↔BBERF/S-GW/e-PDG/any non-3GPP access network gateway: Transfer policy and charging rules
Mx	SIP	IBCF↔I-CSCF, IBCF↔S-CSCF, IBCF↔BGCF Forwarding of SIP signaling between CSCF/BGCF and IBCF
Iq	H.248	IMS-ALG(P-CSCF)↔IMS-AG: Used by IMS-ALG to control IMS-AG, e.g. to request address translation binding.
Ix	H.248	IBCF↔TrGW: Used by IBCF to control TrGW, e.g. to request address translation binding.
Mn	H.248	MGCF↔IMS-MGW: Bearer control
Mp	H.248	MRFC↔MRFP:Bearer control
Ici	SIP	IBCF↔external IBCF: Forwarding of SIP signaling between two IBCF on different network domain.
Izi	Media	TrGW↔external TrGW: Forwarding of media streams between different IMS Core Network domain.
Cs	SS7/TDM	MGCF&MGW↔external network: Interworking with PSTN/PLMN
Mb	RTP	Media path
GIBA	Radius	GGSN↔HSS: Enables GGSN to send accounting info to HSS

Table A.1: 3GPP IMS Interfaces

A.2. IMS Interfaces

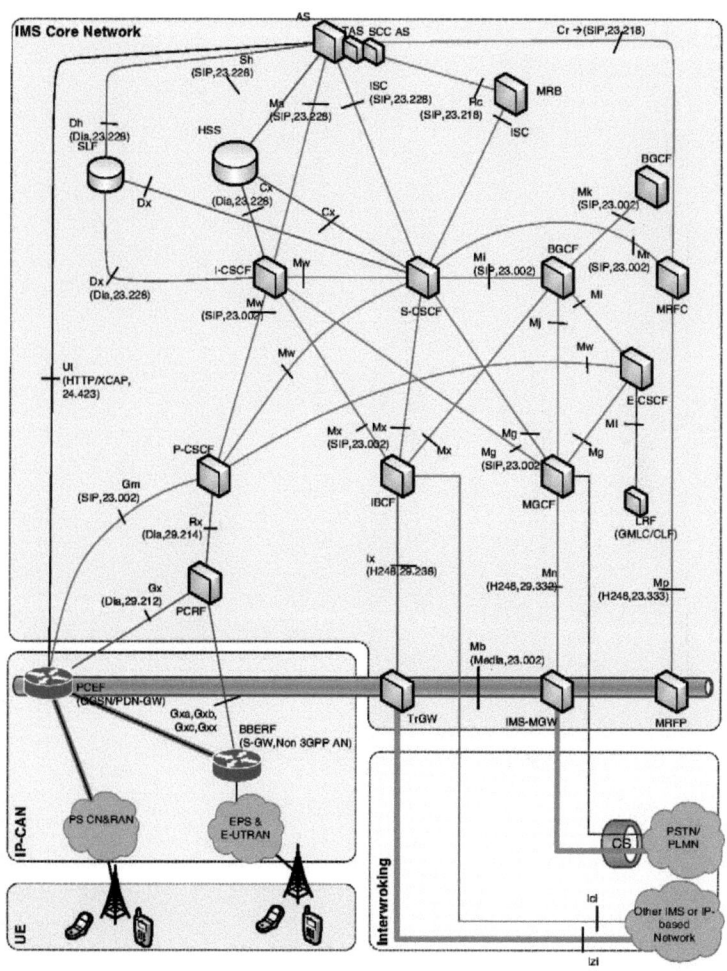

Figure A.1: 3GPP IMS logical architecture

Appendix B
Evaluation of IMS-based IPTV Transactions

B.1 Multicast Switching

The following case study examines the impact of several realization options of multicast switching on the IMS core and the application server. These options have been discussed in 4.2.6, 4.3.2.2 and analyzed in 4.5. We put Equation (4.3), Equation (4.12), Equation (4.13), Equation (4.14) and service flows of 4.3.2.2 into practical exercise, as described in the following table:

Parameters	Reference	Value
Number of IMS subscribers ($SubN$)	Assumption	10000
Percentage of Application usage (AU)	assumption	30%
Percentage of Active Service Usage (ASU) (Note 1)	assumption	70%
Number of Active Users (AUe) $SubN \times AU \times ASU$		2100
Number of Switching per Active User per minute during BH	G. Yu [82]	0.30
Number of Switching per Active User per hour during BH = Pr	G. Yu [82]	7
Number of Switching during BH ($SwPBH$) or Busy Hour Switching Attempts ($BHSwA$)	$AUe \times SwPUBH$	14700
Session Holding Time (SHT) per second	assumption	60
Number of Concurrent Switching during BH ($CSBH$)	$SwPBH \times SHT$	245
Switching Attempts per Second (SwAPS)=Eq. (4.3)	CSBH/3600	10.50
SUBSCRIBE (any) refresh per hour and per active session (Sr)	according to IPTV Spec [68] $>= 12$	6
Number of terminals for a single subscription = Number of PUA	assumption	1
Average number of multimedia services = Ng	assumption	1

Table B.1: IPTV service profile

According to the values defined in B.1 the Number of SIP SUBSCRIBE and NOTIFY messages are as follow:

The number of SIP transactions received by the IMS core and SIP application server according to the above defined parameters are as follows:

224 Appendix B. Evaluation of IMS-based IPTV Transactions

Subscription-notification based	Reference	Value
Subscription	Eq. (4.14)	102900
Notification	Eq. (4.12)	117600
Optimized Notification	Eq. (4.13)	14700

Table B.2: Nr of SIP SUBSCRIBE and NOTIFY messages of an IPTV Service

System Component	Type of signaling message				
	Re-Invite	Info	Sub/Notify	optimized Sub/Notify	Publish
Application Server	14700	14700	220500	117600	14700
IMS Core	14700	14700	220500	117600	14700

Table B.3: Number of SIP transactions for IPTV multicast switching

B.2 Push Delivery Method

The following case study examines the impact of the Push-Use case on the IMS core and the AS. It facilitates the delivery of multimedia content to a set of IMS subscribers as discussed in 4.3.2.3 and 4.3.2.4 and analyzed in 4.5.

Parameters	Reference	Value
average number of applications = Ng Average number of multimedia services	Assumption	1
rate of push request per hour or publish rate = Pr	Assumption	1
average number of users per request = $Npau$	Assumption	10
Average number of multimedia content (watchers) per list (Nw)	Assumption	1
Percentage of active buddies (watchers) (Aul)	Assumption	100%
PUA	Assumption	1
PNA	Assumption	0
Sr per hour	Assumption	1
RLSn	Assumption	1
RLSu	Assumption	0.2
Equation 5	(4.5)	22
Equation 9	(4.9)	40
Optimizing Eq. 9 following Equation 13	(4.13)	20
Equation 2 ($SPU \times SDBH) = Max(Pu, Pr)$	(4.2)	10

Table B.4: Push method service profile

The number of SIP transactions received by the IMS core, the SME, the CIPE and the MDF according to the above defined parameters are as follows:

B.2. Push Delivery Method

Functional Element	Unicast delivery session			Multicast delivery session		
	App-initiated	event-induced	Opt. event-induced	app-initiated	event-induced	Opt. event-induced
IMS core	30	144	104	30	144	104
IMS core (+MDF)	50	164	124	32	164	106
AS (SME)	50	30	30	32	22	22
CIPE	0	124	84	0	124	84
MDF	20	20	20	2	2	2

Table B.5: SIP transactions of different types of unicast and multicast sessions

Appendix C
Specification of Multimedia Service Enablers

In this Appendix, the use cases and the messages flows of the multimedia content delivery framework is illustrated.

C.1 Content Information Provisioning Enabler

C.1.1 CIPE Use Cases

Figure C.1 shows the content provider use case, in which the content provider as either professional or user generated content maintains the content list, which can be a public or private list.

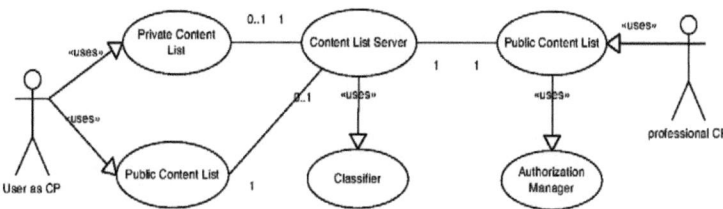

Figure C.1: CIPE content provider use case maintaining own content list

Figure C.2 illustrates the use case of two actors, the content information publisher and content consumer, as depicted in. Furthermore, the use case shows the relationship between both actors and the entire CIPE components for the publishing, the subscription and the notification interactions.

C.1.2 CIPE Message Flows

In order to understand how the CIPE components interact with each other, the following diagrams illustrate the message flows. Figure C.3 shows the content provider maintaining the content list managed by the Content List Server and illustrates the interactions between the main components of the CLS.

Figure C.4 illustrates the message interactions between CIPE entities once the content provider publishes new information related to his content list. However, the publisher

228 Appendix C. Specification of Multimedia Service Enablers

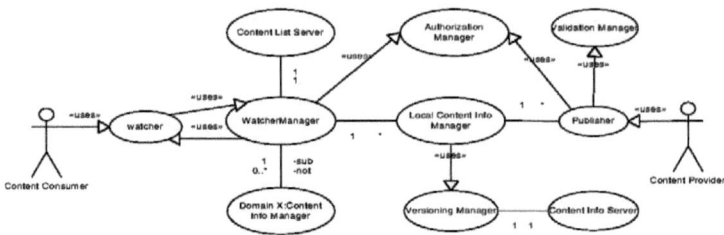

Figure C.2: CIPE content information provisioning use case

can also enable an application or other service enabler like the SME, which may publish information related to the delivery services of certain content information resource.

Figure C.5 shows the message flows between the CIPE entities when content watchers subscribe to any change to content information of a certain content list. Furthermore, the diagram illustrates the successive subscription message for updating the previous subscription message. However, the diagram considers the optimization mechanisms defined in the RFC 5839 [16], while the watcher manager maintains the version of the content information document sent in each notification message. Therefore, the notification message is not issued after receiving the second Subscription message.

Figure C.6 illustrates the case when the CIPE is deployed in several domains. In such a case, the local CIPE (the watcher manager) that serves the related watcher, shall forward the subscription messages of content resources to the corresponding domain. In fact, in an IMS-based network the communication between the watcher manager and the content information manager shall pass the IMS core, which in turn forwards the SIP Subscription messages to the related CIPE (i.e. Content Information Manager, just like the communication between the RLS and the Presence Server as defined in OMA Presence SIMPLE specification [40]).

C.1.3 External Entities

Application or other Service Enabler: Multimedia service enablers (e.g. Multimedia Content Enabler or Session Management Enabler) may act as a watcher or a source of multimedia content information and thus implement the functions of the corresponding system entities (e.g. the content information watcher, the content information source and the XDM client).

In order to provide users with more personalized and recommended content, an application may interact with the CLS and CIS to discover the available content and related status. In this regard, the application may create a new content list with the identified content sources or provide the user with the simple logic to filter content information according to defined criteria.

IMS Core: The IMS core represents all IMS core nodes and is responsible for routing SIP Subscription, Notification and Publish messages among system entities.

Aggregation Proxy: The aggregation proxy authenticates the XDM client requests and delegates the request to the corresponding XDM server.

Remote Content Information Provisioning Enabler: The CIPE may interact

C.1. Content Information Provisioning Enabler

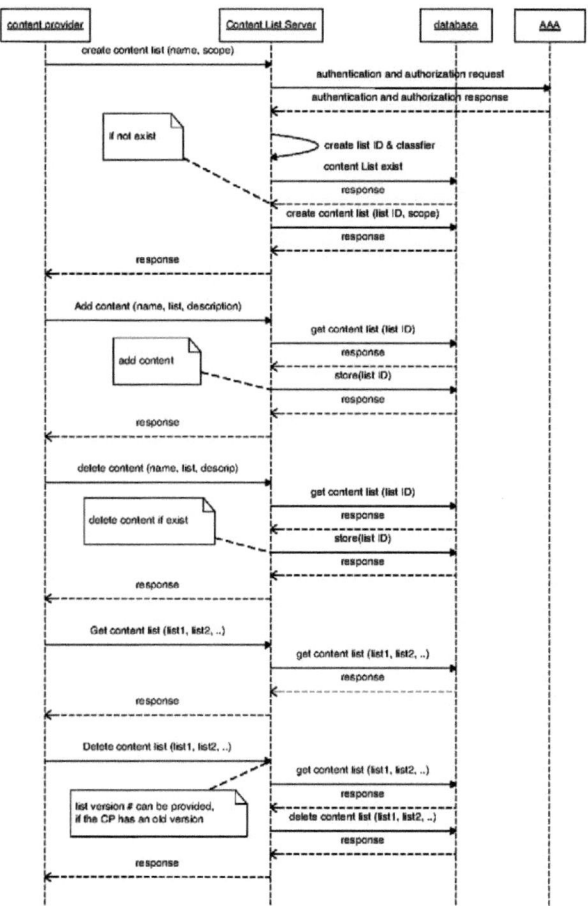

Figure C.3: CIPE message flows for maintaining content list by content provider

with other CIPE deployed in other domains via the IMS core.

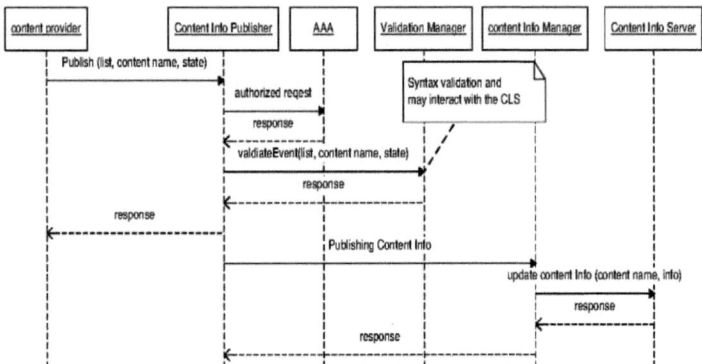

Figure C.4: CIPE Content provider publishing new content information related to his content list

C.1.4 Interfaces

The Reference Points named as CIS and XCI are in the scope of the PSF Architecture. The reference points CIS-1, CIS-2, CIS-3, CIS-4 and CIS-5 use the SIP protocol while CIS-6 and CIS-7 use XCAP over HTTP and CIS-9 and CIS-10 are based on APIs. The reference points XCI-1, XCI-2, XCI-3, XCI-4 and XCI-5 use XCAP over HTTP [11] while the reference points XCI-6 and XCI-7 are based on SIP.

CIS-1 Components and Protocol: CIS - IMS core (SIP)
   Functions:

- Publishing multimedia content information
- Triggering of delivery of the updated multimedia content information from the content provider source

CIS-2 Components and Protocol: Watcher - IMS core (SIP)
   Functions:

- Subscribing to a single multimedia resource of a dedicated multimedia content information and reception of notifications
- Subscribing to multimedia content information and reception of notifications for multimedia content lists

CIS-3 Components and Protocol: IMS core - CLS (SIP)
   Functions:

- Receiving a subscription and sending aggregated notifications for a Multimedia Content List and Request-contained Multimedia Content List and for a Request-contained Watcher Information List

C.1. Content Information Provisioning Enabler 231

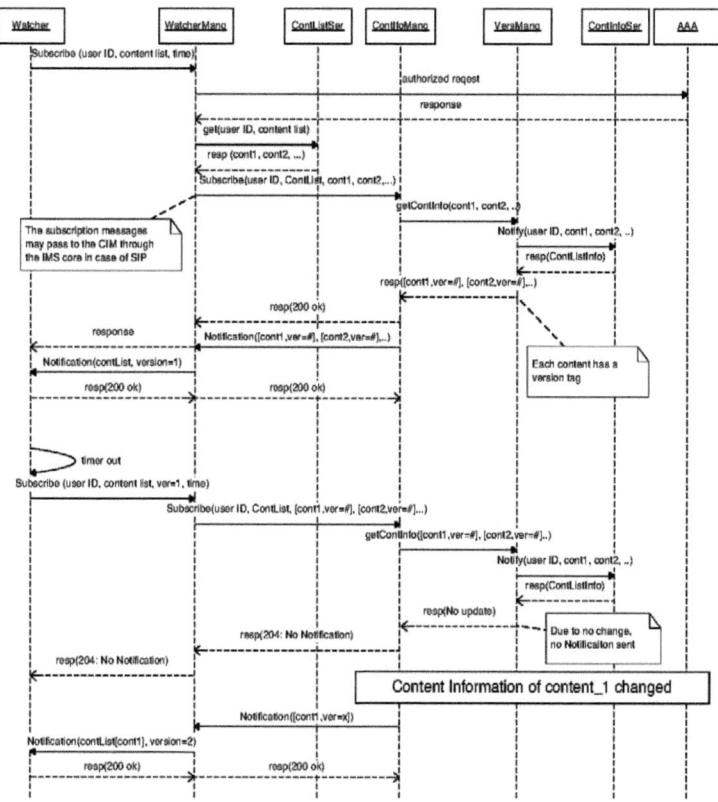

Figure C.5: Content Information Watcher Subscription, single domain

- Subscribing to Multimedia Content Information and receiving notifications for each content resource in a Multimedia Content List and Request contained Multimedia Content List

- Subscribing to Watcher Information and receiving notifications for each content resource in a Request-contained Watcher Information List

- Fetching content lists from the CLS XDMS and subscribing to changes to documents stored in the Content List XDMS and receiving notifications

CIS-4 Components and Protocol: IMS core - CIS (SIP)
Functions:

Appendix C. Specification of Multimedia Service Enablers

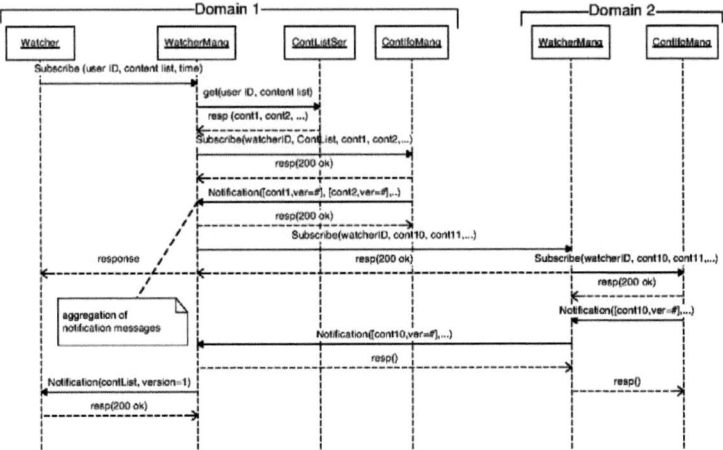

Figure C.6: Information Watcher Subscription, multi domains

- Subscribing to a single content resource's Multimedia Content Information and receiving related notifications
- Subscribing to Watcher Information and receiving notifications
- Subscribing to changes to documents CIS XDMS or CLS XDMS and reception of notifications

CIS-5 Components and Protocol: IMS core - remote PSE
Functions: Communicating with other CIPE deployed in other IMS domains via SIP

CIS-6 Components and Protocol: CIS - CIS XDMS (XCAP)
Functions: Transferring content-specific XML documents (e.g. Multimedia Content Subscription Rules, Permanent Multimedia Content Information) from the CIS XDMS to the CIS

CIS-7 Components and Protocol: CLS - CLS XDMS (XCAP)
Functions: Transferring CLS-specific XML documents (e.g. Multimedia Content Lists) from the CLS XDMS to the CLS

CIS-8 Components and Protocol: CIS - CLS API
Functions: In order to enable a direct communication between the CIS and CLS without the involvement of the IMS core, this interface is used as alternative to the reference points CIS-3 and CIS-4.

CIS-9 Components and Protocol: CIS - other Enabler
Functions: Enabling other enabler (e.g. SME or CME) or application to subscribe to any change to multimedia content information for a single content resource and reception of notification

C.1. Content Information Provisioning Enabler 233

CIS-11 Components and Protocol: CLS - other Enabler
  Functions: Enabling other enabler (e.g. SME or CME) or application to subscribe to any change to multimedia content information for Content Lists and Request-contained Content Lists and reception of notification

XCI-1 Components and Protocol: XDM client in CP (XCAP)
  Functions:

  - Authenticating and authorizing client requests
  - Creating multimedia content resources or multimedia content lists
  - Modifying multimedia content resources or multimedia content lists
  - Fetching multimedia content resources or multimedia content lists

XCI-2 Components and Protocol: XDM client in consumer (XCAP)
  Functions: Authenticating and authorizing client requests and fetching multimedia content resources or multimedia content lists

XCI-3 Components and Protocol: AP - CLS XDMS (XCAP)
  Functions: Forwarding XCM client requests to the dedicated CLS XDMS

XCI-4 Components and Protocol: AP - CIS XDMS (XCAP)
  Functions: Forwarding XCM client requests to the dedicated CIS XDMS

XCI-5 Components and Protocol: AG - Application (XDAP)
  Functions: Applications may act as XDM Client in order to create, modify and fetch individual multimedia content information or multimedia content lists

XCI-6 Components and Protocol: CLS XDMS - IMS core
  Functions: Subscribing to the modification of Multimedia Content specific XML documents pertaining to content lists, and receiving notifications

XCI-7 Components and Protocol: CLS XDMS - IMS
  Functions: Subscribing to the modification of Multimedia Content specific XML documents pertaining to multimedia content, and receiving notifications

C.1.5 Multimedia Content Information Data Model

Content URI: The identifier for multimedia content is a URI. For each unique multimedia content in the network, there is one or more content URIs. A multimedia content may have multiple URIs because they are identified by a protocol-specific URI, such as a SIP URI, HTTP URI, RTSP URI, etc.

When a document is constructed, the content URI is ideally set as the identifier used to request the document in the first place. For example, if a document was requested through a SIP SUBSCRIBE request, the content URI would match the Request URI of the SUBSCRIBE request. This follows the principle of least surprise, since the entity requesting the document may not be aware of the other identifiers for the content.

Content: The content data component models information about the multimedia content that the content data is trying to describe. This information consists of characteristics of the content, and their status. Characteristics of multimedia content are the static information about content that does not change under normal circumstances. Such information is descriptive data that describes the content, such as textual explanation, classification and content types. Another example of content characteristic is an alias. An alias is a URI that identifies the same content, but with a different content URI.

Status information about a multimedia content represents the dynamic information about a multimedia content. This typically consists of a content state that describes the current delivery status of a multimedia content as defined in subsection 4.2.1, the source location the content transmitted from, and target location that the content is transmitted to. Examples of content status are: "*in-production*", "*available-for-trial*", "*available-for-delivery*", "*set-to-schedule*", "*on-air*", "*on-demand*", and "*deleted*".

In the model, there can be only one content component per multimedia content information. In other words, the content component models a single multimedia content, and includes characteristics and statuses related to the content delivery states for a single multimedia content.

Service: Each multimedia content can be delivered with a set of delivery services. Each of these represents a point to obtain the content. Examples of services are linear steaming, on-demand streaming, broadcast streaming, downloading, etc. A service models a system that enables the user to interact with it, in order to request multimedia content. Additional constraints can be applied to define specific content delivery services. For example, such constraint signaling and delivery protocols such as SIP, RTSP or HTTP and RTP, FTP, File Delivery over Unidirectional Transport (FLUTE) or TCP.

Each service is associated with characteristics that identify the nature and capabilities of that service, with reach information that indicates how to connect to the service, with status information representing the state of that service, and relative information that describes the ways in which that service relates to others associated with the multimedia content. Each service is associated with a set of characteristics that describe the delivery capabilities of the multimedia content experienced when a watcher invokes that URI. Examples of such capabilities are the type of content delivery (such as linear or on-demand), transmission mode (unicast or multicast) and media properties (codec, IP, port, language, etc.). Characteristics are important when multiple delivery services are embedded in the multimedia content information document. That is because the purpose of listing multiple delivery services in a multimedia content information document is to give the watcher a choice to select the preferred delivery mechanisms. This can be dependent on several factors, such as device capabilities, price, transmission time, etc.

The reach information for a delivery service provides the instructions for the recipient of a multimedia content document on how to correctly contact that service. A delivery service includes a URI that can be "*hit*" to start content delivery. From an IMS perspective, a delivery service is identified by the PSI, as defined in subsection 4.2.3. When the URI or PSI is insufficient, additional attributes of the service can be present that define the instructions on how the delivery service is to be reached. For instance, if the watcher has to subscribe to a dedicated service delivery, either the URI or additional attribute shall indicate the subscription instructions.

Each delivery service has a status that represents generally dynamic information about the availability of the service. The simplest form of status is the basic status, which is a binary indicator of availability for content delivery using that service delivery. It can have values of either "*closed*" or "*open*". "*Closed*" means that the delivery service is not available for reaching the content. This can be dependent on the characteristics of the delivery session that eventually gets set up or torn down. For example, a status attribute can be defined that indicates that a multicast delivery session is available if the related delivery resources (e.g. on the MDF) have been allocated or released. Services inherently have a lot of dynamic states associated with them. For example, consider a multicast delivery session.

C.2 Content Management Enabler

The status of such a delivery service might include the number of recipients or the time passed. However, not all of this dynamic state is appropriate to include within a delivery service data component of a multimedia content information document.

Device: Device models the physical nodes in which multimedia content is captured, processed or stored and possibly available for delivery. Examples of devices include capture devices (e.g. camera, microphone, mobile phone, etc.), HTTP server or media servers (e.g. MDF).

The mapping of delivery services to devices is many-to-many. A single delivery service can execute on multiple devices. Consider the delivery service of a live multimedia event (e.g. football match). Several capturing devices deployed in the event area can register against a single Address of Record for this delivery service. As a result, the delivery service is associated with all these devices. Similarly, a single device can support a multiplicity of delivery services. A media server can support linear, on-demand and download delivery services.

Devices are identified with a device ID, which shall be unique. In a SIP-based service delivery the device ID might be not provided directly to the end consumer in the multimedia content information document, because the device ID can be obtained during session establishment (i.e. in the SDP part). However, including the device ID in the multimedia content information document might be useful in other delivery services like peer-to-peer or in multicast delivery mode.

Like delivery services and content data components, device data components have generally static characteristics and generally dynamic status. Characteristics of a device include its physical dimensions and capabilities, audio video codec, video resolutions, the speed of its CPU, and the amount of memory. Status information includes dynamic information about the device. This includes whether the device is powered on or off, the geographic location of the device, the amount of battery power that remains in the device, etc.

Encoding and XML Schema: Multimedia Content Information represented according to the data model described above needs to be mapped into an XML schema for simple processing, transport and storage. The Presence Information Data Format (PIDF) representation of presence data specified in the RFC3863 [122] can be used as a basic format for describing Multimedia Content Information. However, the terms <person> and <service> are mapped pertaining to multimedia content provisioning to <content> and <delivery service> as discussed above.

C.2 Content Management Enabler

C.2.1 Use Cases

Figure C.7 illustrates the content provider use case in which CME pulls multimedia content from a dedicated content provider and user of the MDF to store or process the content. Furthermore, the use case shows the content provider using CME to push multimedia content to the network.

Figure C.8 illustrates the relationship between an application and the CME as well as the content provider. In this use case, the application triggers the CME to accept multimedia content from a dedicated content provider.

236   Appendix C. Specification of Multimedia Service Enablers

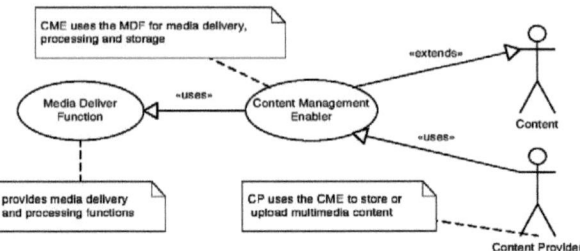

Figure C.7: The use case of content management enabler interacting with the content provider

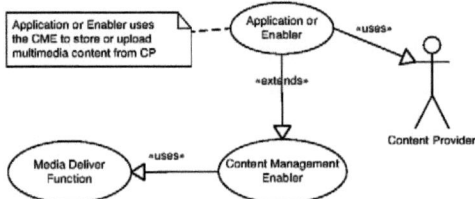

Figure C.8: Relationship between an application and the content management enabler

C.2.2   CME Message Flows

The CME interacts with the Content Provider in two cases. First, the content provider triggers the CME to push multimedia content. Second, the CME pulls multimedia content from the CP.

Figure C.9 shows a content provider pushing multimedia content by issuing a SIP Invite request addressed to the CME, which triggers the MDF to receive or fetch the content.

In the second case, the CME is triggered by either an application or the SME to pull multimedia content from a content provider. The related message flow is depicted in Figure C.10. Once the CME receives a request for a multimedia content that is not available in the MDF, it requests that the CP to deliver the related content to the MDF. In our case, the CME initiates a SIP Invite requests, however, other signaling protocol (e.g. RTSP) can be considered as well.

Once the delivery session has been finalized or an error has occurred, the delivery session between the content provider and the CME (as well as the MDF) should be torn down. The related message interactions between these entities are depicted in Figure C.11, in which either the content provider or the CME initiate the process of the session teardown. Accordingly, the CME issues a SIP Bye message to the MDF and updates the related session information through the ContentHandler.

C.2. Content Management Enabler

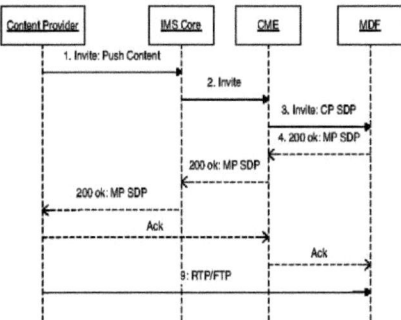

Figure C.9: Setup between the CME and CP, push method

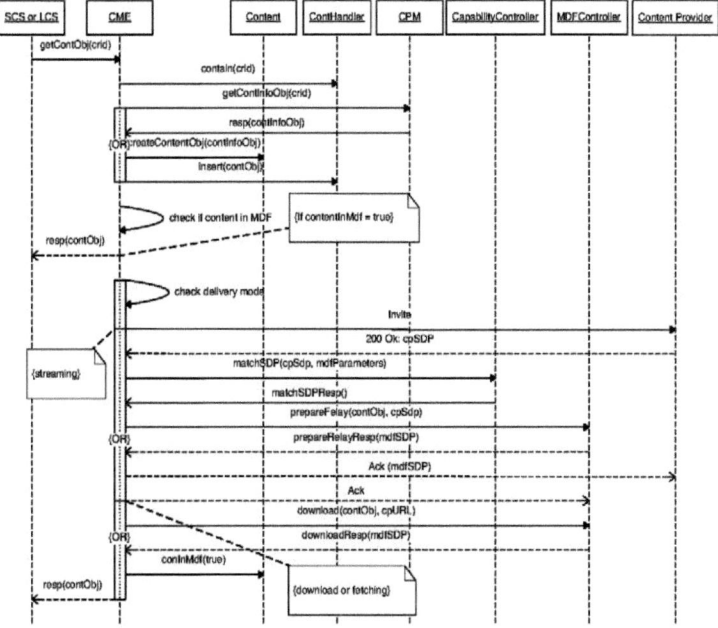

Figure C.10: Session setup between the CME and CP, pull method

Appendix C. Specification of Multimedia Service Enablers

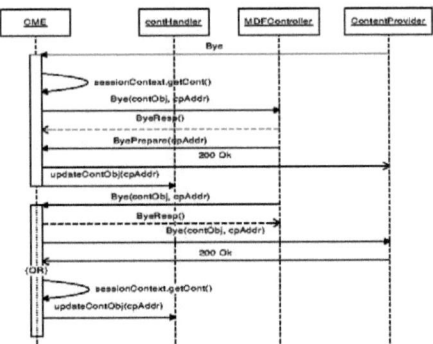

Figure C.11: Session termination between the CME and the content provider

C.2.3 External Entities

Content Information Provisioning Enabler: The CIPE provides content list and multimedia content information to the CME. In case of deploying both CIPE and CME in one domain, the interactions can be based on open APIs instead of using the SIP-based Subscription and Notification model, which leads to an increase of the load on the IMS core.

Aggregation Proxy: The aggregation proxy authenticates the XDM client requests and delegates the request to the corresponding XDM server, namely the XDM CLS server.

Session Management Enabler: The SME interacts with the CME to obtain content information object and check the availability of dedicated multimedia content. The interaction is intended to be based on open APIs. IMS core: The IMS core forwards SIP messages between the CME, the CP and the MDF. The IMS core is in charge of maintaining the SIP registration of the IMS-based CP.

Media Delivery Function: The MDF receives or fetches multimedia content delivery from the CP based on the triggering request issued by the CME.

C.2.4 Interfaces

The reference points named as CME and XCM are in scope of the CME architecture. The reference points CME-1, CME-3, CME-4 and CME-5 use the SIP protocol while CME-2 uses the HTTP or is based on APIs. The reference points CME-6, CME-7, CME-8 and CME-9 are based on open APIs. The reference points XCM-1, XCM-2 and XCM-3 are based on XCAP protocol.

CME-1 Components and Protocol: CP - IMS core SIP
  Functions:

- Registration with the IMS core
- Initiating SIP requests pertaining to multimedia session establishment with the CME

C.2. Content Management Enabler

- Receiving SIP requests initiated by the CME (e.g. Invite requests) via IMS core

CME-2 Components and Protocol: CP - CME (HTTP or APIs)
Functions:

- Enabling session establishment between the CME and the CP in the case that the CP does not support SIP
- The interface may make use of the http or open APIs.

CME-3 Components and Protocol: CP - MDF (SIP)
Functions:

- Fetching multimedia content from CP using HTTP or FTP
- Uploading multimedia content from CP to the MDF using HTTP or FTP
- Streaming multimedia content via RTP

CME-4 Components and Protocol: CME - IMS(SIP)
Functions:

- Initiating SIP requests towards the CP
- Triggering the media delivery and processing functions on the MDF following the RFC4240 [20]
- Receiving SIP requests from the CP

CME-5 Components and Protocol: IMS core - MDF (SIP)
Functions:

- Forwards SIP requests for triggering media delivery functions initiated by the CME
- Forwarding SIP messages initiated by the MDF to the CME

CME-6 Components and Protocol: CME - XDM Client (APIs)
Functions: Fetching content list and related content information obtained from XDMS

CME-7 Components and Protocol: CME - CIPE (APIs)
Functions:

- Subscribing any changes to dedicated multimedia content information
- Receiving notification of changes to multimedia content information

CME-8 Components and Protocol: CME - SME (APIs)
Functions: Enabling the SME to obtain information about the availability of certain multimedia content objects on the MDF

CME-9 Components and Protocol: CME - application (APIs)
Functions:

- Enabling the application to act as CP to push, upload or store multimedia content to the network (i.e. MDF)

240 Appendix C. Specification of Multimedia Service Enablers

- Enabling the application to obtain information about the availability of certain multimedia content objects on the MDF

XCM-1 Components and Protocol: CP XDM client - Aggr. proxy (XCAP)
Functions:

- Creating and modifying content list
- Updating or creating new content information entries

XCM-2 Components and Protocol: CME XDM Client - Aggr. proxy (XCAP)
Functions: Fetching content list of dedicating content provider and Fetching content information of each content list

C.3 Session Management Enabler

C.3.1 Use Cases

Figure C.12 illustrates the use case of a multimedia content consumer who is acting as the main actor by requesting SME for particular multimedia content. The consumer might be aware about such multimedia content and the address of the delivery service supported by the SME through the CIPE. The SME might push multimedia content to the consumer by initiating the request.

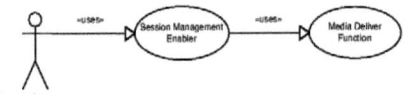

Figure C.12: Use case of delivering multimedia content triggered by a consumer

An application might trigger the SME to deliver a dedicated multimedia content to one or a set of end users, as shown in the use case depicted in Figure C.13.

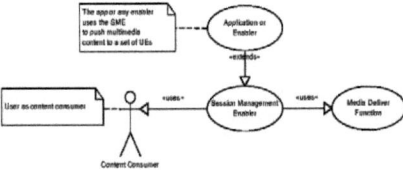

Figure C.13: Use case of delivering multimedia content triggered by an application

The relationship use case between the SME and the CME is depicted in Figure C.14. The SME offers two delivery services, namely the live content streaming and the stored content streaming. Both delivery services interact with the CME to determine the availability of the requested multimedia content.

C.3. Session Management Enabler

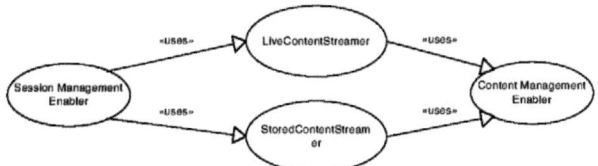

Figure C.14: Relationship use case between the SME and the CME

C.3.2 Message Flows

The SME supports two delivery services, namely the Live Content Streamer (LCS) and the Stored Content Streamer (SCS). A consumer of content can acquire the LCS for delivering a dedicated multimedia content according to provisioning information provided by the CIPE. The corresponding message flows between the LCS components are illustrated in Figure C.15. Upon receiving the SIP Invite request, the LCS checks if the related multimedia content object is available or not. If not, it interacts with CME to retrieve this information and then triggers the MDF controller to deliver the content according to user capabilities and selected bearer (unicast, multicast or broadcast).

After the session establishment of a live delivery session, the LCS might provide the users with a set of delivery channels transmitted over multicast or broadcast (e.g. via DVB-T/H) bearers and publish the related delivery parameters to the users either during the session establishment procedure or via the CIPE as content related information. In such cases, the user can switch among these channels without initiating a new SIP Invite message. In our implementation, we evaluated different signaling mechanisms with the objective of informing the LCS about a user's zapping activities. The corresponding analysis has been provided in subsection 4.3.2 and the measurement results are provided in Chapter 7.

Session termination is triggered by the users or the SME at any time (due to any reasons). Figure C.16 illustrates the associated message flows, in which the user initiates a SIP Bye message to the LCS. The LCS updates the session context according to the transmitted delivery mode (unicast, multicast or broadcast). As a consequence, the LCS triggers the MDF to terminate the unicast or the multicast content delivery and updates the associated session context object.

The session setup for delivering stored multimedia content is almost similar to the previous procedure; however the primary distinction between both is that the delivery of stored content is often based on a unicast transmission mode rather than multicast or broadcast modes. Figure C.17 illustrates the related message flows. Based on user subscription or device capabilities, content streaming can be delivered in a linear or on-demand mode. In the first case, the content stream is transmitted lacking support of trick functions, which are supported in the on-demand mode. In the latter case, the availability of an RTSP stack at the user's and the media server entity's side is required. Activation of content streaming with SIP for session control and RTSP for media control (i.e. for triggering trick functions) is an approach which has an advantage in the probably enormous saving in delay between user action and service reaction. The SCS acts as back-to-back SIP user agent between the user and the MDF. Furthermore, the SCS makes use of the CME in order to obtain the information about content availability on the MDF and the related ID.

Appendix C. Specification of Multimedia Service Enablers

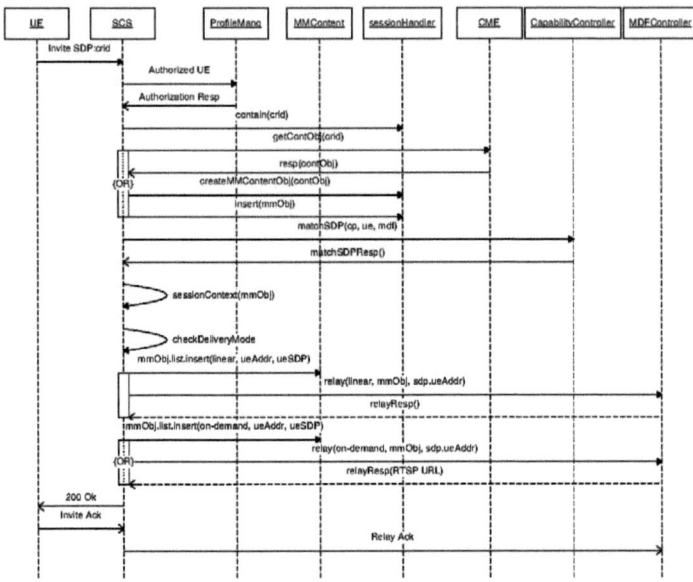

Figure C.15: Message flows of session setup for delivering stored multimedia content

Session teardown can be triggered either by the network or by the end user. The network terminates the session either by the MDF once content delivery is completed or by the SCS due to error or charging issues (e.g. no credit available in the case of on-line charging). Figure C.18 illustrates just two cases of session termination for delivering stored multimedia content. First, the user triggers the termination by issuing a SIP Bye message. Second, the MDF terminates the session by issuing a SIP Bye message for the relay session initiated by the SCS. In both cases the SCS removes the related session context information.

In order to understand how a 3rd party or another service enabler can make use of the LCS or SCS exposed services through open interfaces, Figure C.19 shows one LCS service that allows an application to trigger the delivery of a live multimedia content identified by a unique ID (obtained either from the CIPE or the CME) to a set of IMS subscribers. In fact, in this example the application may obtain the content ID that identifies the live content in the LCS and the MDF. In this regard, the CME has already triggered the MDF to prepare for relaying the corresponding live content stream. Although this step is not depicted in this flow, there are other web service interfaces exposing such capabilities. Furthermore, the IMS core is included in this example between the LCS web service, LCS servlet and the IMS subscriber.

C.3. Session Management Enabler

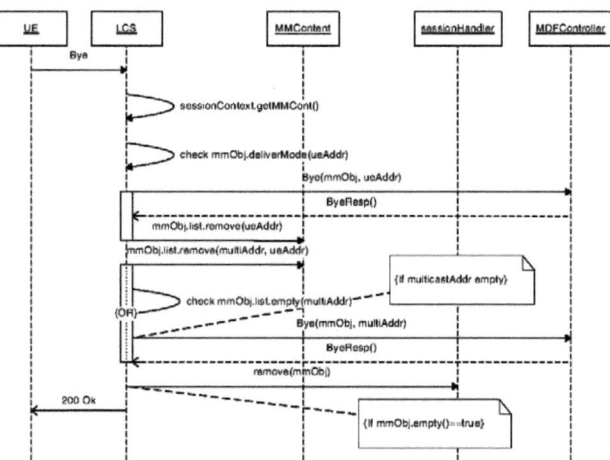

Figure C.16: Message flows of session termination for delivering live multimedia content

C.3.3 External Entities

Content Information Provisioning Enabler: The SME publishes the properties of the live and stored delivery services for each multimedia object. The properties include service ID, service URI, service description, subscription information (if required), media delivery properties (e.g. multicast IP address, scope of the multicast stream, content stream codec, language, transmission time, etc.). If the delivery service (either the live or stored content manager) does not support the delivery of a certain multimedia content, no publish message is generated. For example, a LCS publishes service delivery information pertaining to the live content stream, but the SCS will not issue any publish message related to such a live stream. The interaction between the CIPE and the SME will be based on open APIs. However, the SIP protocol can be used as well.

Content Management Enabler: The SME interacts with the CME in order to obtain content information available on the MDF. CME is in charge of fetching the content list and related content information from the CIPE and providing these to the SME via open APIs.

Consumer: The consumer is the sink of any multimedia content. Either it acts as an originating SIP user agent by issuing a SIP Invite message to the SME or as a terminating SIP user agent by receiving a SIP Invite message initiated by the SME. In the former use case, the consumer initiated request is performed according to previous notification received from the CIPE about the availability of a multimedia content. Consumer and delivery capabilities are negotiated during session establishment followed by content delivery from the MDF to the consumer via RTP, FTP or FLUTE, as discussed in subsection 4.4. Therefore the consumer device shall support the related signaling and transport protocols.

Appendix C. Specification of Multimedia Service Enablers

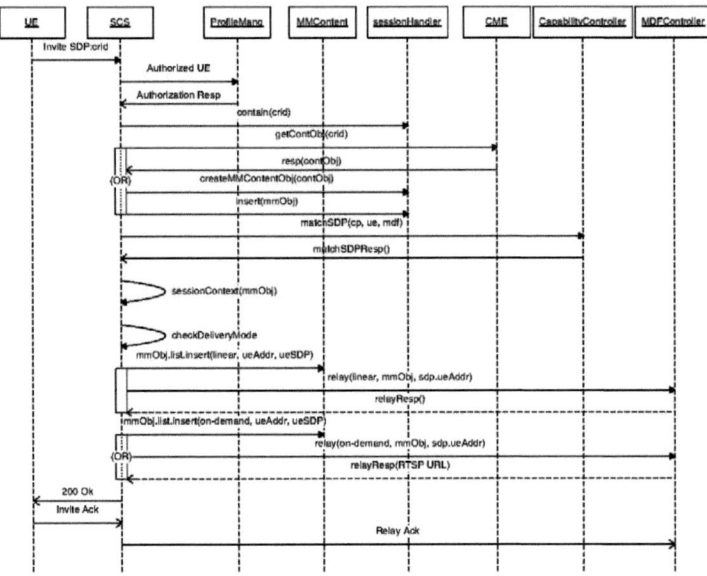

Figure C.17: Message flows of session setup for delivering stored multimedia content

C.3.4 Interfaces

The reference points named as SME are in the scope of the SME architecture. The reference points SME-3, SME-6, SME-7, SME-8 and SME-9 are based on the SIP and SME-4 is based on the RTP, FTP or FLUTE protocols, and the remaining reference points are APIs. We distinguish between external and internal reference points. However, the internal reference points are illustrated with descriptive objectives of the interactions between the internal functional entities without adding architectural constraints to the SME itself.

SME-1 Components and Protocol: SME - CME (APIs)
   Functions: Enabling the SME to obtain the available multimedia content objects in the MDF network and related content information

SME-2 Components and Protocol: SME - CIPE (APIs)
   Functions: Enabling the SME to publish service delivery properties pertaining to certain multimedia objects available in the MDF

SME-3 Components and Protocol: Consumer - IMS core (SIP)
   Functions: User registration with the IMS core

SME-4 Components and Protocol: MDF - Consumer (RTP, FTP or FLUTE)
   Functions:

C.3. Session Management Enabler

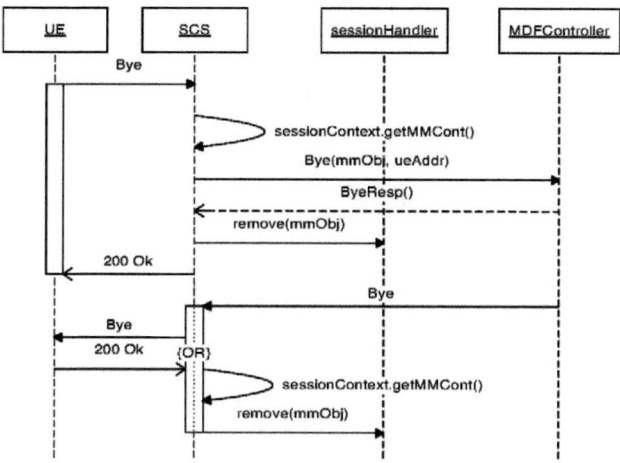

Figure C.18: Message flows of session termination for delivering stored multimedia content

- Streaming multimedia content streaming from the MDF to the end user via RTP over UDP according to the RFC 3550 [22]
- Downloading multimedia content from the MDF to end user(s) via FTP or **FLUTE** protocol

SME-5 Components and Protocol: SME - Application (APIs)
Functions:

- Enabling other service enabler or application to push multimedia content to a set of IMS subscribers
- Enabling the application to trigger any media processing functions (e.g. storing of multimedia content) on available multimedia content delivery content tracks (e.g. live content stream)

SME-6 Components and Protocol: SME - IMS core (SIP)
Functions:

- Receiving SIP messages initiated by the consumers towards the SME (either the SCS, the LCS or the MDF controller)
- Forwarding SIP messages initiated by the SME (either the SCS, the LCS or the MDF controller) towards IMS subscribers (or MDF network)

SME-7 Components and Protocol: SME - IMS core (SIP)
Functions:

- Forwarding SIP messages initiated by the SME towards the MDF network

Appendix C. Specification of Multimedia Service Enablers

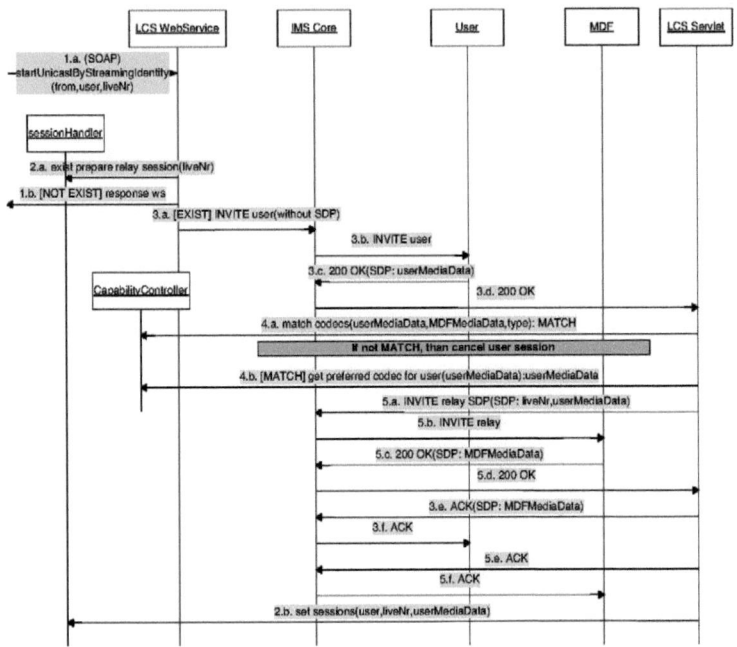

Figure C.19: Pushing live multimedia content triggered by 3rd application

- Forwarding SIP messages initiated by the MDF network to the SME

SME-8 Components and Protocol: SME internal APIs
Functions:

- Bearer selection according to user context and network condition
- Discovering delivery properties according to user capabilities, content properties and MDF capabilities

SME-9 Components and Protocol: SME internal APIs
Functions: Triggering delivery and processing functions on the MDF according to decision making by the bearer and selection controller

C.4 Media Delivery Function

C.4.1 External Entities

Multimedia Service Enabler: The multimedia service enabler or application server is the entity that makes use of the MDF functions for content delivery from the content provider

C.4. Media Delivery Function

to the consumer. The application server or the enabler uses the SIP protocol according to the RFC4240 [20] to trigger the delivery and processing functions either directly or through the IMS core.

IMS core: The IMS core forwards SIP messages initiated by the application server towards the MDF. The IMS core hides the topology of the MDF.

Content Provider: The content provider is in charge of the following functions:

- Streaming live or stored multimedia content to a dedicated MSP port or multicast IP address
- Enabling the MDF to fetch multimedia content via FTP or HTTP
- Uploading multimedia content to a dedicated MSP

Content Consumer: The content consumer is in charge of the following functions:

- Session establishment towards the application server either via SIP or HTTP
- Issuing RTSP control messages in an on-demand content delivery service according to the RFC2326 [18]
- Joining multicast group, in the case of multicast transmission session according to RFC1112, RFC 2236 or RFC 3376 [123, 18, 124]
- Receiving content stream from the MDF via RTP

C.4.2 Interfaces

The reference points named as MDF-n are in the scope of the MDF architecture. The reference points MDF-1, MDF-2 and MDF-3 are based on the SIP protocol, while MDF-7 uses the RTSP to control the media stream. The reference points MDF-5 and MDF-6 are used for content delivery via the RTP, FTP or FLUTE protocol. The MDF-4 is specified as APIs, however any control protocol following client-server, master-slave or peer-to-peer communication model can be applied. Therefore this interface can be considered as a subject for future work.

MDF-1 Components and Protocol: IMS core - AS (SIP)
Functions:

- Discovering MDF delivery and processing capabilities
- Triggering the MDF delivery and processing functions according to the RFC 4042

MDF-2 Components and Protocol: AS - MSC (SIP)
Functions:

- Discovering MDF delivery and processing capabilities
- Triggering the MDF delivery and processing functions according to the RFC 4042
- SIP messages are routed directly to the MSC and do not pass the IMS core

MDF-3 Components and Protocol: IMS core - MSC (SIP)
Functions: Forwarding SIP messages between the AS and the MSC

248 Appendix C. Specification of Multimedia Service Enablers

MDF-4 Components and Protocol: MSC - MSP (APIs)
Functions:
- Controlling delivery functions from the content provider to the MSP
- Controlling delivery functions from the MSP to a set of consumers or a set of multicast groups
- Triggering processing functions according to consumer capabilities and content properties

MDF-5 Components and Protocol: CP - MSP (RTP, FTP or HTTP)
Functions:
- Fetching multimedia content from the CP via FTP or HTTP
- Downloading multimedia content from the CP via FTP or HTTP
- Receiving content streams from the CP via RTP

MDF-6 Components and Protocol: MSP - consumer (RTP, FTP or FLUTE)
Functions:
- " Streaming multimedia content via RTP to a single consumer over a unicast mode or a set of consumers over a multicast mode. However, streaming over HTTP can be considered as well, in the case that the consumer is behind a firewall (i.e. supporting to public Internet)
- Downloading multimedia content via FTP or FLUTE protocol over a single unicast or multicast mode, respectively

MDF-7 Components and Protocol: Consumer - MSC/MSP (RTSP)
Functions:
- Issuing RTSP messages to control the content stream in an on-demand delivery mode
- Either the MSC or the MSP can act as the RTSP server

APPENDIX D
IMS MBMS Integration

Our contribution to the C-Mobile project mainly targeted the integration of the IMS with the MBMS, in order to enhance multimedia delivery session with multicast and broadcast capabilities in 3GPP networks. This section gives an overview of the most important signaling flows regarding IMS-based multicast delivery session using MBMS bearer.

In MBMS the BM-SC maintains functionalities already covered by IMS. In particular, the Membership function is implemented in the S-CSCF and HSS (where service profile is stored) and the S-CSCF and the AS performs the authorization check. The QoS reservation, part of the BMSC Session and Transmission function, is provided by the PCRF and GGSN. In IMS, QoS reservation consists of DiffServ and IntServ mechanisms. The IMS entity MRF (Media Resource Function) is able to combine media streams or to act as a conference bridge. These responsibilities are related to the MBMS Proxy and Transport function. However, the MRF has been extended to support additional MBMS delivery and content processing functions, such as multicast delivery, content relaying, content recording, trans-rating (scaling down the rate of a content stream) and transcoding. Only the Session scheduling function, the Proxy function with Gmb signaling and the Service Announcement function have to be introduced in IMS. Therefore, these required functionalities are considered during the design of the MDF, SME, CIPE and CME.

A simplified version of IMS-MBMS integrated framework is depicted in Figure 7.6 in which the components that we have contributed to are depicted in continuous black line. The Access and Transport Plane corresponds to the RAN and CN. It consists of several 3GPP core nodes. In case of UMTS, this plane contains the GGSN (Gateway GPRS Support Node), the SGSN (Serving GPRS Support Node) and the UTRAN (UMTS Terrestrial RAN). Therefore, the architecture reuses the existing MBMS interfaces Gmb and Gi, which provide access to the control plane functions and to the bearer plane, respectively. The Gmb reference point interfaces with the MDF for MBMS bearer service-specific signaling (i.e. bearer setup and release) and with the PCRF for user-specific signaling (i.e. user authorization and reporting). Session control and session negotiation take place in the IMS-based control plane in collaboration with the Multimedia Service Enablers. This includes security, access control, QoS provisioning and creation of charging records. Therefore, the original MBMS Session and Transmission function is logically split into several sub-functionalities. The lower layered IP transport functionalities (e.g. IP packet scheduling, resource reservation) are maintained by subordinated entities in the control plane.

The high layered functionalities (e.g. SME, CME and CIPE) are realized by service enablers. The Multimedia Service Enablers are, moreover, in charge of service control covering bearer selection and service authorization. It also offers service capabilities such as group management, provisioning, content protection and location-based services. Figure 7.6 shows the IMS-MBMS integrated architecture.

The delivery session goes through different phases. The first phase is the *Content Information Provisioning* phase, in which the user receives information about the service and related parameters (e.g. the IMS Public Service Identifier). The second phase is the IMS session establishment phase, in which the IMS subscriber establishes the session by initiating a SIP Invite request. The third phase is the start transmission phase, in which the SME triggers the content provider and the MDF to start content delivery. The fourth phase is the stop transmission phase, in which the delivery session between the SME and the CP and the MDF are terminated. The final phase is the session termination phase between the IMS subscriber and the network, in which the SIP session as well as MBMS bearer are released.

Figure D.1 illustrates the first two phases; namely the session announcement phase and the session establishment phase. In fact, session establishment can be initiated either by the IMS subscriber or by the SME (application server). In this use case, the IMS subscriber is the one who initiates the session after successful registration with the IMS core and obtaining all available multimedia content services from the network (e.g. CIPE).

One of the C-Mobile usage scenarios, called *"Content Casts"*, was developed. This service provides access to the latest information anytime and anywhere without the need for manual downloads. Users can subscribe to periodically released content such as video podcasts, weather forecasts or the latest news, which is automatically sent to the users' device.

To access the content, the user activates the *"Content Cast"* service and then waits for the start of the data transmission. This corresponds to the Joining and Session Start phases as described in MBMS specification and constitutes the core of the signaling flows. These flows comprise MBMS, DIAMETER as well as SIP signaling. The content is transferred over RTP or FLUTE protocol. The User Subscription, Service announcement, Packet Data Protocol (PDP) and Context Activation procedures remain the same, as specified by the 3GPP MBMS specification in Release 6. However, the service announcement procedure is not specified in details. Then the UE negotiates a session with the SME. The SIP INVITE message is routed by the CSCF to the corresponding AS, which provides the desired MBMS service. The SME triggers the MDF for a multicast relay session (however, the content is not available yet). Thereafter, the SME responds with a 200 ok message covering all related session parameters embedded in the SDP part. Based on the 200 ok message, the P-CSCF requests the PCRF (Policy Control and Charging Rules Function) for authorizing MBMS bearer resource (step 8). The PCRF responds with an authorization token, which is included in the 200 ok message. The UE uses the IP multicast and the authorization token to activate the MBMS context following the MBMS specification. Once the GGSN receives the MBMS authorization request from the SGSN, it interacts with the PCRF to authorize the MBMS context activation based on the authorization token (step 12 and 13)[1]. Thereafter the GGSN registers itself with the MDF for the MBMS bearer service. This step is required, as the traffic between the MDF (acting as the BM-SC) and the GGSN is transmitted over a unicast tunneling mode. However, this procedure is not required in the case that the MDF uses the IP multicast transmission mode.

Finally the UMTS IP core and RAN allocates the required resources and responds to the UE with activate MBMS context response message. This signaling is used to establish a multicast routing tree with the involved GGSNs, SGSNs and RNCs (Radio Network Controller). Every involved entity in this multicast tree creates an MBMS bearer context and changes the context state to *"Standby"*. When the routing tree is established, the SGSN notifies the UE about the success. Then the UE completes the Service Joining procedure with a SIP Acknowledge Message sent to the AS. Afterwards, the UE is able to receive the content and waits for the incoming data transfer (step 22).

---

[1] The authorization for the UE is performed by the PCRF instead of the BM-SC, as in the equivalent MBMS procedure

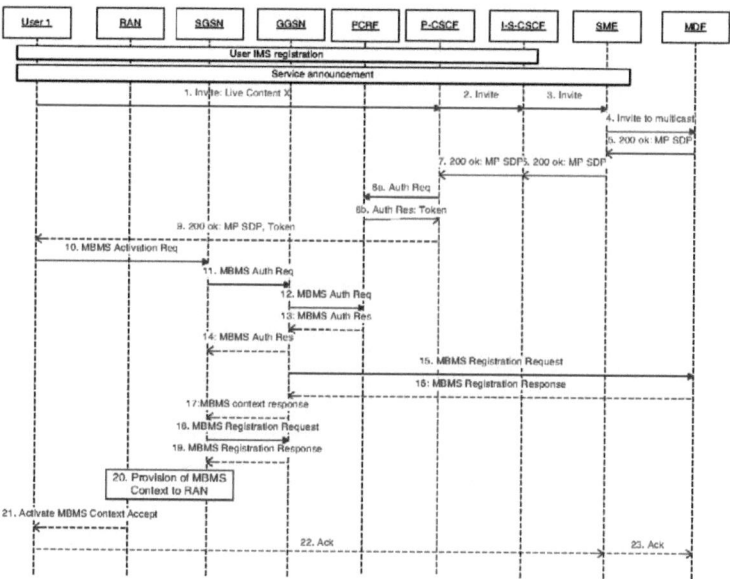

Figure D.1: IMS-MBMS integration, session activation

After a user has joined, specific MBMS service charging records can be created based on the business model. The process of billing is followed by the MBMS Multicast Service Activation.

The signaling of the Session Start phase is depicted in Figure D.2. Opposed to session activation, the start transmission procedure takes place for every data transmission, not for every user. Behaving as a 3rd Party Call Control User Agent, the SME establishes a delivery session to the CP and the MDF (however, the CP may trigger the delivery by issuing the SIP Invite request to the SME). Upon receiving the SIP INVITE message, the MDF begins the MBMS Session Start procedure.

In this procedure the existing 3GPP scheme is reused. All MBMS context states are set to "*Active*" and both CN and RAN resources are reserved. Additional SIP signaling between the IMS core and the UE is avoided, since this would result in network congestion if a large number of users are addressed (Each user would require a point-to-point bearer to be established). A successful MBMS signaling is indicated by a 200 OK Response. Afterward, the SME sends an Acknowledge SIP Message to the CP and to the MDF. The CP waits for a configurable time (e.g. few sec) before it begins to transmit the content. After completing the start transmission signaling, a CP is allowed to send its content. The content is transmitted per unicast to the MDF, where it is optionally transcoded and afterwards transformed to multicast transport for an MBMS bearer.

Appendix D. IMS MBMS Integration

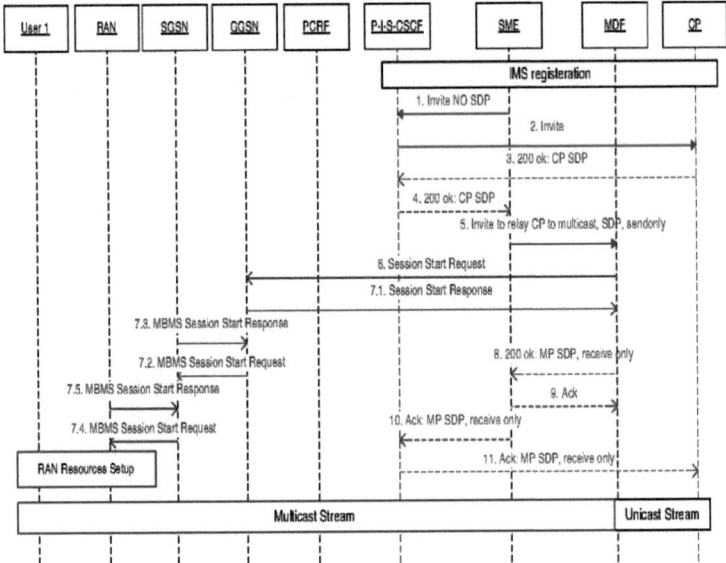

Figure D.2: IMS-MBMS integration, start transmission

When there is no more data to send for a specific period of time, the multicast bearer is released, freeing the network resources. As in the start transmission phase, the SME releases the session by sending a SIP Bye message for both the CP and MDF. The CP may also trigger a stop transmission procedure by sending first the SIP Bye message and, accordingly, the SME releases the session as described before. Consequently, the MDF shuts down the relay session by triggering the MBMS Session Stop Procedure as described in 3GPP MBMS specifications. The network resources are released, although the user SIP dialogs remain active until the user session termination phase takes place, or until the GGSN performs the deregistration, triggering the end of the SIP dialogs with the users.

Die VDM Verlagsservicegesellschaft sucht für wissenschaftliche Verlage abgeschlossene und herausragende

Dissertationen, Habilitationen, Diplomarbeiten, Master Theses, Magisterarbeiten usw.

für die kostenlose Publikation als Fachbuch.

Sie verfügen über eine Arbeit, die hohen inhaltlichen und formalen Ansprüchen genügt, und haben Interesse an einer honorarvergüteten Publikation?

Dann senden Sie bitte erste Informationen über sich und Ihre Arbeit per Email an *info@vdm-vsg.de*.

Sie erhalten kurzfristig unser Feedback!

VDM Verlagsservicegesellschaft mbH
Dudweiler Landstr. 99
D - 66123 Saarbrücken
Telefon +49 681 3720 174
Fax   +49 681 3720 1749
www.vdm-vsg.de

Die VDM Verlagsservicegesellschaft mbH vertritt

Printed by Books on Demand GmbH, Norderstedt / Germany